ice cream

garlic

apple

linguine

haricots verts

the BEST *of*
Gourmet

the BEST of

Gourmet

2003

FROM *the* EDITORS OF GOURMET

CONDÉ NAST BOOKS   •   RANDOM HOUSE, NEW YORK

Copyright © 2002
The Condé Nast Publications Inc. All rights reserved under International and Pan-American Copyright Conventions. Published in the United States by Random House, Inc., New York, and simultaneously in Canada by Random House of Canada Limited, Toronto.
ISBN 1-4000-6057-5
ISSN 1046-1760

Random House website address: www.atrandom.com
Gourmet Books website address: www.Gourmetbks.com

Most of the recipes in this work were published previously in *Gourmet* magazine.

Printed in the United States of America on acid-free paper

98765432
First Edition

All informative text in this book was written by Diane Keitt Abrams and Linda M. Immediato.

The text of this book was set in Times Roman. The four-color separations were done by American Color and Quad/Graphics, Inc. The book was printed and bound at R. R. Donnelley and Sons. Stock is Sterling Ultra Web Gloss, MeadWestvaco.

For Random House
Lisa Faith Phillips, Vice President/General Manager
Tom Downing, Direct Marketing Director
Deborah Williams, Operations Director
Lyn Barris, Direct Marketing Manager
Fianna Reznik, Direct Marketing Associate
Eric Levy, Inventory Assistant
Eric Killer, Direct Marketing Assistant
Molly Lyons, Production Manager

For *Gourmet* Books
Diane Keitt Abrams, Director
Linda M. Immediato, Senior Associate Editor

For *Gourmet* Magazine
Ruth Reichl, Editor-in-Chief
Diana LaGuardia, Creative Director

Zanne Early Stewart, Executive Food Editor
Kemp Miles Minifie, Senior Food Editor
Alexis M. Touchet, Associate Food Editor
Lori Walther Powell, Food Editor/Stylist
Amy Mastrangelo, Food Editor
Katy Massam, Food Editor
Shelton Wiseman, Food Editor
Ruth Cousineau, Food Editor
Gina Marie Miraglia, Food Editor
Melissa Roberts-Matar, Food Editor
Ian McLean Knauer, Recipe Cross-Tester

Romulo A. Yanes, Photographer

Illustrations by Tobie Giddio/CWC International, Inc.

Produced in Association with
Anne B. Wright and John W. Kern

Front Jacket: Berry Tart with Ginger Cream (page 238)
Back Jacket: Sizzle in the City (page 69)
Frontispiece: Steamed Corn Custards with Crab (page 126)

ACKNOWLEDGMENTS

*t*he editors of *Gourmet* Books would like to thank everyone who helped put this volume together—especially our designer Diana LaGuardia, *Gourmet's* Creative Director, for her vigilance, her creativity, and vision. *Gourmet's* Junior Designer, Kevin De Maria, helped retrieve images and other electronic information.

We fell in love with Tobie Giddio's drawings of little teapots, kitchen equipment, vegetables and the like—her stark images make a dramatic impression on the page. Tobie illustrated the entire recipe compendium and endsheets with over 75 original drawings.

Thanks to *Gourmet* Senior Editor Cheryl Brown, for polishing the manuscript, and to *all* the food editors—Alexis Touchet, Lori Powell, Amy Mastrangelo, Katy Massam, Shelton Wiseman, Ruth Cousineau, Gina Miraglia, Melissa Roberts-Matar—for creating the dishes in this book. Also, special thanks to Executive Food Editor Zanne Stewart and Senior Food Editor Kemp Minifie for their guidance.

The photographs that appear throughout are the work of many talented artists (see list on page 263). We'd like to give special acknowledgment to John Kernick for his photos that appear in the Cuisines of the World section, Featuring the Flavors of San Francisco. This section contains two menus—an Italian feast (San Francisco Celebration) created by Ruth Cousineau and a sleek mid-century dinner (Food Noir) by Melissa Roberts-Matar. Both Food Editors were inspired by the meals they ate while on a research trip there. Shelley Wiseman, motivated by the produce of San Francisco area markets, created the artichoke recipes that appear in our Cooking Class section. Artichoke text was written by Jane Daniels Lear.

Thanks to *Gourmet* photographer Romulo Yanes, who photographed the Cooking Class recipes as well as the berry tart with ginger cream (jacket), which captures the essence of summer in its simplicity. To Stephanie Stehofsky, *Gourmet* Production Director, for recipe retrieval we express our sincere gratitude. Molly Lyons, Random House Production Manager, handled production and printing.

And finally, we are truly indebted to Anne Wright, our project director, and John Kern, production editor.

San Francisco Celebration

Cooking Class: Artichokes

Feast of Fancy

Dinner under Glace

CONTENTS

tips for using
GOURMET'S RECIPES

MEASURE LIQUIDS
in glass or clear plastic liquid-measuring
cups.

MEASURE DRY INGREDIENTS
in nesting dry-measuring cups
(usually made of metal or plastic) that
can be leveled off with a knife.

MEASURE FLOUR
by spooning (not scooping) it into a
dry-measuring cup and leveling off with
a knife without tapping or shaking cup.

SIFT FLOUR
only when specified in recipe. If sifted
flour is called for, sift flour before
measuring. (Many brands say "presifted"
on the label; disregard this.)

A SHALLOW BAKING PAN
means an old-fashioned jelly-roll or
four-sided cookie pan.

MEASURE SKILLETS and BAKING PANS
across the top, not across the bottom.

A WATER BATH
for baking is prepared by putting your
filled pan in a larger pan and adding
enough boiling-hot water to reach halfway
up the side of the smaller pan.

METAL PANS
used for baking should be light-colored,
unless otherwise specified. If using
dark metal pans, including nonstick, your
baked goods will likely brown more and
the cooking times may be shorter.

ALL PRODUCE
must be washed and dried before using.

FRESH HERBS or GREENS
are prepped by first removing the leaves
or fronds from the stems. The exception is
cilantro, which has tender stems.

SALTED WATER
for cooking requires 1 tablespoon of salt
for every 4 quarts of water.

BLACK PEPPER
in recipes is always freshly ground.

CHILES
require protective gloves
when handling.

CHEESES
should be grated just before using.

ZEST CITRUS FRUITS
by removing the colored part of
the rind only (avoid the bitter white pith).
For strips, use a vegetable peeler. For
grated zest, we prefer using a rasplike
Microplane zester, which results
in fluffier zest, so pack to measure.

TOAST SPICES
in a dry heavy skillet over moderate
heat, stirring, until fragrant and a
shade or two darker.

TOAST NUTS
in a shallow baking pan in a 350°F oven
until golden, 5 to 10 minutes.

TOAST SEEDS
as you would toast spices or nuts.

PEEL a TOMATO or PEACH
by cutting an X in the end opposite
the stem, then immersing in boiling water
(10 seconds for a tomato or 15 seconds
for a peach). Transfer it to ice water
and then peel.

INTRODUCTION

*L*ast year, hundreds of recipes were developed in *Gourmet's* test kitchens, so even if you're an avid *Gourmet* reader, you've probably overlooked more than a few great dishes. Now that you have a year's worth of recipes in hand, we know you'll be inspired to cook.

As you flip through these pages trying to figure out "what's for dinner?" or "what shall I serve on Saturday night?" you might be surprised to know that *Gourmet's* food editors also have to look for inspiration. Searching for fabulous food ideas is an ongoing quest, but constant "eating out" is only part of the job. Every year, each editor goes on a research trip to study with the best teachers in the world. Recently, Alexis Touchet traveled throughout Thailand with Tony Tan; Lori Powell studied at Darina Allen's Ballymaloe Cooking School in Ireland; and Shelley Wiseman traversed the Spanish Basque countryside, attending home cooking classes as well as two dinners hosted by gastronomic societies. Before heading home, our weary food warriors stuffed their suitcases with the likes of fish sauce, prickly ash (a Thai herb), alcoholic-laced chocolates, cheeses, sea salt, peppercorns, smoked paprika, *Pacharan* (a berry and anise apperitif), and, despite its heft, a Spanish *cazuelas*, and more. Everything landed in *Gourmet's* kitchens for everyone to look over, sniff, taste, and eventually use in their recipes. In fact, *anytime* a food editor goes *anywhere*, there is plenty of such loot. Just this week, Ian Knauer brought in some of his family's honey from their farm in Pennsylvania. No doubt, before long there will be honey dishes to taste.

Aside from ingredients, products, and tools, a constant stream of food experts make their way to our kitchens. Of course, New York City chefs are more than willing to stop by to share their secrets. Back in the fall, Mario Batali left his stove at Babbo in the Village to demonstrate the fine art of making *pappardelle bolognese*, and The Harrison's chef-proprietor, Jimmy Bradley, and his executive chef, Joey Campanaro, came from TriBeCa to cook up some fried clams ("strips, not bellies"). Earlier in the year, Dave Pasternack ambled across Broadway, leaving his kitchen at Esca, to reveal the wonders of Dungeness crabs.

But several other cities act as a constant source of inspiration too. San Francisco is certainly one of them, and this food mecca is featured here in this year's Cuisines of the World section. Everyone in the kitchen and several staff members happily journeyed cross-country to taste their way across town from one gastronomic neighborhood to another. Turn to page 11 to see what they brought home.

Conversely, sometimes it takes a highly unusual, little-known location to get the creative juices flowing. One of this year's wonderful surprises is a menu inspired by Quebec's Ice Hotel, where everything—table, chairs, goblets, and bowls—is made of ice. Turn to Alexis Touchet's *Dinner under Glace* (page 63), where the themes of water (scallops), ice (chilled pea broth with lemon cream in ice bowls), and fire (individual chocolate raspberry baked Alaskas) would make any French Canadian proud.

And you won't want to miss Lori Powell's inspired baked eggs and mushrooms in ham crisps (page 171). When asked how she came up with such a clever idea, she smiled. It seems she made frizzled bacon in muffin cups for another menu and discovered that ham makes a nifty holder. She simply tucked this information away for her next breakfast, this year's *A Grand Rising*.

Yes, perhaps you've missed a few fabulous dishes from 2002. Better have another look. It's all here.

FROM *the* EDITORS OF GOURMET BOOKS

the flavors of SAN FRANCISCO

W E HAVE A SIMPLE METHOD for choosing which cities will be the focus of our special issues at *Gourmet*: We gather around a table and vote on where we want to spend time. It took all of a second to decide that our first one-city issue would be about Paris, and when we determined that the second annual issue should center on an American town, we instantly knew which one it would be. Other cities may have chicer shops, more elegant hotels and fancier restaurants, but when it comes to cooking, no place in America is more exciting than San Francisco.

Climate has something to do with this; few places on earth offer a more nurturing environment. San Francisco, where it is rarely hot and never cold, virtually defines the word "temperate," and plants filled with flavor come leaping out of the ground all year round.

History has played its part as well. The indigenous population had been eating well for centuries when the first settlers arrived. Unlike the austere Puritans who landed at Plymouth Rock, these were more sybaritic people from the south, and they brought with them their native foods. Then, during the nineteenth century, San Francisco was propelled into a food frenzy as people, wild for

gold, hungry for adventure and eager to eat, flooded into the region. This time they came from the far corners of the world, bringing with them soy sauce, chiles, garlic and sourdough, and while most eventually departed, they left a changed city in their wake.

It was a city that insisted on eating well. While less fortunate Americans were content with tough slabs of beef and overcooked vegetables, the people of San Francisco were sitting down to deviled crab, stuffed artichokes and bacon-studded oyster omelets. Most Americans were getting silly on rough distilled alcohol while San Franciscans were cultivating their vines and brewing bountiful harvests into wine. The twentieth century brought a whole new food revolution, called California Cuisine, that has dramatically changed the way America eats. When we contemplated producing an entire issue to honor this wonderful city, we knew it would be pure pleasure.

Still, when *Gourmet*'s staff descended on San Francisco, we found a surprise around every corner. Even though we had heard about the fabulous farmers' markets, we were unprepared for the vast cornucopia that spills across the sidewalks each week. To a cook, San Francisco is a kind of earthly paradise, and as we fanned out across the city, eating in restaurants and romping through the markets, we had a hard time deciding exactly just what to cook.

In the end, we decided to offer a potpourri of the city's history. We began with an homage to the Ligurian immigrants who settled in North Beach at the turn of the century. The food of Liguria is more refined than the raucous southern Italian dishes so often found in eastern American cities, and our San Francisco Celebration is all about elegant restraint and gentle flavors.

There's history in our other menu as well. Wandering the streets, we found ourselves indulging in the old-time restaurants that are so cherished in San Francisco and imagining ourselves in a film noir. The result is a dinner fit for *The Thin Man*, a refined meal that refers to the past while looking forward. It begins, of course, with Martinis and concludes with rum currant ice cream and cinnamon chocolate "cigarettes."

San Francisco is a city so steeped in history that a curious visitor is constantly bumping into the past. Dishes invented 150 years ago are still eaten with great gusto here, and you can still find Hangtown Fry on menus all over town. Every tourist goes down to the Marina to drink Irish coffee and to sit out on the piers to indulge in crab Louis, the great American salad that is one of the city's gifts to the world. And nowhere else on earth can you order Joe's Special, a dish invented on the spur of the moment one hungry night many years ago, which has made people happy ever since.

You'll find recipes for all these dishes in this section. You'll also learn how to deal with one San Francisco native that has been terrorizing American kitchens for years. If you've been suffering from artichoke angst—and who among us has not?—fear no more; our cooking class tames this thorny vegetable once and for all.

One word of warning: These recipes should be taken in small doses. Too much, too soon, and you will soon find yourself looking westward, dreaming of San Francisco.

Ruth Reichl
Editor in Chief

Celebration

Serves 8

CLAMS OREGANATA
Bernardus Monterey County Sauvignon Blanc '00

WALNUT AND PANCETTA
PANSOTI WITH ASPARAGUS
IN PARMESAN BROTH
Valley of the Moon Sonoma County Sangiovese '99

ROAST LEG OF LAMB ON
A BED OF POTATOES
AND WILTED GREENS

STUFFED BABY BELL PEPPERS
Vietti Barbaresco Masseria '98

SNOW EGGS WITH
PISTACHIO CUSTARD AND
CHOCOLATE DRIZZLE

Merryvale Antigua

CLAMS OREGANATA

Serves 8
Active time: 50 min   Start to finish: 1¼ hr

2 garlic cloves, minced
¼ cup extra-virgin olive oil
4 canned whole plum tomatoes, drained, seeded, and coarsely chopped
2 tablespoons minced fresh oregano
3 lb very small (1-inch) hard-shelled clams such as Manila clams or cockles, scrubbed well
½ cup toasted bread crumbs (recipe follows)
1 teaspoon finely grated fresh lemon zest

Cook garlic in oil in a deep 4- to 6-quart heavy pot over moderately low heat, stirring, until garlic is fragrant, about 1 minute. Stir in tomatoes and 1 tablespoon oregano and cook, stirring occasionally, until tomatoes break down, 4 to 5 minutes. Season with pepper. Add clams, stirring well to coat, then cover pot tightly and increase heat to moderately high. Cook, stirring once, until clams open, 5 to 7 minutes. (Discard any clams that have not opened after 7 minutes.)

While clams are cooking, toss together bread crumbs, zest, and remaining tablespoon oregano. Divide clams and pan juices among 8 shallow bowls, then sprinkle with bread crumbs. Serve immediately.

Cooks' note:
• Larger hard-shelled clams such as littlenecks (2 to 2½ inches in diameter) can be used, but cooking time will increase to 8 to 10 minutes.

TOASTED BREAD CRUMBS

Makes about 2 cups
Active time: 10 min   Start to finish: 25 min

These crumbs are used in both the clams oreganata and the stuffed baby bell peppers in this menu. Leftover crumbs are delicious sprinkled over pasta.

3 cups fine fresh sourdough bread crumbs
¼ cup extra-virgin olive oil
   Fine sea salt to taste

Preheat oven to 350°F.
Spread crumbs in a shallow baking pan and bake in middle of oven, stirring occasionally, until golden,

10 to 15 minutes. Transfer crumbs to a bowl, then drizzle with oil and season with sea salt. Stir until crumbs are coated.

Cooks' note:
• Crumbs can be made 1 day ahead and kept, covered, at room temperature.

WALNUT AND PANCETTA PANSOTI WITH ASPARAGUS IN PARMESAN BROTH

Serves 8
Active time: 1¾ hr   Start to finish: 2¾ hr

The plump ravioli called pansoti ("little bellies"), a Ligurian specialty, are often dressed with a walnut sauce. We strayed from tradition a bit and tucked the walnuts into the filling instead.

Be sure to buy pancetta that's well marbled: If it's too lean, it won't render enough fat to flavor the filling. Also, brown the onions well—the caramelization lends a depth and richness that's essential to this dish.

For pansoti *and sauce*
1 (3-oz) piece pancetta (Italian unsmoked cured bacon; not lean), finely chopped (⅔ cup)
1 tablespoon olive oil
1 large onion, finely chopped
¾ teaspoon dried marjoram, crumbled
½ cup walnuts (2 oz), finely chopped
2 tablespoons finely chopped fresh flat-leaf parsley
¼ teaspoon salt
¼ teaspoon black pepper
2 cups water
⅛ teaspoon dried hot red pepper flakes
1 (3- by 2-inch) rind from a wedge of Parmigiano-Reggiano
24 (3½-inch) fresh pasta squares (page 18)
For asparagus
1½ cups asparagus tips (from 2 lb asparagus), halved lengthwise
1 teaspoon extra-virgin olive oil

Accompaniment: **grated Parmigiano-Reggiano**

Make pansoti *filling:*
Cook pancetta in oil in a large heavy skillet over

moderately low heat, stirring frequently, until golden and fat is rendered, 10 to 12 minutes. Add onion and marjoram and cook, stirring occasionally, until onion is well browned, 10 to 15 minutes. Remove from heat and transfer half of mixture to a 2-quart saucepan and remaining half to a bowl. Stir walnuts, parsley, ⅛ teaspoon salt, and pepper into mixture in bowl. Cool filling.

Make sauce:

Add water, red pepper flakes, and cheese rind to pancetta mixture in saucepan and simmer briskly, uncovered, until reduced to about 1 cup, about 12 minutes. Pour through a fine sieve into a bowl and stir in remaining ⅛ teaspoon salt.

Form pansoti*:*

Place 1 level teaspoon filling in center of 1 pasta square, keeping remaining squares covered tightly with plastic wrap. Moisten edges of pasta square with water and fold in half to form a triangle, pressing around filling to force out air (air pockets increase the chance of *pansoti* breaking during cooking) and then pressing edges to seal. Transfer to a dry kitchen towel. Make more *pansoti* in same manner.

Cook asparagus and pansoti*:*

Cook asparagus tips in a small saucepan of salted boiling water (see Tips, page 8) until crisp-tender, about 2 minutes. Drain in a sieve and plunge into a

bowl of ice and cold water to stop cooking. Drain and pat dry.

Bring a 6-quart pot of salted water to a boil, then add *pansoti* and cook at a strong simmer, gently stirring once or twice, until tender, 3 to 5 minutes.

While *pansoti* are boiling, cook asparagus tips in oil in a small skillet over low heat until heated through, 1 to 2 minutes.

Heat sauce in a 12-inch skillet over moderate heat until hot. Transfer *pansoti* with a slotted spoon to sauce and cook over moderate heat, stirring gently, 1 minute. Transfer *pansoti* to plates with slotted spoon, then top with some sauce and sprinkle with asparagus tips.

Cooks' notes:
- *Pansoti* can be formed (but not cooked) 1 day ahead. Arrange in 1 layer in a kitchen-towel-lined shallow baking pan and tightly cover with plastic wrap, then chill.
- If you don't have time to make fresh pasta, you can use wonton wrappers (thawed if frozen), but the flavor and texture won't be as good.
- Sauce can be made 1 day ahead and cooled, uncovered, then chilled, covered.
- Asparagus tips can be boiled and refreshed 1 day ahead and chilled in a sealed plastic bag along with a paper towel to absorb excess moisture. (Asparagus stalks can be used for a puréed soup.)

FRESH PASTA SQUARES

Makes about 24 (3½-inch) squares
Active time: 1 hr   Start to finish: 2 hr

It's important to make this tender fresh pasta into
pansoti *as soon as you have cut the dough into*
squares: The squares dry out quickly and become
difficult to seal.

  1 cup cake flour (not self-rising)
¼ cup all-purpose flour plus additional
     for kneading
½ teaspoon salt
  2 large egg yolks
1½ tablespoons extra-virgin olive oil
  4 tablespoons water

Special equipment: **a pasta maker**

Make dough:
   Blend all ingredients in a food processor until
mixture just begins to form a ball. Knead dough on a
lightly floured surface, incorporating only as much
additional flour as necessary to keep dough from sticking, until smooth and elastic, 6 to 8 minutes. Wrap
dough in plastic wrap and let stand 1 hour.
   Roll out dough:
   Set smooth rollers of pasta machine at widest setting. Cut dough into 4 pieces and keep 3 covered.
Flatten unwrapped piece of dough into a rectangle and
feed through rollers. Fold rectangle in half and feed
through rollers 8 more times, folding in half each time
and dusting with flour as necessary to prevent sticking.
   Turn dial to next (narrower) setting and feed dough
through without folding. Continue to feed dough
through without folding, making space between rollers
narrower each time, until narrowest setting is used. Cut
rolled-out dough into 3½-inch squares. Gather trimmings into a ball and wrap in plastic wrap. Transfer
squares to a wax-paper-lined baking sheet and cover
with plastic wrap. Roll out and cut remaining dough in
same manner, then repeat with trimmings.

   Cooks' note:
• **Pasta dough, though best used immediately, can be**
  made (but not rolled out) 1 day ahead and chilled,
  wrapped in plastic wrap. Bring dough to room
  temperature before rolling out.

ROAST LEG OF LAMB ON A BED OF POTATOES AND WILTED GREENS

Serves 8
Active time: 45 min   Start to finish: 2¾ hr

  1 (6- to 8-lb) leg of lamb, aitchbone removed
     by butcher and leg left untied
  3 large garlic cloves, 2 thinly sliced and
     1 minced
  1 tablespoon chopped fresh thyme
  2 teaspoons chopped fresh rosemary
  4 lb yellow-fleshed potatoes
  7 tablespoons extra-virgin olive oil
  4 teaspoons salt
  1 teaspoon black pepper
  2 tablespoons honey
1¼ lb mixed tender greens (16 cups) such
     as arugula, *mizuna*, kale, or dandelion,
     tough stems or ribs removed

   Preheat oven to 350°F. Trim all fat and silver skin
from lamb. Cut small slits all over lamb with a sharp
knife and put a slice of garlic and a pinch of thyme and
rosemary into each slit.
   Peel potatoes and thinly slice about ¹⁄₁₆ inch thick
with a *mandoline* or other manual slicer, then toss with
4 tablespoons oil, 1½ teaspoons salt, and ½ teaspoon
pepper in a large bowl. Spread potatoes evenly in a
17- by 12- by 2-inch casserole. Put lamb on top of potatoes, then rub with honey and sprinkle with remaining
2½ teaspoons salt and ½ teaspoon pepper.
   Roast lamb in middle of oven 1 hour, then drizzle
with 1 tablespoon oil. Continue to roast until an instant-
read thermometer inserted into thickest part of lamb (do
not touch bone) registers 135°F for medium-rare, 30 to
45 minutes more. Let lamb stand, covered loosely with
foil, 15 minutes.
   While lamb stands, heat remaining 2 tablespoons
oil in a 4- to 6-quart heavy pot over moderately high
heat until hot but not smoking, then sauté minced garlic, stirring, until fragrant, about 30 seconds. Add a
handful of greens and sauté, tossing with tongs, then
add more greens as preceding ones wilt and sauté until
all greens are wilted and tender, 5 to 6 minutes total.
Season with salt and pepper.
   Transfer lamb to a cutting board and carve, then
serve with potatoes and greens.

STUFFED BABY BELL PEPPERS

Serves 8
Active time: 50 min   Start to finish: 2 hr

You can use 4 small regular bell peppers (1½ lb total) instead of the 24 baby bell peppers, but you'll need to halve them lengthwise and make 1½ times the filling.

For filling
- 1 medium onion, chopped
- 2 anchovy fillets, rinsed, patted dry, and finely chopped
- 2 tablespoons olive oil
- ¾ cup toasted bread crumbs (page 16)
- 1 cup whole-milk ricotta
- ⅓ cup finely grated Parmigiano-Reggiano (1 oz)
- 2 tablespoons drained capers, rinsed, patted dry, and chopped
- 2 large eggs, lightly beaten
- 3 tablespoons finely chopped fresh flat-leaf parsley

For peppers
- 1½ lb baby red and yellow bell peppers (2 inches in diameter; 24)
- ½ cup water
- 1 tablespoon olive oil

Make filling:

Cook onion and anchovies in oil in a heavy skillet over moderate heat, stirring frequently, until onion is golden, about 8 minutes. (Anchovies will dissolve.) Transfer to a bowl and stir in bread crumbs, cheeses, capers, eggs, and parsley until combined well.

Stuff and bake peppers:

Preheat oven to 350°F.

Cut tops from baby peppers (keep stems on tops) and reserve. Cut a very thin slice from bottom of each pepper so it can stand upright (don't worry if you make a hole in bottom). Scoop out and discard seeds, then divide filling among peppers. Cover with reserved tops and arrange peppers upright in an oiled baking dish. Add water to dish and drizzle peppers with oil.

Bake, uncovered, in middle of oven until peppers are tender and filling is puffed, 50 to 60 minutes.

Cooks' note:
• Peppers can be stuffed 1 day ahead and chilled, covered. Bring to room temperature before baking.

SNOW EGGS WITH PISTACHIO CUSTARD AND CHOCOLATE DRIZZLE

Serves 8 (makes 16 meringue "eggs")
Active time: 2 hr   Start to finish: 10½ hr (includes chilling)

This dessert, called sciummette *("little sponges") in Liguria, is the Italian version of the French* oeufs à la neige. *One look at these fluffy ovals of meringue will tell you where the name comes from.*

- ½ cup plus 2 tablespoons shelled unsalted pistachios (not dyed red, preferably raw)
- 1 cup sugar
- 1 qt whole milk
- 4 large eggs, separated
- 1 teaspoon fresh lemon juice
- 3 drops almond extract
- 2 oz fine-quality bittersweet chocolate (not unsweetened), finely chopped

Peel and dry pistachios:

Preheat oven to 350°F.

Drop nuts into boiling water and cook 2 minutes. Drain in a colander and transfer to a bowl of ice and water to stop cooking. Drain in colander again. Peel off skins and pat nuts dry, then spread in 1 layer in a shallow baking pan.

Bake pistachios in middle of oven until dry and lightly toasted, about 7 minutes, then cool. Coarsely chop 2 tablespoons nuts and leave remaining nuts whole.

Make pistachio cream:

Finely grind whole pistachios with 2 tablespoons sugar in a food processor. Add 3 tablespoons milk and process to a paste. Blend in 5 tablespoons milk and transfer pistachio cream to a bowl. Chill, covered, 8 hours.

Make "eggs":

Whisk together 2 tablespoons sugar and remaining 3½ cups milk in a deep 12-inch skillet and bring to a bare simmer (milk should steam but not bubble).

While milk is heating, beat whites with lemon juice and a pinch of salt in a large bowl with an electric mixer at medium speed until they just hold soft peaks. Gradually beat in ½ cup plus 2 tablespoons sugar, a little at a time, and beat until meringue just holds stiff peaks.

Using an oval-shaped ice cream scoop or an oval soupspoon, form 8 meringue "eggs," gently dropping them as formed into milk mixture (keep milk at a bare simmer). Poach meringues until set on bottom, about 2 minutes, then carefully turn over and poach until set throughout, about 2 minutes more. Transfer with a slotted spoon to a plastic-wrap-lined shallow baking pan and make 8 more meringues in same manner.

Make custard:

Pour poaching liquid through a very fine sieve into a large glass measure. Whisk together yolks, remaining 2 tablespoons sugar, and a pinch of salt in a 2-quart heavy saucepan, then slowly add poaching liquid, whisking constantly. Cook custard over moderately low heat, stirring constantly with a wooden spoon, until it's thick enough to coat back of spoon and registers 170 to 175°F on an instant-read thermometer (do not boil).

Pour custard into a metal bowl and stir in pistachio cream and almond extract. Set bowl in a larger bowl of ice and cold water and cool custard, stirring occasionally. Pour custard through very fine sieve into another bowl, pressing on and discarding solids.

Assemble dessert:

Melt chocolate in a small metal bowl set over a small saucepan of barely simmering water, stirring occasionally, until smooth.

Pour custard into 8 shallow bowls or rimmed plates and arrange meringues on top. Drizzle chocolate over meringues and custard and sprinkle with chopped pistachios.

Cooks' notes:
- Using raw (not roasted) pistachios gives the custard the best color and a true pistachio flavor.
- Meringues and custard can be made 6 hours ahead and chilled separately, covered. Bring to room temperature before serving.
- The egg whites in this recipe will not be fully cooked. If salmonella is a problem in your area, you can use reconstituted powdered egg whites such as Just Whites.

Food Noir

Serves 6

CLASSIC MARTINIS

RUMAKI

DEVILED CRAB
WITH SHERRY SAUCE

Charles Krug Family Reserve Napa Valley
Chardonnay '99

PANCETTA-STUDDED BEEF
TENDERLOIN

WILD RICE
AND TOASTED ALMOND
PILAF

SNOW PEAS WITH
LEMON HERB
BUTTER

Beaucanon Napa Valley Reserve Cabernet
Sauvignon '99

RUM CURRANT
ICE CREAM

CINNAMON CHOCOLATE
"CIGARETTES"

CLASSIC MARTINIS

Makes 2 drinks
Active time: 5 min   Start to finish: 5 min

6 oz gin (¾ cup)
¾ oz vermouth (1½ tablespoons)
3 cups ice cubes

Garnish: **pimiento-stuffed green olives**
or lemon twists
Special equipment: **a cocktail shaker**

Fill 2 (4-ounce) Martini glasses with ice water and let stand 1 minute (to chill glasses). Discard ice water and dry glasses. Shake together gin, vermouth, and ice cubes in cocktail shaker, then strain into glasses.

RUMAKI

Makes 24 hors d'oeuvres
Active time: 20 min   Start to finish: 1½ hr

We can thank Vic Bergeron—owner of Trader Vic's restaurant, in San Francisco—for bringing rumaki into mainstream dining culture. He claimed that this delicious hors d'oeuvre came from Hawaii, with Chinese roots and a Japanese name.

¼ lb chicken livers, trimmed and rinsed
¼ cup soy sauce
1 tablespoon finely grated peeled
fresh ginger
2 tablespoons packed light brown sugar
½ teaspoon curry powder
12 canned water chestnuts, drained
and halved horizontally
8 bacon slices (½ lb), cut crosswise
into thirds

Special equipment: **24 wooden toothpicks**

Cut chicken livers into 24 (roughly ½-inch) pieces. Stir together soy sauce, ginger, brown sugar, and curry powder. Add livers and water chestnuts and toss to coat. Marinate, covered and chilled, 1 hour.

While livers marinate, soak toothpicks in cold water 1 hour. Drain well.

Preheat broiler.

Remove livers and chestnuts from marinade and discard marinade. Place 1 piece of bacon on a work surface and put 1 piece of liver and 1 chestnut in center. Wrap bacon around liver and chestnut and secure with a toothpick. Make 23 more rumaki in same manner.

Broil rumaki on rack of a broiler pan 2 inches from heat, turning once, until bacon is crisp and livers are cooked but still slightly pink inside (unwrap 1 to check for doneness), 5 to 6 minutes. Serve immediately.

DEVILED CRAB WITH SHERRY SAUCE

Serves 6
Active time: 20 min   Start to finish: 25 min

2 lb cooked king crab legs in shell, thawed
if frozen and shells split lengthwise
½ stick (¼ cup) unsalted butter
2 tablespoons all-purpose flour
1 cup whole milk
1 large garlic clove, lightly crushed
2 large egg yolks
⅓ cup medium-dry Sherry
½ teaspoon dry mustard
⅛ teaspoon freshly grated nutmeg
⅛ teaspoon cayenne
½ teaspoon salt
2 tablespoons finely chopped fresh
flat-leaf parsley
¼ cup fine dry bread crumbs
¼ cup finely grated
Parmigiano-Reggiano (½ oz)

Preheat oven to 450°F.

Remove crabmeat from shell, discarding cartilage, and cut meat into ½-inch pieces.

Melt 2 tablespoons butter in a 1½-quart heavy saucepan over moderately low heat, then add flour and cook, whisking, 2 minutes. Add milk in a slow stream, whisking, then add garlic and bring to a boil, whisking. Reduce heat and simmer, whisking, until béchamel is thickened, about 3 minutes. Remove from heat and discard garlic.

Whisk together yolks, Sherry, mustard, nutmeg, cayenne, and salt in a bowl. Add hot béchamel in a slow stream, whisking. Pour mixture into saucepan and cook over very low heat, whisking constantly, until an instant-read thermometer registers 160°F, about 2 min-

PANCETTA-STUDDED BEEF TENDERLOIN

Serves 6
Active time: 20 min   Start to finish: 1¼ hr

For beef
> 1 (3-lb) trimmed and tied beef tenderloin
>   at room temperature
> 2 oz thinly sliced pancetta (Italian unsmoked
>   cured bacon), cut into ⅓-inch pieces
> 2 teaspoons kosher salt
> 2 teaspoons black pepper
> 2 tablespoons vegetable oil

For sauce
> ¼ cup finely chopped shallot
> ½ cup dry red wine
> ¼ cup dry Marsala wine
> ¾ cup beef or veal *demiglace*
> 2 tablespoons red currant jelly
> 1½ tablespoons unsalted butter, cut into bits
> ¼ teaspoon salt
> ⅛ teaspoon black pepper

Roast beef:
Preheat oven to 425°F.

Pat beef dry and cut ½-inch-deep slits at 1-inch
intervals all over roast, then insert 1 piece of pancetta
into each slit. Sprinkle beef with kosher salt and pepper. Heat oil in a 12-inch heavy skillet over high heat
until just smoking, then brown beef on all sides,
5 minutes. Transfer to a roasting pan, reserving skillet.

Roast beef in middle of oven until an instant-read
thermometer inserted diagonally 2 inches into center
registers 120°F, about 25 minutes. Transfer beef to a
cutting board and let stand, loosely covered with foil,
25 minutes. (Beef will continue to cook as it stands,
reaching 130°F for medium-rare.)

Make sauce while beef stands:
Heat reserved skillet over moderately high heat
until oil is hot but not smoking, then sauté shallot until
golden, about 2 minutes. Add red wine and Marsala
and deglaze skillet by boiling, stirring and scraping up
brown bits, until liquid is reduced by one third. Add
demiglace and jelly and briskly simmer, whisking, until
jelly is incorporated, about 2 minutes. Add butter, 1 bit
at a time, whisking until incorporated, then remove
from heat. Whisk in salt and pepper. Pour sauce
through a fine-mesh sieve into a bowl, pressing
on solids.

utes. Remove from heat and gently stir in crabmeat and
parsley. Divide mixture among 6 (4-ounce) ramekins.

Melt remaining 2 tablespoons butter and cool
slightly. Stir together melted butter, bread crumbs, and
cheese with a fork, then sprinkle over crab. Put
ramekins in a shallow baking pan and bake in upper
third of oven until crab is bubbling and crumbs are
golden brown, about 5 minutes.

Cooks' note:
• Deviled crab can be prepared (but not baked) 4 hours
  ahead and chilled, covered. Bring to room temperature
  before baking.

WILD RICE AND TOASTED ALMOND PILAF

Serves 6
Active time: 10 min   Start to finish: 1½ hr

2 cups wild rice (12 oz)
2 tablespoons olive oil
1 medium onion, finely chopped
3 cups chicken broth
4 cups water
2 teaspoons unsalted butter
1 cup sliced almonds (3½ oz)
1 teaspoon salt
¼ teaspoon black pepper

Rinse rice in a large sieve under cold water, then drain. Heat oil in a 5-quart heavy pot over moderate heat until hot but not smoking, then cook onion, stirring occasionally, until golden, about 5 minutes. Add rice and cook, stirring, until fragrant, about 3 minutes. Stir in broth and water and bring to a boil. Reduce heat to low and simmer, covered, until rice is tender (grains will split open), 1 to 1¼ hours. Drain well in sieve and transfer to a bowl.

While rice is cooking, melt butter in a 10-inch skillet over moderate heat until foam subsides, then cook almonds, stirring, until golden, about 3 minutes.

Add almonds, salt, and pepper to rice and stir gently to combine.

SNOW PEAS WITH LEMON HERB BUTTER

Serves 6
Active time: 15 min   Start to finish: 20 min

1½ tablespoons unsalted butter, softened
1 teaspoon finely grated fresh lemon zest
1 teaspoon finely chopped fresh tarragon
1 teaspoon finely chopped fresh
   flat-leaf parsley
½ teaspoon salt
¼ teaspoon black pepper
1 lb snow peas, trimmed

Stir together butter, zest, tarragon, parsley, salt, and pepper.

Cook snow peas in a 5-quart pot of boiling salted water (see Tips, page 8) until crisp-tender, about 1½ minutes, then drain well. Transfer hot snow peas to a bowl, then add lemon herb butter and toss to coat.

RUM CURRANT ICE CREAM

Makes about 1 quart
Active time: 15 min   Start to finish: 8 hr
(includes chilling and freezing)

⅓ cup dark rum
¾ cup dried currants
2 cups heavy cream
1 cup half-and-half
⅛ teaspoon salt
2 large eggs
¾ cup packed light brown sugar

Special equipment: **an ice cream maker**

Heat rum in a small saucepan until just warm, then remove from heat. Add currants and let stand, covered, 1 hour.

Bring cream, half-and-half, and salt just to a boil in a 2-quart heavy saucepan. Whisk together eggs and brown sugar in a large bowl, then add hot cream mixture in a slow stream, whisking. Pour custard into saucepan and cook over moderately low heat, stirring constantly with a wooden spoon, until thick enough to coat back of spoon and an instant-read thermometer registers 170 to 175°F, about 5 minutes (do not let boil).

Pour custard through a sieve into a bowl, then add rum and currants and cool completely, stirring occasionally. Chill, covered, until cold, at least 3 hours.

Freeze custard in ice cream maker. Transfer ice cream to an airtight container and put in freezer to harden. (Due to rum, this ice cream will have a slightly softer texture than others.)

CINNAMON CHOCOLATE "CIGARETTES"

Makes about 24 cookies
Active time: 30 min   Start to finish: 1¼ hr

- **3 large egg whites**
- **¾ cup confectioners sugar**
- **½ cup all-purpose flour**
- **5⅓ tablespoons (⅓ cup) unsalted butter, melted**
- **¼ teaspoon salt**
- **¼ teaspoon cinnamon**
- **4 oz bittersweet chocolate (not unsweetened), finely chopped**

Special equipment: **a nonstick baking pad such as Silpat (optional); a small metal offset spatula; a pencil or a chopstick**

Preheat oven to 350°F.

Whisk together all ingredients except chocolate until combined well. Working in batches of 4, drop 1 level teaspoon of batter for each cookie about 3 inches apart onto nonstick-pad-lined or buttered baking sheet, then spread each dollop of batter into a 3-inch round with offset spatula or back of a spoon.

Bake cookies 1 baking sheet at a time in middle of oven until edges are golden, 6 to 8 minutes. Working quickly, lift 1 cookie off sheet with a long flexible spatula, then roll it around pencil or chopstick to form a narrow cylinder. Immediately slide "cigarette" off pencil or chopstick and transfer to a rack to cool. Make more "cigarettes" in same manner. (If cookies become too brittle to roll, return to oven for 1 minute to soften.)

Melt chocolate in a double boiler or a metal bowl set over a saucepan of barely simmering water, stirring occasionally, then remove top of double boiler or bowl from heat.

When cookies are cool, working with 1 cookie at a time, dip ¼ inch of tip of 1 end into melted chocolate ("ash"), letting excess drip off, and place on a parchment- or wax-paper-lined baking sheet. Let stand at room temperature until chocolate sets.

Cooks' notes:
- After rolling up each cookie, press the pencil in place for a few seconds to seal the seam.
- For a professional look, after dipping the cookies into chocolate "ash," scrape that end on the side of the bowl to prevent a blob from forming.
- Cookies can be made 2 days ahead and kept in an airtight container.

CIOPPINO
San Francisco–Style Seafood Stew

Serves 6

Active time: 45 min   Start to finish: 1½ hr

*This dish was created by San Francisco's Italian and Portuguese fishermen, who "chipped in" (*cioppino*) from their daily catch to make a communal stew. Use whatever seafood looks best at the market.*

    4 large garlic cloves, minced
    2 medium onions, finely chopped
    1 Turkish bay leaf or ½ California bay leaf
    1 teaspoon dried oregano, crumbled
    1 teaspoon dried hot red pepper flakes
 1½ teaspoons salt
    ½ teaspoon black pepper
    ¼ cup olive oil
    1 green bell pepper, cut into ¼-inch dice
    2 tablespoons tomato paste
 1½ cups dry red wine
    1 (28- to 32-oz) can whole plum tomatoes,
        drained, reserving juice, and chopped
    1 cup bottled clam juice
    1 cup chicken broth
    1 (1-lb) king crab leg, thawed if frozen
   18 small (2-inch) hard-shelled clams
        (1½ lb) such as littlenecks, scrubbed
    1 lb skinless red snapper or halibut fillets,
        cut into 1½-inch pieces
    1 lb large shrimp (16 to 20), shelled
        (tails and bottom segment of shells
        left intact) and deveined
    ¾ lb sea scallops, tough muscle removed
        from side of each if necessary
    ¼ cup finely chopped fresh flat-leaf parsley
    3 tablespoons finely chopped fresh basil

Garnish: shredded fresh basil leaves and
    small whole leaves
Accompaniment: focaccia or sourdough bread

Cook garlic, onions, bay leaf, oregano, and red pepper flakes with salt and pepper in oil in an 8-quart heavy pot over moderate heat, stirring, until onions are softened, about 5 minutes. Stir in bell pepper and tomato paste and cook, stirring, 1 minute. Add wine and boil until reduced by about half, 5 to 6 minutes. Add tomatoes with their juice, clam juice, and broth and simmer, covered, 30 minutes. Season with salt and pepper.

While stew is simmering, hack crab leg through shell into 2- to 3-inch pieces with a large heavy knife. Add crab pieces and clams to stew and simmer, covered, until clams just open, 5 to 10 minutes, checking every minute after 5 minutes and transferring opened clams to a bowl with tongs or a slotted spoon. (Discard any unopened clams after 10 minutes.) Lightly season fish fillets, shrimp, and scallops with salt and add to stew, then simmer, covered, until just cooked through, about 5 minutes. Discard bay leaf, then return clams to pot and gently stir in parsley and basil.

Serve *cioppino* immediately in large soup bowls.

Cooks' note:
• The stew—without seafood—can be made 1 day ahead. Cool, uncovered, then chill, covered. Bring to a simmer before adding seafood.

GREEN GODDESS DRESSING

Makes about 1¼ cups

Active time: 10 min   Start to finish: 10 min

The William Archer play The Green Goddess *had a run in San Francisco in the 1920s. Star George Arliss, dining at the Palace Hotel, was served a specially created salad with this green-hued dressing.*

    1 cup mayonnaise
    3 minced flat anchovy fillets
    1 chopped scallion
    2 tablespoons chopped fresh flat-leaf parsley
    2 tablespoons chopped fresh chives
    1 tablespoon tarragon vinegar
    1 teaspoon chopped fresh tarragon

Purée all ingredients in a food processor until smooth and season with salt and pepper.

CHOP SUEY

Serves 6
Active time: 1¼ hr   Start to finish: 1¼ hr

Chinese viceroy Li Hung Chang, while visiting
San Francisco's Palace Hotel in the 1890s, requested
vegetables with a bit of meat "job suey," or
"in fine pieces," and chef Joseph Herder obliged.

  2 minced garlic cloves
  1 tablespoon plus 1 teaspoon oyster sauce
  ½ tablespoon soy sauce
  1 teaspoon salt
1½ teaspoons cornstarch
  1 lb pork tenderloin, halved lengthwise,
     then cut crosswise into ⅛-inch-thick strips
  4 tablespoons vegetable oil
  2 celery ribs, cut diagonally into
     ¼-inch-thick slices
  6 oz snow peas, cut diagonally into
     ¼-inch-thick slices
  ¼ lb mushrooms, cut into
     ¼-inch-thick slices
  1 onion, halved lengthwise and cut
     lengthwise into ¼-inch thick strips
  1 green bell pepper, cut lengthwise
     into ¼-inch-thick strips and halve
     strips crosswise
  1 (5-oz) can sliced water chestnuts,
     rinsed and drained
  1 (5-oz) can sliced bamboo shoots,
     rinsed and drained
  ¼ lb mung bean sprouts, rinsed
     and drained
  ½ lb bok choy, leaves and ribs separated,
     and each cut into ¼-inch-thick slices
  1 tablespoon water
  ¼ cup chicken broth

Accompaniment: **cooked rice**

Stir together garlic, 1 tablespoon oyster sauce, soy
sauce, salt, and ½ teaspoon cornstarch in a large bowl,
then add pork and marinate 15 minutes.
Heat a wok over high heat until a bead of water
dropped onto cooking surface evaporates immediately.
Drizzle 1 teaspoon oil around side of wok, then stir-fry
celery, seasoning with salt, until crisp-tender, about
2 minutes and transfer to a large bowl.

Cook remaining vegetables in batches:
Reheat wok and stir-fry each remaining vegetable
separately in same manner, adding 1 teaspoon oil to
wok before each batch and seasoning with salt as
cooked. (Allow only 1 minute for bean sprouts to
cook, and when stir-frying bok choy, begin with ribs,
then add leaves and water after 1 minute.) Transfer
vegetables as cooked to bowl with celery.
Stir together broth, remaining teaspoon oyster
sauce, and remaining teaspoon cornstarch.
Reheat wok over high heat until a bead of water
dropped onto cooking surface evaporates immediately.
Drizzle remaining tablespoon oil around side of wok,
then stir-fry pork until just cooked through, about
2 minutes.
Return all vegetables to wok and toss. Make a well
in center, then stir broth mixture and add to well. Bring
sauce to a boil, undisturbed, then stir to combine
with pork and vegetables. Serve immediately with
cooked rice.

CRAB LOUIS

Serves 4 (main course)
Active time: 20 min   Start to finish: 30 min

At least two San Francisco establishments—
Solari's restaurant and the St. Francis Hotel—have
laid claim to this classic. Both places reportedly
started serving crab Louis around 1915.

  1 cup mayonnaise
  ¼ cup ketchup-based chili sauce
  ¼ cup minced scallion
  2 tablespoons minced green olives
  2 teaspoons fresh lemon juice
  1 teaspoon Worcestershire sauce
  1 teaspoon drained bottled horseradish
1½ lb jumbo lump crabmeat, picked over
     Shredded iceberg lettuce

Garnish: **capers, tomato wedges, hard-boiled**
   egg, and lemon

Whisk together mayonnaise, chili sauce, scallion,
olives, lemon juice, Worcestershire sauce, horseradish,
and salt and pepper to taste in a bowl.
Divide crabmeat among 4 plates lined with
shredded lettuce. Top with garnishes and serve
with dressing.

IRISH COFFEE

Makes 1 drink
Active time: 5 min   Start to finish: 15 min

Created at an Irish airport by chef Joe Sheridan for passengers who made an emergency landing there, this recipe was then passed along to a bartender at San Francisco's old Buena Vista Hotel.

¼ **cup chilled heavy cream**
2 **teaspoons sugar**
1½ **oz Irish whiskey (3 tablespoons)**
¾ **cup hot strong brewed coffee**

Whip cream with sugar in a small bowl until it just holds stiff peaks.

Pour whiskey into a mug or Irish coffee glass, then add enough coffee to fill it three-fourths full. Spoon whipped cream on top.

HANGTOWN FRY
Fried-Oyster Omelet

Serves 1
Active time: 15 min   Start to finish: 15 min

This omelet hails from Hangtown, a town northeast of Sacramento that was named for the notorious hangings once held there (it's now called Placerville). The dish seems to have come into existence during the Gold Rush, as the high-priced breakfast of a lucky miner, and later became a specialty at San Francisco's Tadich Grill. It is traditionally served with bacon.

¼ **cup all-purpose flour**
¼ **cup ground saltine crackers (about 8)**
4 **large eggs**
4 **shucked oysters**
2 **tablespoons unsalted butter**

Put flour and ground crackers in 2 separate bowls and season flour with salt and pepper. Beat 1 egg with a fork in a small bowl and season with salt and pepper.

Pat oysters dry and coat 1 at a time, in flour, then egg, and then cracker crumbs, shaking off excess between each coating. Transfer oysters to a plate.

Beat remaining 3 eggs with a fork in a bowl. Heat butter in an 8-inch nonstick skillet over moderate heat until foam subsides, then fry oysters, turning over once, until golden, about 2 minutes total, transferring with tongs to paper towels to drain.

Reduce heat to moderately low, then add eggs to skillet and cook, stirring gently, until half set, about 1 minute. Season with salt and pepper. Arrange oysters over half of eggs opposite skillet handle, then cook until eggs are just set, about 1 minute more. Fold omelet over oysters and invert onto a plate.

JOE'S SPECIAL
Scrambled Eggs and Beef

Serves 4 to 6 (brunch or supper)
Active time: 45 min   Start to finish: 45 min

This meal was supposedly concocted at a spot called New Joe's, on Columbus Street, as late-night fuel for 1920s musicians.

2 **medium onions, finely chopped**
3 **garlic cloves, finely chopped**
2 **tablespoons olive oil**
½ **teaspoon dried oregano, crumbled**
1½ **teaspoons salt**
½ **teaspoon black pepper**
½ **lb sliced mushrooms**
1 **lb lean ground beef chuck**
10 **oz fresh spinach, trimmed**
    and coarsely chopped
6 **large eggs**

Sauté onions and garlic in oil in a 12-inch heavy skillet over moderately high heat, stirring, until golden, about 10 minutes. Add oregano, salt, black pepper, and mushrooms and sauté, stirring, until mushrooms are golden and any liquid they give off is evaporated, about 5 minutes. Add beef and sauté, stirring and breaking up lumps, until browned, 3 to 5 minutes.

Add spinach and cook, stirring, until wilted, about 2 minutes. Beat eggs with a fork in a bowl and add to skillet, then cook, stirring, until just set, about 2 minutes.

*a*RTICHOKES stuffed with soppressata and provolone. Artichoke bottoms *alla romana* —braised, that is, in olive oil with garlic and mint. Tiny sweet ones fried to a delicate, crackly crunch. Reasons enough, we think, to tackle what might be the world's least user-friendly vegetable. Technically, it's the unopened flower bud of a giant thistle—complete with thorns; armorlike leaves (bracts); and a clump of bristly purplish petals in the middle that's called, appropriately enough, the choke. (Unharvested, an artichoke will develop into an enormous blue-violet flower.) But the artichoke's allure is obvious: an odd, haunting, sweet—almost nutty—flavor; a dense, meaty texture; and the slow ceremonial aspect of eating it leaf by leaf.

Green Globe is an old standard artichoke variety; most of the new sorts being grown today are "globe" types. In the late nineteenth century, Italian immigrants planted artichokes around Castroville, California, where they have flourished ever since. March through May is peak season, although there is another harvest in October.

The size of an artichoke, incidentally, depends on where it is on the plant. The one at the top of the central stem can be huge. So-called "baby" artichokes are a

1. We prefer this tapered shape of artichoke to the fat, round ones that you sometimes see. It should be heavy for its size, a sign of freshness. The leaves (bracts) seen here should be more tightly closed— also signifying freshness. 2. When preparing the carciofi alla romana *(page 34), begin by cutting 1 inch off the top with a knife. Use scissors to snip off the thorny tips from remaining leaves. 3. Snap off leaves until you reach the pale yellow layer. 4. Cut remaining leaves flush with top of artichoke bottom. 5. Scoop out choke. We use a melon-ball cutter because it's sharper than a spoon. 6. Trim all fibrous parts from base and side. Keep stem attached, but trim it down to its pale inner core. (To see where the core is, cut ¼-inch off the end to expose it).*

bonus crop; once the main flower bud is harvested, growers can force smaller buds to form on lateral shoots. The meaty base and tender yellow leaves of the little ones are what's sold as "artichoke hearts."

Even though regular artichokes are picked for tenderness, show no mercy when trimming them. It may seem wasteful, but you have to get down to the inner succulent leaves. Our favorite way to prepare whole artichokes is in a pressure cooker. Think twice, however, before using the one you stashed in the attic years ago. The rubber gasket deteriorates over time, which means you won't be able to seal the cooker properly. Either order a new gasket or splurge on a new cooker.

One last thing. It's commonly held that artichokes are death to wines because an enzyme they contain makes wines taste sweet. And they are often served with a vinaigrette or mayonnaise, also a problem with wine. Gerald Asher, *Gourmet*'s wine editor, suggests a moderately full-textured white Rhône varietal like a Viognier, a Marsanne, or a Roussanne, or even California's ubiquitous white Zinfandel, which usually has some sweetness anyway. —*Jane Daniels Lear*

SHAVED RAW ARTICHOKE SALAD

Serves 2 (first course)
Active time: 15 min   Start to finish: 15 min

For this salad choose a very fresh, tightly closed artichoke with no brown edges and do all the prep work right before serving to prevent discoloration.

  1 large artichoke (12 oz)
  1 lemon, halved
  1 large (2-inch-wide) very fresh *cremino* or
     white mushroom
1½ teaspoons mild extra-virgin olive oil plus
     additional for drizzling
  1 teaspoon chopped fresh flat-leaf parsley
  ¼ teaspoon kosher salt
  ⅛ teaspoon black pepper
  1 wedge Parmigiano-Reggiano for curls

Special equipment: **a melon-ball cutter and**
    a *mandoline* or other adjustable
    manual slicer

Cut off artichoke stem and discard. Cut off top inch of artichoke with a serrated knife. Bend back outer leaves until they snap off close to base, then discard several more layers of leaves in same manner until you reach pale yellow leaves with pale green tips.

Cut remaining leaves flush with top of artichoke bottom with a sharp knife, then pull out purple leaves and scoop out fuzzy choke with melon-ball cutter. Rub cut surfaces with a lemon half. Trim remaining dark green fibrous parts from base and sides of artichoke with a sharp paring knife, then rub cut surfaces with same lemon half.

Trim mushroom stem flush with cap, then rub mushroom with same lemon half. Squeeze ½ teaspoon juice from remaining lemon half into a bowl. Shave artichoke and mushroom as thinly as possible with slicer and toss immediately with lemon juice, then with oil, parsley, salt, and pepper.

Shave a few pieces of cheese on top of salads with slicer or a vegetable peeler, then drizzle with olive oil.

CARCIOFI ALLA ROMANA
Artichoke Bottoms Braised in Olive Oil
with Garlic and Mint

Serves 6 (first course or antipasto)
Active time: 1 hr   Start to finish: 1½ hr

6 large artichokes (10 to 12 oz each)
1 lemon, halved
1 cup water
⅓ cup extra-virgin olive oil
1 tablespoon finely chopped garlic
2 teaspoons kosher salt
1 tablespoon finely chopped fresh mint

Garnish: **chopped fresh mint**
Special equipment: **a melon-ball cutter**

Keep stem attached and, at opposite end, cut off top inch of 1 artichoke with a serrated knife. Bend back outer leaves until they snap off close to base, then discard several more layers of leaves in same manner until you reach pale yellow leaves with pale green tips.

Cut remaining leaves flush with top of artichoke bottom using a sharp knife, then pull out purple leaves and scoop out fuzzy choke with melon-ball cutter. Trim dark green fibrous parts from base and sides of artichoke with a sharp paring knife, then rub cut surfaces with a lemon half.

Cut ¼ inch from end of stem to expose inner core. Trim sides of stem (still attached) down to pale inner core. Rub cut surfaces with same lemon half.

Trim remaining artichokes in same manner.

Put water and oil in a 4-quart heavy pot.

Mince and mash garlic with 1 teaspoon kosher salt, then mix in mint. Rub one sixth of garlic paste into cavity of each artichoke, then stand artichokes upside down in liquid in pot. Sprinkle remaining teaspoon salt over artichokes, then simmer, covered, over low heat, until tender, 20 to 30 minutes.

Transfer artichokes to a serving dish and boil cooking liquid, whisking, until emulsified and reduced to about ⅓ cup. Pour sauce over artichokes and serve warm or at room temperature.

Cooks' note:
- Artichokes with sauce keep, covered and chilled, 2 days.

CREAM OF ARTICHOKE AND JERUSALEM ARTICHOKE SOUP

Serves 6
Active time: 30 min   Start to finish: 1 hr

This recipe calls for both artichokes and Jerusalem artichokes, which are actually an unrelated root vegetable (also called Sun Chokes).

1 lemon, halved
1½ lb artichokes (2 or 3)
½ lb Jerusalem artichokes
1 cup chopped onion
1 tablespoon chopped garlic
3 tablespoons unsalted butter
¾ teaspoon salt
½ cup dry white wine
3½ cups chicken broth
¾ cup heavy cream

Garnish: **sliced almonds, toasted**
(see Tips, page 8)

Trim regular artichokes:

Squeeze juice from 1 lemon half into a large bowl of water, then drop same half into water.

Cut off stem of 1 artichoke, then trim ¼ inch from end of stem to expose inner core. Trim sides of stem down to pale inner core, then rub with other lemon half. Drop stem into acidulated water.

Cut off top inch of same artichoke with a serrated knife. Bend back outer leaves until they snap off close to base, then discard several more layers of leaves in same manner until you reach pale yellow leaves with pale green tips. Cut off green tips.

Trim dark green fibrous parts from base and sides of artichoke with a sharp paring knife, then rub cut surfaces with lemon half.

Cut artichoke into 8 wedges, then cut out fuzzy choke and purple leaves with paring knife. Rub all cut surfaces with lemon half, then drop artichoke into acidulated water.

Prepare remaining artichokes in same manner.

Trim Jerusalem artichokes:

Peel Jerusalem artichokes with a sharp paring knife and cut into ¼-inch-thick slices.

Prepare soup:

Cook Jerusalem artichokes, onion, and garlic in butter in a 4-quart heavy pot over moderately low heat, covered, stirring occasionally, 5 minutes. Drain regular artichokes and add to pot along with salt. Cook, covered, stirring occasionally, until Jerusalem artichokes are crisp-tender, about 5 minutes. Add wine and boil, uncovered, until reduced by half, about 3 minutes. Add broth and simmer, covered, until vegetables are very tender, 20 to 25 minutes.

Purée soup in batches in a blender until very smooth, about 2 minutes (use caution when blending hot liquids). Return soup to pot and stir in cream and pepper to taste. Reheat soup, stirring.

Cooks' note:
- Soup keeps 3 days. Cool completely, uncovered, and then chill, covered.

DEEP-FRIED BABY ARTICHOKES STUFFED WITH PEPPER JACK CHEESE

Makes 24 hors d'oeuvres
Active time: 45 min   Start to finish: 1 hr

For trimming and cooking artichokes
  1 lemon, halved, plus 1 tablespoon fresh lemon juice
  12 baby artichokes (1 to 1½ lb)
  1 tablespoon all-purpose flour
  1 tablespoon olive oil
  1 tablespoon salt

For stuffing and frying artichokes
  About 1½ qt vegetable oil for deep-frying
  3 oz pepper Jack cheese, grated (¾ cup)
  2 large eggs, lightly beaten
  1 cup fine fresh bread crumbs
  ½ teaspoon salt
  ¼ teaspoon black pepper

Special equipment: a melon-ball cutter and a deep-fat thermometer

Trim and cook artichokes:

Squeeze juice from 1 lemon half into a large bowl of water, then drop same half into water.

Cut off artichoke stems and discard. Cut off top ½ inch of 1 artichoke with a serrated knife. Bend back outer leaves until they snap off close to base, then discard several more layers of leaves in same manner until you reach pale yellow leaves with pale green tips. Cut off green tips.

Trim dark green fibrous parts from base and sides of artichoke with a sharp paring knife, then rub cut surfaces with other lemon half. Drop artichoke into acidulated water.

Trim remaining artichokes in same manner.

Put 2 quarts water in a 4-quart pot and whisk in flour. Whisk in oil, salt, and remaining tablespoon lemon juice and bring to a simmer.

Add trimmed artichokes and simmer, partially covered, until just tender when pierced with a knife, 8 to 12 minutes. Drain in a colander, then invert onto paper towels to drain thoroughly. Pat dry.

When artichokes are cool enough to handle, pull out all pointed inner leaves and scoop out fuzzy choke with melon-ball cutter (see cooks' note, at right).

Stuff and fry artichokes:

Heat 2 inches oil in a 4-quart heavy pot over moderate heat until thermometer registers 350°F.

While oil is heating, stuff each artichoke with 2 packed teaspoons pepper Jack cheese, pressing leaves around cheese.

Put eggs and bread crumbs in separate shallow bowls and divide salt and pepper between them, stirring them in. Dip each artichoke in egg, turning to coat and letting excess drip off, then in crumbs, turning to coat. Transfer to a tray.

Fry artichokes in 2 batches (returning oil to 350°F between batches) until golden brown, about 2 minutes. Transfer artichokes as fried to paper towels to drain, then cut in half.

Cooks' notes:
• Unless they are purplish in color, it's not necessary to remove chokes from very small artichokes because they are edible at this stage. But removing them will create more room for cheese stuffing.
• Artichokes may be stuffed, but not coated, 1 day ahead and chilled, covered. Bring to room temperature before frying.

WHOLE STUFFED ARTICHOKES
BRAISED IN WHITE WINE

Serves 4 (first course)
Active time: 1½ hr   Start to finish: 2 hr

In these stuffed artichokes, based on a recipe by Marie Miraglia—mother of one of our food editors, Gina—the provolone melts into each bite, and the soppressata adds more depth of flavor. Though we've given a regular-pot method in our recipe, there's nothing like the tenderness the leaves acquire in a pressure cooker—and the artichokes are done in a fraction of the time.

For stuffing artichokes
   2 cups fine fresh bread crumbs from an Italian loaf (4 oz)
   ½ cup finely grated Parmigiano-Reggiano (1½ oz)
   1½ tablespoons finely chopped garlic
   ¼ cup finely chopped fresh flat-leaf parsley
   ¼ cup minced sweet soppressata (dried Italian sausage; 1¼ oz)
   1 teaspoon finely grated fresh lemon zest (optional)
   1 teaspoon salt
   ¼ teaspoon black pepper
   ¼ cup olive oil
   4 medium artichokes (8 to 9 oz each)
   1 lemon, halved
   4 thin slices provolone cheese
For cooking artichokes
   1½ cups water
   ½ cup dry white wine
   ¼ cup olive oil
   ½ cup finely chopped onion
   1½ teaspoons finely chopped garlic
   ½ teaspoon salt
   ¼ teaspoon black pepper

Special equipment: **a 6- to 8-quart pressure cooker or a wide 4- to 6-quart heavy pot with a tight-fitting lid; a melon-ball cutter**

   Make stuffing:
   Preheat oven to 350°F.
   Spread crumbs in a shallow baking pan and bake in middle of oven until pale golden, about 10 minutes. Cool crumbs completely, then toss with parmesan, garlic, parsley, soppressata, zest if using, salt, and pepper. Drizzle oil over crumbs and toss to coat evenly.

   Trim and stuff artichokes:
   Cut off artichoke stems and discard. Cut off top ½ inch of 1 artichoke with a serrated knife, then cut about ½ inch off all remaining leaf tips with kitchen shears. Rub cut leaves with a lemon half.
   Separate leaves slightly with your thumbs and pull out purple leaves from center and enough yellow leaves to expose fuzzy choke. Scoop out choke with melon-ball cutter, then squeeze some lemon juice into cavity.
   Trim remaining artichokes in same manner.
   Spoon about 2 tablespoons stuffing into cavity of each artichoke and, starting with bottom leaves and spreading leaves open as much as possible without breaking, spoon a rounded ½ teaspoon stuffing inside each leaf. Top each artichoke with a slice of provolone.
   Cook artichokes:
   Put water, wine, oil, onion, garlic, salt, and pepper in pressure cooker (without insert) or pot and arrange stuffed artichokes in liquid in 1 layer.
   Seal pressure cooker with lid and cook at high pressure, according to manufacturer's instructions, 10 minutes. Put pressure cooker in sink (do not remove lid) and run cold water over lid until pressure goes down completely.
   If using a regular pot, simmer artichokes, covered, until leaves are tender, about 50 minutes.
   Transfer artichokes with tongs to 4 soup plates and spoon cooking liquid around them.

the menu
COLLECTION

*i*ssue after issue, menu after menu, the editors of *Gourmet* stress the importance of using fresh seasonal ingredients. Although many items can be found in the supermarket year round, we feel it's better to use locally grown produce in season. Simply—freshness makes all the difference, and the less time it takes an ingredient to travel, the fresher it will be. The menus in this collection have been arranged to take you through the year, season by season.

Winter—is for fireside meals and spending time with friends and family. We've created an entire *Weekend in the Country* set of menus for doing just that. Welcome your guests with a warming bowl of kale and white bean soup with provolone toasts. Next morning, rise-and-shine to baked eggs and mushrooms cooked in ham crisps. Then, after a day out in the snow, sit down to an elegant and hearty meal of pork chops brined with Riesling wine and pickling spices and upside down gingerbread cake for dessert. Finally, send them on their way with cheddar shortcakes and corned beef hash. We've taken care of everything, including a game plan for cooking.

Spring—is for blossom decked tables and enjoying the fruits and vegetables of the season in a *Cook Me a Rainbow* alfresco dinner. Bowls of asparagus soup with parmesan custards, herbed bean ragout with fresh *haricot verts*, meringue napoleons stacked with blackberries, and lime ice cream are sublime. You'll also find a fantasy *Dinner under Glace*, set in a real ice castle, with smoked duck toasts topped with gingered rhubarb, chilled pea broth with lemon cream, and a wilted baby spinach salad that makes great use of the tender young green.

Summer—is the time to get outdoors. The season is short so whether you throw a *Sizzle in the City* rooftop soirée (with pink daiquiris and grilled spinach stuffed flank steak), an *All-American* backyard feast (of grilled chicken with lemon and oregano and a berry cream tart), or simply throw down a blanket for a *Splendor in the Grass* picnic (with a choice of two sandwiches—carrot and goat cheese or chicken and roasted pepper) be sure to enjoy the great outdoors while you can.

Fall—is for watching the leaves change color and hosting holiday parties. Our *Thanksgiving with a Twist* is just what you've been waiting for—a spin on the traditional meal. We've modernized it, making it sleek and elegant. The turkey is plum-glazed, stuffed with spinach, bacon, and cashews, and drizzled with plum gravy. Mashed potatoes are made a vibrant green from the addition of chives and parsley, and individual maple pumpkin *pots de crème* top it all off. We've even included a vegetarian meal, *The Peaceable Feast*, to make use of the fall harvest with dishes like beet carpaccio, mushroom filled crêpes with Brussels sprouts and toasted pecans, and fruit gratin with apple brandy and mascarpone.

Finally, we say farewell to the year with a huge celebration— a stunning, decadent *Feast of Fancy* masquerade ball—where the star of the banquet is a prime rib of buffalo with a sweet orange balsamic glaze, followed by a host of trimmings, and if that wasn't enough, *five* desserts.

And not to worry, there are plenty of year-round everyday meals too. We've included two Low-Fat Menus packed with flavor, not calories, and six One-Dish Dinners. This edition also includes a few Dinners for One. Now one isn't the loneliest number—not with roasted salmon and chocolate rum pudding to keep you company.

With *The Best of Gourmet*, there's always a season to look forward to.

out of AFRICA

Serves 6

less
IS MORE

Serves 8
Each serving about 788 calories and 17 grams fat

Mushroom barley soup; banana Boston cream pie; salt and pepper grissini. Opposite: Veal piccata; buttered noodles with chives; and spicy sautéed Broccolini with garlic.

A WEEKEND IN THE COUNTRY

the
WELCOMING
TABLE

Serves 6

KALE AND WHITE
BEAN SOUP

page 135

PROVOLONE
TOASTS

page 135

Caparzo Sangiovese di Toscana '99

OATMEAL COCONUT
RASPBERRY BARS

page 230

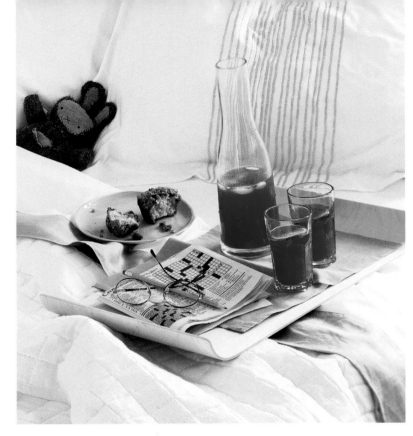

a GRAND RISING

Serves 6

A WEEKEND IN THE COUNTRY

one enchanted EVENING

Serves 6

**CAMEMBERT CARAWAY SPREAD
ON PUMPERNICKEL TOASTS**

page 128

Kuentz-Bas Pinot Blanc '00

BRINED PORK CHOPS

page 154

**MASHED POTATOES AND TURNIPS
WITH HORSERADISH**

page 198

ROASTED BEETS AND CARROTS

page 190

Domaine Zind-Humbrecht Wintzenheim
Clos Häuserer Riesling '99

**UPSIDE-DOWN PEAR
GINGERBREAD CAKE**

page 229

Domaine Schlumberger Grand Cru Kitterlé Gewürztraminer '97

GAME PLAN

You'll want to spend as much of
the weekend as possible relaxing,
so here's how to organize
your time and break up the work:

3 days ahead
Make oatmeal coconut
    raspberry bars.

2 days ahead
Make kale and
    white bean soup.
Prepare toasts for
    Camembert caraway spread.
Brine pork chops.
Roast beets.

1 day ahead
Make coffee cakes.
Prepare Camembert caraway spread.
Make tomatillo salsa.
Prepare fruit in mint syrup.

sunday SEND-OFF

Serves 6

CHEDDAR SHORTCAKES WITH CORNED BEEF HASH
page 172

TOMATILLO SALSA
page 220

PINEAPPLE, KIWIFRUIT, AND ORANGE IN MINT SYRUP
page 250

Roederer Estate
Anderson Valley Brut

cook me
A RAINBOW

Serves 6

**MINIATURE CRAB CAKES WITH
TOMATO GINGER JAM**

page 120

**ASPARAGUS SOUP WITH
PARMESAN CUSTARDS**

page 134

Freiherr Heyl zu Herrnsheim Niersteiner
Brudersberg Riesling '99

**PROSCIUTTO-WRAPPED
SALMON**

page 143

HERBED BEAN RAGOUT

page 188

Clos Du Val Gran Val Vineyard Pinot Noir '99

**MERINGUE NAPOLEONS
WITH LIME ICE CREAM AND
BLACKBERRIES**

page 243

Dr. Loosen Wehlener Sonnenuhr
Riesling Auslese Goldkapsel '99

Prosciutto-wrapped salmon and herbed bean ragout; asparagus soup with parmesan custards. Opposite: Meringue napoleons with lime ice cream and blackberries.

plain good
AMISH COOKING

Serves 6

**QUICK CUCUMBER PICKLES WITH
RYE BREAD AND CHEESE**

page 123

Sierra Nevada Pale Ale

**APPLE, CURRANT, AND CARAWAY
STUFFED CHICKEN BREASTS**

page 164

WHEAT BERRIES WITH PECANS

page 185

HONEY-GLAZED WAX BEANS

page 189

**DANDELION SALAD WITH
WARM BACON DRESSING**

page 205

Schneider Weisse Hefeweizen

MAPLE BUTTERMILK PIE

page 235

Brooklyn Brewery Black Chocolate Stout

Apple, currant, and caraway stuffed chicken breasts; wheat berries with pecans; honey-glazed wax beans; and dandelion salad with warm bacon dressing. Opposite: Maple buttermilk pie.

dinner UNDER GLACE

Serves 6

FRAISES DES BOIS ROYALES

page 257

**SMOKED-DUCK TOASTS
WITH GINGERED
RHUBARB**

page 119

**CHILLED PEA BROTH
WITH LEMON CREAM**

page 137

**SEARED SCALLOPS
WITH TOMATO
BEURRE BLANC**

page 146

WILTED BABY SPINACH

page 198

STRAW POTATOES

page 198

Morgan Monterey Chardonnay '00

**INDIVIDUAL
CHOCOLATE RASPBERRY
BAKED ALASKAS**

page 242

Inniskillin Niagara Peninsula
Riesling Ice Wine '99

Chilled pea broth with lemon cream; smoked-duck toasts with gingered rhubarb; seared scallops with tomato beurre blanc. Opposite: Individual chocolate raspberry baked Alaskas.

tropic of CASUAL

Serves 8

sizzle
IN THE CITY

Serves 6

Opposite: Grilled matambre *(spinach and carrot stuffed flank steak); herbed quinoa; and grilled bell peppers with criolla sauce. This page: Coconut tuile cones with passion-fruit ice cream.*

a new way TO GRILL

Serves 8

Opposite: Grilled brined salmon and eggplant with fennel cucumber relish. This page: Potato salad with mustard vinaigrette; coffee granita with sambuca cream and chocolate shavings.

all AMERICAN

Serves 16

**FIZZY SOUR
CHERRY LEMONADE**
page 257

**SHRIMP WITH
ORANGE TOMATO
COCKTAIL SAUCE
AND GREEN
GODDESS DIPPING SAUCE**
page 125

**BELL PEPPER AND
ONION CROSTINI
WITH PESTO**
page 116

**GRILLED CHICKEN WITH
LEMON, GARLIC,
AND OREGANO**
page 166

**GRILLED SWEET POTATOES
WITH LIME CILANTRO
VINAIGRETTE**
page 199

**CREAMY CORN
WITH SUGAR SNAP PEAS
AND SCALLIONS**
page 192

**TOMATO, CUCUMBER,
AND PITA SALAD**
page 212
Handley Anderson Valley Pinot Noir Rosé '01

**BERRY TART WITH
GINGER CREAM**
page 238
Schramsberg Crémant Demi-Sec '98

Grilled chicken with lemon, garlic, and oregano; creamy corn with sugar snap peas and scallions; grilled sweet potatoes with lime cilantro vinaigrette; and fizzy sour cherry lemonade. Opposite: Berry tart with ginger cream.

the art of
COOL

Serves 4

Abbazia Monte Oliveto, La Gentilesca,
Vernaccia di San Gimignano '00

Steamed corn custards with crab.
Opposite: Green tea ice cream
with a vanilla thin.

it's a
BREEZE

Serves 4

*Lobster with tarragon Vermouth sauce; and parsley
potatoes. Opposite: Mocha cake with malted semifreddo.*

splendor
IN THE GRASS

Serves 6

SALT AND PEPPER POTATO CHIPS

page 123

CURRIED VEGETABLE DIP

page 129

**MOROCCAN CARROT AND
GOAT CHEESE SANDWICHES
WITH GREEN OLIVE TAPENADE**

page 174

**CHICKEN AND ROASTED PEPPER
SANDWICHES WITH
CILANTRO ALMOND RELISH**

page 175

HEIRLOOM TOMATO SALAD

page 210

Claiborne & Churchill Central Coast Dry
Gewürztraminer '00

NECTARINE CAKE SQUARES

page 229

Chicken and roasted pepper sandwich with cilantro almond relish; heirloom tomato salad; and salt and pepper potato chips with curried vegetable dip. Opposite: Nectarine cake square.

a trip to BOUNTIFUL

Serves 6

Spiced fillet of beef with mizuna salad; and pearl couscous with oli[v]
and roasted tomatoes. Left: Lobster salad canapés; zucchini and saf[fron]
vichyssoise with scallops; and peach praline bombe with peach syru[p.]

welcome
TO THE
FUTURE

Serves 4

thanksgiving
WITH A TWIST

Serves 8 to 10

GAME PLAN

1 week ahead

Make kumquat and
cranberry compote.

4 days ahead

Make chive and parsley oil.

2 days ahead

Make celery-root bisque.
Make turkey giblet stock.
Make tart shells.
Make Port glaze for tarts.
Make *pots de crème*.

1 day ahead

Prepare stuffing.
Roast and stuff onion shells.
Make mashed potatoes.
Roast squash.

Thanksgiving Day

Assemble grape tarts.
Make turkey glaze and
roast turkey.
Bake stuffing and
stuffed onions.
Cook beans and heat with
roasted squash.
Make Sherry soy butter.
Reheat mashed potatoes.
Make gravy.
Reheat bisque and
sauté mushrooms.

101

the peaceable
FEAST

Serves 6

BEET CARPACCIO
page 126

**SCALLION WILD RICE CRÊPES
WITH MUSHROOM FILLING AND
RED PEPPER SAUCE**
page 186

**FRISÉE AND ENDIVE SALAD
WITH WARM BRUSSELS SPROUTS
AND TOASTED PECANS**
page 207

Columbia Crest Reserve Syrah '00

**FRUIT GRATIN
WITH CALVADOS
AND MASCARPONE**
page 249

FEAST OF *fancy*

Lime custard tart; chocolate chestnut torte with chocolate Cognac mousse; chocolate Earl Grey truffles; and panforte. Opposite: Buffalo prime rib with orange balsamic glaze; and roasted carrots and parsnips with herbs.

low-fat: PLAY IT COOL

Serves 6

Each serving about 737 calories and 13 grams fat

low-fat:
FALL HARVEST
DINNER

Serves 6

BITTER GREENS
AND GRAPES
WITH BLUE CHEESE
DRESSING

page 206

ROAST PORK TENDERLOIN
WITH APPLES
AND CIDER SAUCE

page 153

SWEET-POTATO AND
PARMESAN CAKE

page 200

DRIED CHERRY AND
RAISIN RICE PUDDING

page 254

Each serving about 637 calories and 17 grams fat

Eggplant and spinach lasagne spirals

Moroccan-style roast Cornish hens

Red wine-braised short ribs with vegetables

Layered Cobb salad

"Paella" couscous salad

six
ONE-DISH
DINNERS

Duck and wild rice salad

dinner for one:
HOME ALONE

Serves 1

**GRILLED NEW YORK STRIP STEAK
WITH SALSA VERDE**

**ORZO WITH TOMATOES
AND ARUGULA**

GRILLED CORN

**CHOCOLATE RASPBERRY
ICEBOX CAKE**

dinner for one:
BE YOUR GUEST

Serves 1

**BABY GREENS WITH
WARM GOAT CHEESE**

page 206

ROASTED SALMON

page 142

**CAULIFLOWER
PURÉE**

page 192

**CHOCOLATE RUM
PUDDING**

page 255

the recipe
COMPENDIUM

*e*ven before the baked eggs and mushrooms in ham crisps photo (on the left) landed on *Gourmet*'s February 2002 cover, we knew that we wanted it to appear here. Not only is it a feast for the eyes, the dish is a treat for the taste buds, too. Since the recipe (page 171) takes a bit of time to prepare and bake, you'll want to earmark it for relaxed weekends, ideally when company's around. Until then, our sausage and egg sandwiches (page 171) will do nicely. While they might not be quite so photogenic, they take only fifteen minutes to assemble and are immensely satisfying.

Here we've gathered hundreds of recipes that were created in our test kitchens during 2002—recipes from featured *Gourmet* Entertains menus and Every Day Low-Fat Dinners, One-Dish Dinners, and Dinners for One, as well as a staggering number of dishes from various other *Gourmet* columns. The most pleasant way to find those that you'll want to try is to leaf through these pages. After all, there's nothing like skimming through a recipe's ingredient list to really savor what's in store. But if your lifestyle at the moment doesn't allow such luxury, simply turn to our comprehensive index. Quick recipes—those that can be prepared in 30 minutes or less—are accompanied by a clock symbol; while leaner/lighter dishes (calorie and fat information included) are indicated by a feather.

The majority of recipes in this collection come from Gourmet Every Day, a section of the magazine dedicated to harried cooks who need to put dinner on the table quickly and without a lot of fuss. Dishes like pork chops with golden onions and wilted tomatoes; potato, Italian sausage, and arugula salad; peas with spinach and shallots; and apple, prune, and brandy crisp defy ordinary fare by combining easy-to-find ingredients in extraordinary combinations. Sprinkled throughout the compendium, you'll also find several special dishes from our Five Ingredients column. You may think that simple cooking compromises on taste, but that's not the case. Sole *goujons* with paprika salt, sour cherry strudels, and New Orleans praline pieces are just too good (and easy) to pass up.

And, since cooking with the freshest ingredients is always best, we've included many recipes that were developed for our Seasonal Kitchen column. This winter you'll want to stock up on grapefruit for fabulous desserts, such as a grapefuit and mascarpone cheese tart laced with candied ginger and an unforgettable grapefruit ambrosia with sweetened flaked coconut, a tad of Campari, and a sprinkling of toasted pistachios. Then, in the spring, load up on mussels for an elegant (and beautiful) creamy chowder with finely chopped leeks, shallots, carrots, and orange bell peppers. Or combine mussels with tomatoes, *crème fraîche*, basil, and garlic for an easy gratin. Come apricot season, the roast pork with apricot and shallot stuffing and the roasted apricot sorbet are musts.

But that's not all. From our ever-popular The Last Touch column comes a host of new ideas for old favorites: Cheddar cheese plays the lead in Cheddar scallion drop biscuits and Cheddar garlic stuffed potatoes; slaws come in many new guises, like fig and carrot slaw; and basil gets whirled into pesto goat cheese spread, basil lime syrup, and creamy basil dressing.

As *Gourmet's* appetite for all good foods continues to grow, you'll want to keep an eye on what's coming out of our kitchens. These pages promise wonderful combinations that you just might never think of on your own. And once you taste them, they'll be yours for life. Come and savor all that is new in *The Best of Gourmet*.

APPETIZERS

hors d'oeuvres

SWEET-POTATO GAUFRETTES WITH DUCK CONFIT

Makes about 24 hors d'oeuvres
Active time: 55 min   Start to finish: 1¼ hr

A well-sharpened French mandoline *with a fluted blade is the secret to these paper-thin wafers.*

> 2 large sweet potatoes (1½ lb total)
> 6 cups vegetable oil
> 1 confit duck leg (5½ oz), skin and bone discarded and meat finely shredded
> Cranberry black pepper chutney (recipe follows)

Special equipment: **a mandoline fitted with fluted blade; a deep-fat thermometer**

Adjust fluted blade of *mandoline* to an opening of slightly more than ⅛ inch. Peel sweet potatoes, then slice crosswise on *mandoline*, turning each potato at a 90-degree angle after each slice to produce a waffle pattern. (It may take a few tries to get the pattern right.)

Heat oil in a 4-quart heavy saucepan over moderate heat until it registers 300°F on thermometer. Fry potatoes, 6 to 8 slices at a time, stirring and turning them frequently, until golden and crisp, 2½ to 3 minutes. Transfer with a slotted spoon to paper towels to drain and return oil to 300°F between batches. Season *gaufrettes* lightly with salt while still warm.

Heat a 10-inch nonstick skillet over moderate heat until hot and cook duck, stirring, until any excess fat is melted and edges are slightly crisp, about 2 minutes.

Top each *gaufrette* with some duck and a scant ½ teaspoon chutney.

Cooks' notes:
· *Gaufrettes* can be made 1 day ahead and kept in an airtight container at room temperature.
· Hors d'oeuvres can be assembled 30 minutes ahead and kept at room temperature.
PHOTO ON PAGE 104

CRANBERRY BLACK PEPPER CHUTNEY

Makes about 1 cup
Active time: 10 min   Start to finish: 30 min

> ⅓ cup finely chopped shallot
> 1 tablespoon unsalted butter
> 6 oz fresh or frozen cranberries (not thawed; 2 cups)
> ½ cup sugar
> ⅓ cup water
> 1 tablespoon cider vinegar
> ¾ teaspoon cracked black pepper
> ¼ teaspoon salt

Cook shallot in butter in a 1½-quart heavy saucepan over moderate heat, stirring occasionally, until golden, 3 to 5 minutes. Stir in remaining ingredients and simmer, uncovered, stirring occasionally, until berries have burst and chutney is thickened, about 20 minutes. Cool to room temperature.

Cooks' note:
· Chutney can be made 1 week ahead and chilled, covered.

BELL PEPPER AND ONION CROSTINI WITH PESTO

Makes 60 crostini
Active time: 1 hr   Start to finish: 1½ hr

For toasts
> 1 (18- to 22-inch-long) baguette, cut into 60 (¼-inch-thick) slices
> ¼ cup extra-virgin olive oil
For peppers and onions
> 6 assorted red, yellow, and orange bell peppers (3 lb), cut into ¼-inch-wide strips
> 2 large onions (1½ lb), cut lengthwise into ¼-inch-thick slices
> 1 teaspoon finely chopped garlic
> ½ teaspoon salt
> 2 tablespoons extra-virgin olive oil
> 1 tablespoon red-wine vinegar
For pesto
> 1 cup coarsely chopped fresh basil
> ¼ cup pine nuts, toasted (see Tips, page 8)

¼ cup finely grated parmesan (1 oz)
2 teaspoons chopped garlic
2 tablespoons water
¼ teaspoon salt
⅛ teaspoon black pepper
⅓ cup olive oil

Make toasts:

Preheat oven to 350°F. Put baguette slices on 2 large baking sheets, then brush tops with oil and season with salt and pepper. Bake in batches in middle of oven until pale golden, about 10 minutes. Cool on a rack.

Cook peppers and onions:

Cook bell peppers, onions, and garlic with salt in oil in a wide 4- to 6-quart heavy pot over moderately low heat, uncovered, stirring occasionally, until softened, 20 to 25 minutes. Cover pot and continue to cook, stirring occasionally, until vegetables are very tender and just beginning to brown, 20 to 25 minutes more. Stir in vinegar and remove from heat.

Make pesto while peppers cook:

Pulse all pesto ingredients except oil in a food processor until finely chopped. With motor running, add oil in a slow stream and blend until combined well.

Assemble crostini:

Put about 1 tablespoon pepper mixture on each toast and top with about ¼ teaspoon pesto.

Cooks' note:
• **Pepper mixture and pesto can be made 1 day ahead and chilled separately, covered. Bring to room temperature before serving.**

BLACK-EYED PEA FRITTERS WITH HOT PEPPER RELISH

Makes about 36 fritters

Active time: 45 min   Start to finish: 9 hr (includes soaking)

These fritters are called akara *in Nigeria and Sierra Leone, and* akla *or* koosé *in Ghana. They're eaten as a snack, side dish, or breakfast, served with a hot pepper relish (*ata*). We think they make a great hors d'oeuvre.*

For fritters
1 cup dried black-eyed peas
1 medium onion, chopped
½ teaspoon minced fresh *habanero* chile
   (including seeds)
1 large egg
1 teaspoon salt

3 to 4 tablespoons water
6 cups vegetable oil
For relish
4 red bell peppers (1½ lb), chopped
1 medium onion, chopped
2 plum tomatoes, chopped
1 tablespoon minced fresh *habanero* chile
   (including seeds)
1½ teaspoons salt
¼ cup peanut or vegetable oil

Special equipment: **a deep-fat thermometer**

Soak peas for fritters:

Put peas in water to cover by 2 inches and soak 8 hours. Drain in a colander.

Make relish:

Purée bell peppers, onion, tomatoes, chile, and salt in 2 batches in a food processor.

Heat oil in a 12-inch heavy skillet over moderately high heat until hot but not smoking, then stir in purée (use caution). Reduce heat and simmer, stirring occasionally, until most of liquid is evaporated, 8 to 10 minutes. Cool to room temperature.

Make fritters:

Purée peas, onion, and chile in food processor until as smooth as possible, then blend in egg and salt. With motor running, add 3 tablespoons water and blend until smooth and fluffy (add remaining tablespoon water if necessary to form a batter just thin enough to drop from a spoon).

Fry fritters:

Heat oil in a 4-quart heavy pot (preferably cast-iron) until thermometer registers 360°F. Working in batches of 8, gently drop tablespoons of batter into hot oil, using a small spoon to scrape batter from tablespoon. Fry, stirring constantly (to prevent fritters from browning too quickly), until golden, about 2 minutes, then transfer to paper towels to drain. Return oil to 360°F between batches.

PHOTO ON PAGE 40

GINGER-GLAZED ALMONDS

Makes 2 cups
Active time: 10 min   Start to finish: 40 min

 2 tablespoons unsalted butter
 3 tablespoons packed brown sugar
 2 tablespoons water
 1 tablespoon finely grated peeled fresh ginger
 1¼ teaspoons kosher salt
 ¼ teaspoon ground ginger
 ¼ teaspoon cayenne
 2 cups whole almonds with skins (9 oz)

Preheat oven to 300°F.

Melt butter in a 12-inch nonstick skillet over moderate heat. Add remaining ingredients except almonds and cook, stirring, until sugar is dissolved. Remove from heat, then add almonds and stir until coated.

Spread almonds in a lightly oiled shallow baking pan (1 inch deep) and bake, stirring occasionally, until insides of nuts are golden (cut 1 open to test), about 25 minutes. Cool completely.

Cooks' note:
• Glazed almonds can be made 2 days ahead and kept in an airtight container at room temperature.

CHEDDAR PECAN CRISPS

Makes about 50 crackers
Active time: 15 min   Start to finish: 1 hr

 1 stick (½ cup) unsalted butter, softened
 8 oz Cheddar, coarsely grated (2 cups)
 1 large egg yolk
 ½ teaspoon salt
 ½ teaspoon cayenne
 ⅔ cup all-purpose flour
 ⅔ cup pecans, finely chopped

Preheat oven to 350°F.

Beat together butter and Cheddar in a bowl with an electric mixer until smooth, then beat in remaining ingredients.

Roll rounded teaspoons of dough into balls and arrange about 3 inches apart on buttered baking sheets. Flatten each ball into a 1½-inch disk and bake in batches in middle of oven until golden, 15 to 18 minutes.

LOBSTER SALAD CANAPÉS

Makes about 36 hors d'oeuvres
Active time: 45 min   Start to finish: 1½ hr

 1 (1½-lb) live lobster
 2 thick seedless cucumbers (usually plastic-
    wrapped; at least 1¾ inches in diameter),
    cut into 36 (¼-inch-thick) slices
 2 tablespoons mayonnaise
 2 to 3 teaspoons fresh lime juice
 1½ teaspoons minced fresh jalapeño chile
    (including seeds)
 ¼ teaspoon salt
 ⅓ cup finely diced peeled mango
 ¼ cup finely chopped celery
 2 tablespoons finely chopped red onion
 2 tablespoons finely chopped fresh cilantro

Garnish: **thinly sliced fresh cilantro**
Special equipment: **a 1½-inch scalloped round cookie cutter (optional)**

Plunge lobster headfirst into a 6- to 8-quart pot of boiling salted water (see Tips, page 8). Cook lobster, partially covered, over moderately high heat 9 minutes from time it enters water, then transfer with tongs to sink to cool.

While lobster is cooling, cut each cucumber slice with scalloped cutter (if using), discarding trimmings. Whisk together mayonnaise, lime juice (to taste), jalapeño, salt, and a pinch of pepper.

When lobster is cool, remove meat from claws, joints, and tail, discarding tomalley, roe, and shells, then cut meat into ¼-inch pieces. Add lobster, mango, celery, onion, and cilantro to dressing and toss well.

Top each cucumber round with 1 rounded teaspoon lobster salad.

Cooks' notes:
• Instead of using scalloped cutter, you can simply peel cucumber before slicing.
• Lobster can be cooked and removed from shell 1 day ahead and chilled, covered.
• Lobster salad can be made 6 hours ahead and chilled, covered.

PHOTO ON PAGE 94

FRESH CORN MADELEINES WITH SOUR CREAM AND CAVIAR

Makes about 36 hors d'oeuvres
Active time: 25 min   Start to finish: 45 min

For madeleines
  1 tablespoon unsalted butter, melted, plus
     additional for brushing molds
  ⅓ cup yellow cornmeal (not coarse)
  2 tablespoons all-purpose flour
  ½ teaspoon sugar
  ¼ teaspoon baking soda
  ¼ teaspoon salt
  ⅛ teaspoon black pepper
  1 large egg
  ⅓ cup well-shaken buttermilk
  ½ cup corn (from 1 ear), chopped
For topping
  ⅓ cup sour cream
  50 g caviar (1¾ oz; preferably sevruga)

Garnish: **chopped fresh chives**
Special equipment: **a madeleine pan with
     20 miniature (½-tablespoon) molds
     (preferably nonstick); a small pastry bag
     fitted with small star or leaf tip (optional)**

Make madeleines:
Preheat oven to 400°F. Brush molds with some melted butter.

Whisk together cornmeal, flour, sugar, baking soda, salt, and pepper in a bowl. Whisk together egg, buttermilk, 1 tablespoon melted butter, and corn in another bowl, then add to dry ingredients, stirring until just combined.

Spoon 1 teaspoon batter into each mold and bake in middle of oven until madeleines are golden around edges and spring back when pressed lightly, 5 to 6 minutes. Turn madeleines out onto a rack to cool and make more in same manner.

Top madeleines:
Put sour cream in pastry bag (if using) and pipe (or spoon) about ½ teaspoon onto each madeleine, then top with a rounded ¼ teaspoon caviar.

Cooks' note:
• Madeleines (without topping) are best when made no more than 6 hours ahead. Once cooled, keep in an airtight container at room temperature.

PHOTO ON PAGE 93

SMOKED-DUCK TOASTS WITH GINGERED RHUBARB

Serves 6 (hors d'oeuvre)
Active time: 30 min   Start to finish: 30 min

  18 (¼-inch-thick) diagonal slices of baguette
     (preferably sourdough)
  1½ tablespoons unsalted butter, melted
   6 oz rhubarb stalks, trimmed and cut into
     ¼-inch dice
  1½ teaspoons finely grated peeled fresh ginger
  ⅓ cup water
   2 tablespoons plus ¾ teaspoon sugar
  ¼ cup mayonnaise
   1 (¾-lb) smoked duck breast half
  18 fresh cilantro sprigs

Preheat oven to 450°F.

Brush 1 side of each bread slice lightly with butter, then toast on a baking sheet in middle of oven until golden, about 6 minutes, and cool.

Simmer rhubarb, ginger, water, and sugar in a small heavy saucepan, uncovered, stirring gently, until rhubarb is just tender, 2 to 3 minutes, then set pan in a bowl of ice and cold water to stop cooking. Drain rhubarb in a medium-mesh sieve set over a bowl, reserving rhubarb, then whisk together 2 teaspoons rhubarb liquid and mayonnaise. Discard remaining cooking liquid.

Remove skin and fat from duck breast. Carve 18 (⅛-inch-thick) slices from duck, cutting across the grain. Trim slices to fit toasts, reserving any remaining duck for another use.

Spread about 1 teaspoon rhubarb mayonnaise on buttered side of each toast and top with 1 slice of duck, 1 teaspoon rhubarb, and a cilantro sprig.

PHOTO ON PAGE 64

FRICO CUPS WITH HERBED GOAT CHEESE

Makes 24 hors d'oeuvres
Active time: 40 min   Start to finish: 40 min

It's very important to use freshly shredded Parmigiano-Reggiano—preferably shredded with a Microplane—for these parmesan crisps (called frico*).*

  1 cup finely shredded fresh
      Parmigiano-Reggiano (3 oz)
  1 tablespoon all-purpose flour
  4 oz soft mild goat cheese (⅓ cup) at
      room temperature
  3 tablespoons heavy cream
  1½ teaspoons finely chopped fresh chives
  1½ teaspoons finely chopped fresh
      flat-leaf parsley
  ⅛ teaspoon salt
  ⅛ teaspoon black pepper

Garnish: **tiny mesclun leaves such as baby romaine, arugula, and red mustard**
Special equipment: **a flexible heatproof plastic spatula; a mini-muffin pan with 12 (1¾-inch) cups; a pastry bag fitted with ½-inch plain tip (optional)**

Stir together parmesan and flour with a fork. Heat an 8- to 10-inch nonstick skillet over moderately low heat until hot. Sprinkle 2 teaspoons parmesan mixture into a 2½-inch free-form round in skillet and cook until cheese is set, about 10 seconds. Loosen edge of *frico* with plastic spatula, then turn over and cook 5 seconds more. Immediately transfer *frico* to a muffin cup, lightly pressing it in, and remove from cup once crisp, about 30 seconds. Make more *frico* cups in same manner.

Stir together goat cheese, cream, chives, parsley, salt, and pepper and transfer to pastry bag (if using). Tuck a mesclun leaf inside each cup, then pipe (or spoon) in herbed goat cheese to fill two thirds of each cup.

Cooks' notes:
• *Frico* cups can be made (but not filled) 2 days ahead and kept in an airtight container at room temperature.
• Herbed goat cheese can be made 2 days ahead and chilled in pastry bag or covered with plastic wrap. Bring to room temperature before proceeding.
• Hors d'oeuvres can be assembled 30 minutes ahead and kept at room temperature.
PHOTO ON PAGE 104

MINIATURE CRAB CAKES WITH TOMATO GINGER JAM

Makes about 36 hors d'oeuvres
Active time: 1¾ hr   Start to finish: 5 hr

  ½ cup mayonnaise
  1 large egg
  1 tablespoon Dijon mustard
  ¾ teaspoon Old Bay Seasoning
  1½ teaspoons fresh lemon juice
  ¼ teaspoon salt
  ⅛ teaspoon black pepper
  ⅛ teaspoon Tabasco
  1 lb jumbo lump crabmeat, picked over
  4 cups cornflakes

Accompaniment: **tomato ginger jam (recipe follows)**
Garnish: **thinly sliced fresh cilantro**

Whisk together mayonnaise, egg, mustard, Old Bay, lemon juice, salt, pepper, and Tabasco, then gently stir in crabmeat. Chill, covered, 2 hours.

Pulse cornflakes in a food processor until coarsely ground and put in a shallow dish. Form 1 heaping teaspoon crab mixture into a 1½-inch-diameter cake (mixture will be very moist), then gently dredge in cornflakes. Make more crab cakes in same manner, transferring to buttered baking sheets. Chill, covered, at least 1 hour and up to 4 hours.

Preheat oven to 400°F.

Bake crab cakes in batches in middle of oven until crisp and golden, 8 to 10 minutes. Transfer with a spatula to a platter and top each with about ½ tablespoon tomato ginger jam.
PHOTO ON PAGE 55

TOMATO GINGER JAM

Makes about 1¼ cups
Active time: 30 min   Start to finish: 1 hr

  ¼ cup minced shallot
  1 tablespoon finely grated peeled fresh ginger
  1 large garlic clove, minced
  ¾ teaspoon salt
  ¼ teaspoon black pepper
  ⅛ teaspoon dried hot red pepper flakes
  2 tablespoons unsalted butter

1 tablespoon sugar
1½ lb plum tomatoes, seeded and finely
   chopped
1½ tablespoons fresh lime juice
2 tablespoons finely chopped fresh cilantro

Cook shallot, ginger, garlic, salt, black pepper, and red pepper flakes in butter in a 10-inch heavy skillet over moderately low heat, stirring, until shallot is softened, about 5 minutes. Add sugar and cook, stirring, until dissolved. Add tomatoes and simmer over moderate heat, stirring occasionally, until thickened, 10 to 15 minutes.

Cool jam to room temperature, then stir in lime juice and cilantro.

Cooks' note:
• Jam can be made 2 days ahead and chilled, covered. Stir in lime juice and cilantro just before serving.

FRIED BEER-BATTER MUSSELS WITH TWO SAUCES

Serves 8 to 10 (hors d'oeuvre)
Active time: 40 min   Start to finish: 1 hr

For sauces
1 cup mayonnaise
3 tablespoons coarse-grain mustard
2 tablespoons finely chopped fresh cilantro
2 teaspoons fresh lime juice
½ teaspoon curry powder
For fried mussels
8 oz beer (not dark; 1 cup)
1 cup all-purpose flour
1½ qt vegetable oil for frying
2 lb mussels (preferably cultivated), cleaned
   and steamed (procedures follow), then
   shucked

Accompaniment: **lemon wedges**
Special equipment: **a deep-fat thermometer**

Make sauces:
Put ½ cup mayonnaise into each of 2 small serving bowls and whisk mustard into 1 bowl. Whisk cilantro, lime juice, and curry powder into other bowl. Season dipping sauces with salt and pepper and keep chilled, covered.

Make batter and fry mussels:
Whisk beer into flour in a bowl until combined well.

Heat oil in a 4-quart heavy saucepan over moderate heat until thermometer registers 375°F.

While oil is heating, pat mussels dry between layers of paper towels, pressing lightly.

Dredge 10 mussels in batter, letting excess drip off, and fry in oil, stirring, until golden brown, 1 to 2 minutes. Transfer mussels as fried with a slotted spoon to paper towels to drain, then season with salt. Fry remaining mussels in batches in same manner, returning oil to 375°F between batches.

Serve mussels immediately, with dipping sauces.

mussels

TO CLEAN AND STEAM MUSSELS

1½ to 4½ lb cultivated mussels
1 cup liquid (water, or a mix of water
   and white wine or beer)

Scrub each mussel shell with a brush under cold water, scraping off any barnacles with a knife. If byssus (beard) is still attached, remove it just before cooking by pulling it from tip to hinge or cutting it off with a knife.

Bring liquid to a boil in a 4- to 6-quart heavy pot, then reduce heat to moderate and cook mussels, covered, stirring occasionally, until mussels are opened, 3 to 6 minutes, checking frequently after 3 minutes and transferring as opened to a bowl. (Discard any unopened mussels after 6 minutes.)

SMOKED SALMON BARQUETTES

Makes 24 tartlets
Active time: 30 min   Start to finish: 2 hr

Barquettes *are small, boat-shaped pastry shells that can be filled with sweet or savory ingredients.*

For pastry dough
  1½ cups all-purpose flour
  1¼ sticks (10 tablespoons) cold unsalted butter, cut into ½-inch cubes
  ½ teaspoon salt
  3 to 5 tablespoons ice water
For filling
  ¼ cup finely diced red onion
  2 teaspoons fresh lemon juice
  3½ oz sliced fine-quality smoked salmon, finely chopped (1¼ cups)
  1 tablespoon sour cream at room temperature
  ½ tablespoon unsalted butter, melted
  1 teaspoon finely grated fresh lemon zest
  ¼ teaspoon black pepper
  1 oz salmon roe (caviar)

Garnish: **fresh dill sprigs**
Special equipment: **a pastry or bench scraper; 24 (3½-inch)** *barquette* **molds; parchment paper; pie weights or raw rice**

  Make dough:
  Blend together flour, butter, and salt in a bowl with your fingertips or a pastry blender (or pulse in a food processor) just until most of mixture resembles coarse meal with small (roughly pea-size) butter lumps. Drizzle evenly with 3 tablespoons ice water and gently stir with a fork (or pulse in processor) until incorporated.
  Squeeze a small handful: If it doesn't hold together, add remaining ice water, ½ tablespoon at a time, stirring (or pulsing) until just incorporated, then test again. (Do not overwork mixture, or pastry will be tough.)
  Turn out mixture onto a lightly floured surface and divide into 4 portions. With heel of your hand, smear each portion once or twice in a forward motion to help distribute fat. Gather dough together with scraper and divide into 2 pieces, then flatten each piece into a 4-inch square. Chill squares, wrapped in plastic wrap, until firm, at least 1 hour.
  Make barquette shells:
  Keeping remaining dough chilled, roll out 1 piece

on a lightly floured surface into a 13-inch square. Arrange 12 *barquette* molds close together on a work surface and drape rolled-out dough over molds. Roll a lightly floured rolling pin over molds to cut dough, then lightly press into molds. Repeat with remaining dough, then prick each shell several times with a fork and chill all shells in a shallow baking pan until firm, about 30 minutes.
  Preheat oven to 375°F.
  Arrange *barquette* molds close together in shallow pan and cover with parchment. Put pie weights on top of parchment (over molds) and bake in middle of oven until edges of shells are pale golden, about 15 minutes. Carefully remove parchment and weights and bake shells until golden, 7 to 10 minutes more. Cool shells in molds on a rack 10 minutes, then remove from molds and cool completely.
  Prepare filling while shells bake and cool:
  Stir together onion, lemon juice, and a pinch of salt in a bowl and let stand at room temperature 30 minutes. Stir in salmon, sour cream, butter, zest, and pepper.
  Assemble barquettes:
  Fill each *barquette* shell with a scant teaspoon salmon mixture and top with a scant ¼ teaspoon caviar.

  Cooks' notes:
  • Dough can be chilled up to 1 day. Before rolling out, let stand at room temperature until slightly softened, about 20 minutes.
  • *Barquette* shells can be baked 2 days ahead and kept in an airtight container at room temperature.
  • Hors d'oeuvres can be assembled 30 minutes ahead and kept at room temperature.
  PHOTO ON PAGE 104

PETITES PISSALADIÈRES
Miniature Onion Tartlets

Makes 36 tartlets
Active time: 1 hr   Start to finish: 1¼ hr

  1 frozen puff pastry sheet (from a 17¼-oz package), thawed
  3 tablespoons olive oil
  1 large onion (12 oz), halved lengthwise and cut crosswise into ⅛-inch-thick slices
  ½ teaspoon salt
  ¼ teaspoon black pepper
  3 to 4 flat anchovy fillets, patted dry and finely chopped
  2 teaspoons chopped fresh thyme

¼ cup Kalamata or other brine-cured
　　black olives, pitted and very thinly
　　sliced lengthwise

Preheat oven to 400°F.

Roll out puff pastry on a lightly floured surface into
a 12½-inch square, then trim edges to form a 12-inch
square. Prick sheet all over with a fork. Cut into 36
(2-inch) squares and transfer to 2 buttered large baking
sheets, arranging about 2 inches apart.

Bake in upper and lower thirds of oven, switching
position of sheets halfway through baking, until puffed
and golden, 12 to 15 minutes total. Transfer squares to
a rack and cool until just warm.

While pastry is baking, heat 2 tablespoons oil in a
12-inch nonstick skillet over moderate heat until hot but
not smoking, then cook onion with salt and pepper, stirring occasionally, until golden brown, 15 to 20 minutes.
Stir in anchovies (to taste) and 1 teaspoon thyme and
keep warm, covered.

Lightly brush tops of pastry squares with remaining
tablespoon oil. Make a small indentation in center of
each square with your finger, then top each with
1 teaspoon onion mixture and a few olive slivers.
Sprinkle squares with remaining teaspoon thyme.

Cooks' notes:
- Pastry squares can be baked 1 day ahead, cooled
  completely, and kept in an airtight container at
  room temperature. Reheat in a 350°F oven 6 minutes
  before topping.
- Onion mixture can be made 1 day ahead and
  chilled, covered. Reheat over moderate heat, stirring,
  until heated through, about 10 minutes.
PHOTO ON PAGE 85

SALT AND PEPPER POTATO CHIPS

Makes about 12 dozen chips
Active time: 15 min　Start to finish: 50 min

¼ cup olive oil
2 large russet (baking) potatoes (1 lb total),
　　scrubbed
¾ teaspoon coarse salt
1 teaspoon coarsely ground black pepper

Special equipment: **a Japanese Benriner
　　or other adjustable-blade slicer**

Preheat oven to 375°F.

Brush 2 large shallow baking pans (1 inch deep)
generously with some olive oil. Cut 1 potato crosswise
into ¹⁄₁₆-inch-thick slices with slicer and immediately
arrange in 1 layer on baking sheets. Lightly brush
slices with more oil and sprinkle with half of coarse
salt and pepper.

Bake in upper and lower thirds of oven, switching
position of sheets halfway through baking, until golden,
10 to 20 minutes (check frequently after 10 minutes),
and transfer as cooked with a metal spatula to a rack
to cool. Make more chips with remaining potato in
same manner.

Cooks' note:
- Chips can be made 3 days ahead and kept in an
  airtight container at room temperature.
PHOTO ON PAGE 88

QUICK CUCUMBER PICKLES
WITH RYE BREAD AND CHEESE

Serves 6 (hors d'oeuvre)
Active time: 10 min　Start to finish: 30 min

2 seedless cucumbers (usually plastic-
　　wrapped)
2 teaspoons kosher salt
½ cup cider vinegar
¼ cup sugar
1 tablespoon dry mustard
2 teaspoons drained bottled horseradish
1 tablespoon chopped fresh dill
1 loaf rye bread (1 lb)
2 (6- to 8-oz) pieces semisoft cheese
　　(preferably German, such as Cambozola
　　or Mirabo)

Cut cucumbers crosswise into ⅛-inch-thick slices,
then toss with kosher salt in a bowl and let stand
15 minutes. Rinse and drain cucumbers and pat dry
with paper towels.

Whisk together vinegar, sugar, mustard, horseradish, and dill until sugar is dissolved. Stir in cucumber
and let marinate at room temperature at least 5 minutes.

Slice bread and serve with pickles and cheese.

Cooks' note:
- Pickles can marinate up to 4 hours, covered
  and chilled.
PHOTO ON PAGE 59

SARDINE PUFFS

Makes 120 hors d'oeuvres
Active time: 25 min   Start to finish: 40 min

**15 slices firm white sandwich bread, lightly
    toasted**
1 (3¾- to 4⅜-oz) can sardines in oil, drained
½ cup mayonnaise
3 tablespoons minced onion
2 tablespoons chopped fresh flat-leaf parsley

Preheat oven to 375°F.

Trim crusts from bread and cut each slice into
8 triangles.

Mash sardines with mayonnaise in a bowl with a
fork, then stir in onion and parsley. Spread on toasts
and bake on a large baking sheet in middle of oven
until puffed and golden, 10 to 15 minutes.

COCONUT SHRIMP
WITH TAMARIND GINGER SAUCE

Serves 8 (hors d'oeuvre)
Active time: 1 hr   Start to finish: 1½ hr

For sauce
1 teaspoon tamarind concentrate
1½ tablespoons fresh lime juice
⅔ cup mayonnaise
1½ tablespoons mild honey
2 teaspoons Dijon mustard
1 teaspoon finely grated peeled fresh ginger
¼ teaspoon salt
For shrimp
**4 cups sweetened flaked coconut (10 oz),
    coarsely chopped**
1 cup all-purpose flour
¾ cup beer (not dark)
¾ teaspoon baking soda
½ teaspoon salt
1 teaspoon cayenne
1 large egg
6 cups vegetable oil
**48 medium shrimp in shell (1½ lb), peeled,
    leaving tail and first segment of shell
    intact, and, if desired, deveined**

Special equipment: **a deep-fat thermometer**

Make sauce:

Whisk together tamarind concentrate and lime juice
in a small bowl until concentrate is dissolved. Stir in
remaining sauce ingredients and chill, covered.

Prepare shrimp:

Transfer half of coconut to a shallow soup bowl or
pie plate. Whisk together flour, beer, baking soda, salt,
cayenne, and egg in a small bowl until smooth.

Heat oil in a 4- to 6-quart deep heavy pot over
moderately high heat until it registers 350°F on
thermometer.

While oil is heating, coat shrimp: Hold 1 shrimp
by tail and dip into batter, letting excess drip off, then
dredge in coconut, coating completely and pressing
gently to help adhere. Transfer to a plate and coat
remaining shrimp in same manner, adding remaining
coconut to bowl as needed.

Fry shrimp in oil in batches of 8, turning once, until
golden, about 1 minute. Transfer with a slotted spoon
to paper towels to drain and season lightly with salt.
Skim any coconut from oil and return oil to 350°F
between batches.

Serve shrimp with sauce.

Cooks' note:
• Tamarind ginger sauce can be made 6 hours ahead
  and chilled, covered. Bring to room temperature
  before serving.
PHOTO ON PAGE 66

SHRIMP WITH ORANGE TOMATO COCKTAIL SAUCE AND GREEN GODDESS DIPPING SAUCE

Serves 16
Active time: 1¼ hr   Start to finish: 1¼ hr

For shrimp
**3 lb large shrimp in shell
(21 to 25 per pound)**
For cocktail sauce
**¾ cup ketchup
¼ teaspoon finely grated fresh orange zest
¼ cup fresh orange juice
1 to 1½ tablespoons fresh lemon juice
3 tablespoons drained bottled horseradish
¼ teaspoon Tabasco**
For Green Goddess dipping sauce
**½ cup mayonnaise
½ cup sour cream
¼ cup chopped scallion
2 tablespoons chopped fresh chives
2 tablespoons chopped fresh flat-leaf parsley
2 teaspoons chopped fresh tarragon
3 flat anchovy fillets or 1 tablespoon
anchovy paste
1 tablespoon fresh lemon juice
¼ teaspoon salt
⅛ teaspoon black pepper**

Prepare shrimp:
Bring a 6- to 8-quart pot two-thirds full of salted water (see Tips, page 8) to a boil, then simmer shrimp, stirring occasionally, until pink and almost cooked through (they will still be translucent in very center but will continue to cook from residual heat), about 3 minutes. Drain and cool. Peel shrimp, leaving tail and first segment of shell intact.

Make cocktail sauce:
Stir together all cocktail sauce ingredients until combined well.

Make Green Goddess sauce:
Purée all sauce ingredients in a food processor until smooth and light green.

Serve shrimp with sauces for dipping.

Cooks' notes:
• **Shrimp can be cooked and peeled 1 day ahead and chilled, covered.**
• **Sauces can be made 1 day ahead and chilled separately, covered.**

SESAME WONTON CRISPS

Makes 24 crisps
Active time: 10 min   Start to finish: 20 min

**1 tablespoon vegetable oil
2 teaspoons cornstarch
12 square wonton wrappers, thawed if frozen
2 tablespoons sesame seeds, toasted
(see Tips, page 8)
1 teaspoon kosher salt**

Preheat oven to 375°F.
Stir together oil and cornstarch in a small bowl until combined.
Stack wonton wrappers and halve diagonally. Arrange in 1 layer on a large baking sheet and brush tops with oil mixture. Sprinkle evenly with sesame seeds and kosher salt and bake in middle of oven until golden brown, 5 to 6 minutes. Transfer crisps as browned to a rack to cool.

Cooks' note:
• **Crisps can be made 1 day ahead and kept in an airtight container at room temperature.**

Each serving (4 crisps) about 80 calories and 3 grams fat

first courses

SARDINE AND BEAN BRUSCHETTA

Serves 4 (first course)
Active time: 15 min   Start to finish: 15 min

**1 (16- to 19-oz) can *cannellini* beans, rinsed
and drained
1 (3¾- to 4⅜-oz) can sardines in oil, drained
1½ tablespoons fresh lemon juice
3 tablespoons extra-virgin olive oil
1 garlic clove, minced
4 (½-inch-thick) slices country-style bread
2 oz arugula or watercress (5 cups)**

Mash beans and half of sardines in a bowl with a fork. Stir in lemon juice, 1 tablespoon oil, garlic, and salt and pepper to taste.

Toast bread, then brush with remaining 2 tablespoons oil. Top toasts with arugula, bean mixture, and remaining sardines.

BEET CARPACCIO

Serves 6
Active time: 40 min   Start to finish: 2½ hr

6 large or 12 medium beets (3 lb with greens),
  trimmed, leaving 1 inch of stems attached
3 medium onions (1 lb), halved lengthwise
  and thinly sliced crosswise
3 tablespoons unsalted butter
½ teaspoon salt
½ teaspoon sugar
2 teaspoons balsamic vinegar
⅓ cup dry white wine
¼ cup extra-virgin olive oil
1 (½-lb) piece Parmigiano-Reggiano

Special equipment: **a Japanese Benriner or
    other adjustable-blade slicer; a small
    offset spatula**

Preheat oven to 400°F.

Tightly wrap beets in double layers of foil to make
3 packages (2 large beets or 4 medium per package)
and roast on a baking sheet in middle of oven until tender, 1¼ to 1½ hours. Cool to warm in foil packages (the
steam makes beets easier to peel), about 30 minutes.

While beets are roasting, cook onions in butter in a
12-inch heavy skillet, covered, over moderately low
heat, stirring occasionally, until soft, about 20 minutes.
Add salt, sugar, and vinegar and cook, uncovered, stirring occasionally, until onions are very tender and
caramelized to deep brown, about 20 minutes more.
Add wine and boil, stirring occasionally, until liquid
is reduced to about 2 tablespoons, 3 to 5 minutes.

Transfer mixture to a food processor and pulse to a
coarse purée. Return to skillet and season with salt and
pepper, then reheat onion marmalade, covered, over
low heat.

While marmalade is reheating, peel beets, discarding stems and root ends. Cut crosswise into ⅛-inch-thick
slices with slicer.

Divide warm marmalade among 6 dinner plates and
spread evenly in a very thin layer to cover bottom of
each plate using offset spatula. Arrange beet slices in
1 layer over onion, overlapping them only enough to
cover onions. Drizzle 2 teaspoons oil over each serving
and season with pepper. Shave 4 to 6 curls of
Parmigiano-Reggiano with a vegetable peeler over
beets on each plate. Serve immediately.

Cooks' notes:
• Beets can be roasted and peeled 1 day ahead and
  chilled in a sealed plastic bag. Slice beets, then stack
  slices in 2 piles, wrap in foil, and reheat in a 400°F
  oven until warm, about 10 minutes.
• Onion marmalade can be made 1 day ahead and
  chilled, covered. Reheat before using.
PHOTO ON PAGE 103

STEAMED CORN CUSTARDS WITH CRAB

Serves 4
Active time: 20 min   Start to finish: 40 min

For custard
  1 cup fresh corn kernels (from 2 ears)
    or thawed frozen
  ⅓ cup whole milk
  1 large egg, lightly beaten
    Rounded ¼ teaspoon salt
For crab topping
  1 (¾-lb) king crab leg, thawed if frozen
    and shell discarded
  1 tablespoon unsalted butter
  1 tablespoon chopped fresh chives

Special equipment: **4 (2-oz) ramekins**

Make custard:

Cook corn in a 1-quart saucepan of boiling salted
water (see Tips, page 8) until very tender, 3 to
5 minutes, and drain in a medium-mesh sieve.

Purée milk and hot corn in a blender until almost
smooth, then force through a fine-mesh sieve into a

bowl, discarding solids. Whisk in egg and salt and divide custard among ramekins.

Steam custards in a steamer set 1 inch above simmering water, covered with lid, until centers are set and a thin knife inserted into center of 1 custard comes out clean, 6 to 8 minutes. Remove ramekins from steamer with tongs and cool custards slightly on a rack.

Make crab topping while custards cool:

Coarsely chop ¼ cup crabmeat and reserve remainder for another use. Heat butter in a small heavy skillet over moderate heat until foam subsides, then cook crab, stirring constantly, until heated through, about 2 minutes. Stir in chives.

Serve custards topped with crab.

Cooks' note:
• Custard mixture can be prepared and poured into ramekins 1 day ahead and chilled, surfaces covered with plastic wrap. Bring to room temperature before steaming.

PHOTO ON PAGE 82

SWISS CHARD AND CRISP SHALLOT ROLLS WITH CILANTRO RAITA

Serves 4 (first course or side dish)
Active time: 1 hr   Start to finish: 1½ hr

The raita—a type of Indian yogurt sauce—makes a terrific dip for the rolls.

For rolls
   1 cup vegetable oil
   ½ lb shallots, thinly sliced (2 cups)
   8 medium Swiss chard leaves, stems
      trimmed flush with leaves
For raita
   1 small garlic clove
   ½ teaspoon fine sea salt
   ½ cup chopped fresh cilantro
   1 cup whole-milk yogurt

Special equipment: a deep-fat thermometer

Fry shallots for rolls:

Heat oil in a 1-quart saucepan over moderately high heat until it registers 365°F on thermometer, then fry shallots in 3 batches, stirring occasionally, until golden brown, 2 to 3 minutes. Transfer with a slotted spoon to paper towels to drain, spreading evenly, then cool.

Assemble rolls:

Cook chard leaves in a large pot of boiling salted water (see Tips, page 8) until tender, about 2 minutes. Transfer with tongs to a bowl of ice and cold water to stop cooking. Drain well and pat dry with paper towels.

Halve each leaf lengthwise, discarding rib. Place 1 tablespoon shallots at 1 end of a chard strip and firmly roll up, forming a cigar shape. Make 15 more rolls in same manner.

Make raita:

Mash garlic to a paste with sea salt using a mortar and pestle (or mince and mash with a large heavy knife). Purée cilantro with garlic paste and ¼ cup yogurt in a blender, scraping down sides occasionally. Transfer to a bowl and stir in remaining ¾ cup yogurt.

Serve chard rolls with raita.

Cooks' notes:
• Shallots can be fried 1 day ahead, cooled, and kept at room temperature (do not cover or they will become soggy).
• Chard leaves can be cooked 1 day ahead and chilled, layered between paper towels in a sealed plastic bag.

PHOTO ON PAGE 96

dips and spreads

ROASTED PEPPER AND WHITE BEAN SPREAD

Makes about 1⅓ cups
Active time: 10 min   Start to finish: 10 min

   1 cup drained bottled roasted red peppers
      (8 oz), rinsed
   1 cup drained canned white beans (6 oz),
      rinsed
   ½ cup coarse fresh white bread crumbs
      (1 slice bread)
   1½ teaspoons chopped flat anchovy fillets
      (optional)
   ¼ cup extra-virgin olive oil
   ½ teaspoon salt
   ¼ teaspoon black pepper

Purée all ingredients in a food processor until smooth.

CAMEMBERT CARAWAY SPREAD ON PUMPERNICKEL TOASTS

Serves 6
Active time: 15 min   Start to finish: 20 min

1 (10-oz) ripe Camembert wheel with rind, quartered and at room temperature
3 oz cream cheese at room temperature
5 tablespoons sour cream
3 tablespoons chopped shallot
1 teaspoon caraway seeds
½ teaspoon black pepper
¼ cup chopped fresh chives
8 (⅓- to ½-inch-thick) slices pumpernickel bread, each cut into thirds
½ stick (¼ cup) unsalted butter, melted

Garnish: **fresh chives**

Make spread:
Purée Camembert, cream cheese, sour cream, shallot, and caraway seeds in a food processor. Stir in pepper and chives.
Make toasts:
Preheat oven to 425°F.
Brush 1 side of bread with butter and season with salt and pepper. Toast bread, buttered sides up, on a baking sheet in middle of oven until crisp, about 7 minutes, then transfer to a rack to cool.

Cooks' notes:
• Spread can be made 1 day ahead and chilled, covered. Bring to room temperature before serving.
• Toasts can be made 2 days ahead, then cooled completely and kept in an airtight container.

GARLIC ANCHO CHILE JAM

Makes about 1 cup
Active time: 20 min   Start to finish: 1¼ hr

This recipe was adapted from chef Robert del Grande of Cafe Annie, in Houston.

2 medium heads garlic, left whole
3 tablespoons olive oil
2 oz dried *ancho* chiles, stems, seeds, and veins discarded
2 tablespoons cider vinegar
2 tablespoons mild honey

Preheat oven to 400°F.
Cut off and discard tops of garlic heads to expose cloves and rub each head with ½ tablespoon oil. Wrap heads together in foil and bake in middle of oven until tender, about 45 minutes. Cool to warm.
While garlic is roasting, toast chiles in a dry heavy skillet over moderate heat, turning, until fragrant, about 1 minute. Soak chiles in hot water until softened, about 20 minutes, then drain.
Squeeze garlic from skins into a food processor and purée with chiles, vinegar, honey, remaining 2 tablespoons oil, and salt to taste. Force purée through a sieve into a bowl.

CHICKPEA CILANTRO DIP WITH GRILLED PITA AND CARROT STICKS

Serves 4
Active time: 30 min   Start to finish: 45 min

1 cup canned chickpeas, rinsed and drained
¼ cup low-fat plain yogurt
½ cup chopped fresh cilantro
1 small garlic clove, chopped
1½ tablespoons fresh lemon juice
1 tablespoon water
¼ teaspoon salt
2 (7-inch) pita loaves with pockets, split horizontally
½ lb carrots, trimmed and cut into sticks

Prepare charcoal or gas grill for cooking. If using charcoal, open vents on bottom of grill.
Slip skins from chickpeas with your fingers, then purée chickpeas with yogurt, cilantro, garlic, lemon juice, water, and salt in a food processor until smooth.
When fire is hot (you can hold your hand 5 inches above rack for 1 to 2 seconds), grill pitas on lightly oiled grill rack, uncovered, turning once, until golden, about 2 minutes total.
Serve dip with pitas and carrots.

Cooks' notes:
• Dip can be made 1 day ahead and chilled, covered. Bring to room temperature before serving.
• Pitas can also be grilled in a lightly oiled well-seasoned ridged grill pan over moderately high heat.

Each serving about 168 calories and 1 gram fat

CURRIED VEGETABLE DIP

Makes about 1½ cups
Active time: 15 min   Start to finish: 15 min

½ cup sour cream
¼ cup mayonnaise
3 oz cream cheese at room temperature
1 teaspoon fresh lemon juice, or to taste
1 teaspoon curry powder
½ teaspoon ground cumin
½ teaspoon salt
¼ teaspoon turmeric
⅓ cup finely chopped celery
⅓ cup finely chopped peeled and seeded
    cucumber
1 scallion, trimmed and finely chopped

Garnish: **scallion greens, sliced diagonally**

Whisk together all ingredients except celery, cucumber, and scallion until smooth, then stir in vegetables.

Cooks' note:
• Dip can be made 2 days ahead and chilled, covered.
PHOTO ON PAGE 88

AVOCADO JICAMA SALSA WITH YUCA CHIPS

Makes about 3 cups
Active time: 30 min   Start to finish: 30 min

2 firm-ripe California avocados, pitted,
    peeled, and cut into ¼-inch dice
6 oz jicama, peeled and cut into ¼-inch dice
    (1½ cups)
1 small red onion, finely chopped
⅓ cup finely chopped fresh cilantro
2 fresh *serrano* chiles, minced (including seeds)
¼ cup fresh lime juice
2 tablespoons olive oil

Accompaniment: **yuca chips (recipe follows)**

Stir together all ingredients and season with salt.

Cooks' note:
• Salsa can be made 6 hours ahead and chilled, its
  surface covered with plastic wrap.
PHOTO ON PAGE 69

YUCA CHIPS

Serves 6
Active time: 30 min   Start to finish: 30 min

2 to 2½ lb fresh yuca (cassava), trimmed
About 7 cups vegetable oil
Kosher salt for sprinkling

Special equipment: **a Y-shaped vegetable peeler; a deep-fat thermometer; a Japanese Benriner or other adjustable-blade slicer**

Peel yuca with vegetable peeler, removing all waxy brown skin and pinkish layer underneath, then cut flesh crosswise into 3-inch sections.

Heat 1½ inches oil in a 5-quart heavy pot over moderately high heat until it registers 375°F on thermometer.

While oil is heating, shave as many very thin lengthwise strips as possible from yuca sections with peeler or slicer.

Fry yuca strips a handful at a time, stirring and turning with a slotted spoon, until golden, 30 to 45 seconds, transferring to paper towels to drain. Sprinkle immediately with kosher salt.

Cooks' note:
• Yuca chips can be made 3 days ahead and kept in an
  airtight container at room temperature.

PESTO GOAT CHEESE SPREAD

Makes about 1 cup
Active time: 5 min   Start to finish: 5 min

4 oz soft mild goat cheese at room
temperature
2 oz cream cheese at room temperature
¼ cup pesto (recipe follows)

Stir together all ingredients with salt and pepper to taste until smooth.

Cooks' notes:
- Use spread as an hors d'oeuvre (with crackers or toasts) or as a sandwich spread.
- Spread keeps, covered and chilled, 1 week.

PESTO

Makes about 1⅓ cups
Active time: 15 min   Start to finish: 15 min

3 large garlic cloves
½ cup pine nuts
2 oz Parmigiano-Reggiano, coarsely grated
(⅔ cup)
1 teaspoon salt
½ teaspoon black pepper
3 cups loosely packed fresh basil
⅔ cup extra-virgin olive oil

With food processor running, drop in garlic cloves and finely chop. Stop motor and add nuts, cheese, salt, pepper, and basil, then process until finely chopped. With motor running, add oil, blending until incorporated.

Cooks' notes:
- For pasta with pesto: Put ⅔ cup pesto in a large bowl and cook 1 pound linguine or spaghetti until al dente, then whisk about ⅓ cup pasta cooking water into pesto. Add drained pasta to thinned pesto with salt and pepper to taste and toss well. Serve with additional grated Parmigiano-Reggiano.
- Pesto keeps, its surface covered with plastic wrap, chilled, 1 week.

OLIVE AND EGGPLANT SPREAD

Makes about 1 cup
Active time: 15 min   Start to finish: 1 hr

1 (1-lb) eggplant, halved lengthwise and
flesh scored in a crosshatch pattern
4 tablespoons extra-virgin olive oil
¼ cup Kalamata or other brine-cured
black olives, rinsed, patted dry,
and pitted
1 tablespoon drained bottled capers, rinsed

Preheat oven to 375°F.
Rub eggplant with 2 tablespoons oil and bake, cut sides down, in a small baking pan in middle of oven until flesh is browned and very tender, about 50 minutes.
Scoop flesh from eggplant into a food processor, discarding skin, and purée with olives, capers, remaining 2 tablespoons oil, and salt and pepper to taste.

Basil leaves

BREADS

CHIVE BLINI

Makes 6 *blini*
Active time: 45 min   Start to finish: 2¼ hr

1 (¼-oz) package active dry yeast
  (2½ teaspoons)
2½ cups warm whole milk (100–110°F)
1 teaspoon sugar
⅔ cup rice flour
3 large eggs, separated
¼ cup sour cream
¾ stick (6 tablespoons) unsalted butter,
  melted and cooled
1⅔ cups all-purpose flour
1 teaspoon fine sea salt
⅓ cup chopped fresh chives

Stir together yeast, ¼ cup milk, and sugar in a large bowl until sugar is dissolved, then let stand until foamy, about 10 minutes. (If yeast doesn't foam, discard and start over with new yeast.) Add 1¼ cups milk and rice flour, whisking until smooth. Cover bowl with plastic wrap and let sponge rise in a warm place until bubbly, about 1 hour.

Meanwhile, whisk together yolks, sour cream, 2 tablespoons butter, and remaining cup milk in a bowl.

Whisk yolk mixture into bubbly sponge, then add all-purpose flour and sea salt, whisking until smooth. Stir in chives. Beat egg whites in a bowl with an electric mixer until they just hold stiff peaks, then fold into batter. Let stand 30 minutes.

Put a buttered large baking sheet in oven and preheat oven to 200°F.

Brush some of remaining butter onto bottom of a 10-inch nonstick skillet and heat over moderate heat until hot but not smoking. Add 1 cup batter and cook until underside is lightly browned and surface is covered with holes, about 2 minutes. Turn over with a wide spatula and cook until golden on bottom and puffed, about 1 minute more. Brush top with some melted butter, then transfer to buttered baking sheet. Cover loosely with foil and keep warm in middle of oven. Make 5 more *blini* in same manner (you'll have 2 extra), stacking them on baking sheet in 2 piles with sheets of foil between *blini*.

Cooks' note:
· *Blini* can be made 1 day ahead and chilled, covered. Reheat, wrapped in 2 foil packages (3 *blini* per package), in a 350°F oven 30 minutes.
PHOTO ON PAGE 96

GARLIC BREAD

Serves 4 to 6
Active time: 10 min   Start to finish: 30 min

The secret to garlic bread that's neither too greasy nor too dry is having the correct proportion of butter to bread, so we give specific dimensions for the Italian loaf. If yours is a different size, you'll need to adjust the amount of garlic butter accordingly.

2 teaspoons finely chopped garlic
¼ teaspoon salt
½ stick (¼ cup) unsalted butter, softened
1 tablespoon extra-virgin olive oil
2 tablespoons finely chopped fresh
  flat-leaf parsley
1 (15- by 3½-inch) loaf Italian bread

Preheat oven to 350°F.

Mince and mash garlic to a paste with salt using a heavy knife. Stir together butter, oil, and garlic paste in a bowl until smooth, then stir in parsley.

Without cutting completely through bottom, cut bread diagonally into 1-inch-thick slices with a serrated knife, then spread garlic butter between slices.

Wrap loaf in foil and bake in middle of oven 15 minutes. Open foil and bake 5 minutes more.

Cooks' notes:
· Bread can be spread with garlic butter 8 hours ahead and chilled, wrapped in foil. Let stand at room temperature 30 minutes before baking.
· For a brighter flavor, you can substitute 1 tablespoon finely chopped fresh basil for 1 tablespoon of parsley.

CHEDDAR SCALLION DROP BISCUITS

Makes 12 biscuits
Active time: 15 min   Start to finish: 35 min

2¼ cups all-purpose flour
2½ teaspoons baking powder
2 teaspoons sugar
¾ teaspoon baking soda
1 teaspoon salt
6 tablespoons (¾ stick) cold unsalted butter
6 oz Cheddar, coarsely grated (1½ cups)
3 scallions, finely chopped
1 cup well-shaken buttermilk

Preheat oven to 450°F.

Whisk together flour, baking powder, sugar, baking soda, and salt in a bowl. Cut butter into ½-inch cubes, then blend butter into mixture with your fingertips until it resembles coarse meal. Stir in Cheddar and scallions. Add buttermilk and stir until just combined.

Drop dough in 12 equal mounds about 2 inches apart onto a buttered large baking sheet. Bake in middle of oven until golden, 18 to 20 minutes.

FRESH CORN SPOON BREAD

Serves 6
Active time: 15 min   Start to finish: 35 min

2 cups whole milk
⅓ cup yellow cornmeal
1½ cups fresh corn kernels (from 2 to 3 ears)
1 tablespoon unsalted butter
1 teaspoon salt
4 large eggs, separated

Preheat oven to 425°F.

Bring milk, cornmeal, corn kernels, butter, and salt to a boil in a 3-quart heavy saucepan over moderately high heat, stirring frequently, then simmer, stirring constantly, until thickened, 3 to 4 minutes. Remove from heat and cool 5 minutes, stirring occasionally, then whisk in yolks.

Beat whites and a pinch of salt with an electric mixer at medium speed just until soft peaks form. Whisk one fourth of whites into cornmeal mixture to lighten, then fold in remaining whites gently but thoroughly. Spread mixture in a buttered 9½-inch deep-dish glass pie plate or 1½-quart shallow casserole and bake in middle of oven until puffed and golden, 15 to 20 minutes. Serve immediately (bread collapses).

SALT AND PEPPER GRISSINI

Makes 16 breadsticks
Active time: 20 min   Start to finish: 1 hr

¼ cup rye flour
¼ cup plus 1 tablespoon all-purpose flour
½ teaspoon baking powder
¼ teaspoon baking soda
½ teaspoon sugar
1½ to 1¾ teaspoons kosher salt
¼ cup well-shaken low-fat buttermilk
2 teaspoons unsalted butter, melted
   and cooled
1 large egg white, lightly beaten with
   1 teaspoon water
1 teaspoon coarsely ground black pepper

Special equipment: **parchment paper**

Whisk together flours, baking powder, baking soda, sugar, and ¼ teaspoon kosher salt, then stir in buttermilk and butter with a fork. Transfer to a lightly floured surface and gently knead 5 or 6 times.

Preheat oven to 350°F.

Form dough into a log and cut into 16 pieces. Roll each piece into a 10-inch-long rope (if dough sticks, lightly flour work surface) and arrange ½ inch apart on 2 parchment-lined large baking sheets.

Brush breadsticks with beaten egg white and sprinkle with pepper and remaining kosher salt (to taste). Bake in upper and lower thirds of oven, switching position of sheets halfway through baking, until golden and crisp, 20 to 22 minutes total. Transfer to racks to cool.

Cooks' note:
• *Grissini* can be made 1 day ahead and kept in an airtight container at room temperature.

Each serving (2 breadsticks) about 42 calories and 1 gram fat
PHOTO ON PAGE 44

SOUPS

ZUCCHINI AND SAFFRON VICHYSSOISE WITH SCALLOPS

Makes about 8½ cups
Start to finish: 1 hr   Active time: 5½ hr

   2 lb small (5-inch-long) zucchini
   1 lb boiling potatoes
   1 medium onion, chopped
   3 tablespoons unsalted butter
   1 teaspoon chopped garlic
   ¼ teaspoon finely crumbled saffron threads
   5 cups chicken broth
   1 Turkish or ½ California bay leaf
   ½ teaspoon packed fresh thyme leaves
   ½ cup chilled heavy cream
   2 teaspoons fresh lemon juice
  1¼ teaspoons salt
   ¼ teaspoon black pepper
   4 large sea scallops (4 oz total), tough muscle
      removed from side of each if necessary
   1 tablespoon vegetable oil

Special equipment: **a Japanese Benriner or
      other adjustable-blade slicer fitted with
      julienne blade**

Thinly julienne zucchini lengthwise with slicer,
working around core, into ¼-inch-thick ribbons. Cut
zucchini cores into ½-inch pieces.

Peel potatoes and cut into ½-inch pieces. Cook
onion in butter in a 5-quart heavy pot over moderate
heat, stirring occasionally, until softened, about
10 minutes. Add potatoes, garlic, and saffron and cook,
stirring, 1 minute. Add broth, bay leaf, and thyme
and simmer, uncovered, until potatoes are tender, about
20 minutes. Add chopped zucchini cores and simmer,
uncovered, until zucchini is very tender, about
8 minutes.

Purée soup in batches in a blender until very
smooth (use caution when blending hot liquids) and
pour through a fine-mesh sieve into a bowl. Stir in
cream, lemon juice, salt, and pepper, then cool to room
temperature, uncovered. Chill soup, covered, until cold,
at least 4 hours.

While soup is chilling, cook julienned zucchini
in boiling salted water until crisp-tender, about
30 seconds, then drain and transfer to a bowl of ice
and cold water. Drain and pat dry with paper towels.
Season with salt and pepper and chill, covered.

Before serving soup, cut each scallop horizontally
into 3 rounds and pat dry. Heat oil in a large nonstick
skillet over high heat until hot but not smoking, then
sear scallops, turning once, until golden brown, 40 seconds to 1 minute total, and season with salt.

Serve soup with zucchini mounded in center,
topped with scallop rounds.

   Cooks' note:
 • Soup can be chilled up to 2 days.
   PHOTO ON PAGE 94

CHINESE EGG DROP SOUP WITH NOODLES

Serves 4
Active time: 10 min   Start to finish: 20 min

*Though egg drop soup is not traditionally made with
noodles, we love the texture and substance they add.*

   5 cups chicken stock, or 4 cups chicken broth
      plus 1 cup water
   1 teaspoon soy sauce
   2 tablespoons medium-dry Sherry
   1 (2-inch) piece fresh ginger, thinly sliced
   1 garlic clove, smashed
   1 cup dried fine egg noodles (1 oz)
   2 large eggs, lightly beaten
   1 to 2 scallions, thinly sliced
  1½ teaspoons Asian sesame oil, or to taste

Bring stock, soy sauce, Sherry, ginger, and garlic to
a boil in a 2-quart heavy saucepan. Remove ginger and
garlic with a slotted spoon and discard. Stir in noodles
and simmer, uncovered, until tender, about 4 minutes.
Stirring soup in a circular motion, add eggs in a slow,
steady stream. Simmer, undisturbed, until strands of
egg are cooked, about 1 minute. Remove from heat
and stir in scallions (to taste) and sesame oil. Season
with salt.

ASPARAGUS SOUP WITH PARMESAN CUSTARDS

Serves 6
Active time: 45 min   Start to finish: 2½ hr

For custards
2½ oz Parmigiano-Reggiano, coarsely grated
    (1¼ cups)
  1 cup heavy cream
  ½ cup whole milk
  1 whole large egg
  2 large egg yolks
  ⅛ teaspoon salt
    Pinch of white pepper
For soup
  1 large leek (white and pale green parts only),
    finely chopped (1¼ cups)
  ½ cup finely chopped shallot
  ¼ teaspoon black pepper
  ¾ teaspoon salt
  2 tablespoons unsalted butter
2½ lb asparagus, trimmed and cut into
    1½-inch pieces
3½ cups low-sodium chicken broth
1½ cups water
  ¼ cup heavy cream

Garnish: **Parmigiano-Reggiano curls, shaved
    from a wedge with a vegetable peeler**
Special equipment: **6 (2-oz) ramekins**

Make custards:
  Bring cheese, cream, and milk just to a boil in a small heavy saucepan over moderate heat, stirring occasionally. Remove from heat and steep, covered, 30 minutes.
  Preheat oven to 300°F.
  Pour steeped cream through a fine-mesh sieve into a bowl, pressing lightly on cheese solids and discarding them. Whisk together whole egg, yolks, salt, and white pepper in another bowl, then add steeped cream in a stream, whisking until smooth. Divide among well-buttered ramekins.
  Set ramekins in a baking pan and bake in a hot water bath (see Tips, page 8) in middle of oven until centers of custards are completely set, 40 to 45 minutes. Transfer ramekins with tongs to a rack and cool 5 minutes (do not allow to cool longer, or custards will stick to ramekins).

Make soup while cream steeps and custards bake:
  Wash chopped leek in a bowl of cold water, then lift out and drain well. Cook leek, shallot, pepper, and ½ teaspoon salt in butter in a 4- to 6-quart heavy pot over moderately low heat, stirring, until leek is softened, about 3 minutes. Add asparagus, broth, and water and simmer, covered, until asparagus is just tender, 10 to 12 minutes. After 2 to 4 minutes, remove 6 asparagus tips, halve lengthwise and reserve for garnish.
  Purée soup in batches in a blender until smooth (use caution when blending hot liquids). Transfer to a large bowl, then pour through a medium-mesh sieve into cleaned pot. Stir in cream, remaining ¼ teaspoon salt, and pepper to taste and heat over moderately low heat until hot.

Serve soup with custards:
  Working with 1 custard at a time, run a thin knife around edge of each to loosen it, then invert a soup bowl over ramekin and invert custard into bowl. Repeat with remaining custards. Ladle soup around custards and garnish with reserved asparagus tips and parmesan curls.

  Cooks' note:
• Soup can be made 1 day ahead and cooled, uncovered, then chilled, covered.

PHOTO ON PAGE 56

GARLIC SOUP WITH POACHED EGGS

Serves 4
Active time: 30 min   Start to finish: 30 min

  1 medium head of garlic, cloves peeled and
    thinly sliced
  3 tablespoons olive oil
  8 (½-inch-thick) baguette slices
  1 qt chicken stock or broth
  ½ teaspoon dried hot red pepper flakes
  4 large eggs
  ½ cup packed small fresh cilantro sprigs
  4 lime wedges

  Cook garlic in oil in a deep 10-inch heavy skillet over low heat, stirring occasionally, until tender and pale golden, 8 to 10 minutes. Transfer garlic to a bowl with a slotted spoon. Add bread slices to skillet and cook over moderate heat, turning once, until browned, about 4 minutes total. Divide toasts among 4 large soup bowls.

Add stock, red pepper flakes, and garlic to skillet and bring to a simmer.

Break 1 egg into a cup and slide egg into simmering stock. Repeat with remaining eggs. Poach eggs at a bare simmer until whites are firm but yolks are still runny, 3 to 4 minutes. Transfer eggs with slotted spoon to toasts and season with salt. Ladle soup into bowls and top with cilantro. Serve with lime wedges.

asparagus

KALE AND WHITE BEAN SOUP

Serves 6 (main course)
Active time: 1 hr   Start to finish: 3 hr

1 lb dried white beans such as Great
    Northern, *cannellini*, or navy
2 onions, coarsely chopped
2 tablespoons olive oil
4 garlic cloves, finely chopped
5 cups chicken broth
2 qt water
1 (3- by 2-inch) piece Parmigiano-Reggiano
    rind
2 teaspoons salt
½ teaspoon black pepper
1 Turkish or ½ California bay leaf
1 teaspoon finely chopped fresh rosemary
1 lb smoked sausage such as kielbasa
    (optional), sliced crosswise ¼ inch thick
8 carrots, halved lengthwise and cut crosswise
    into ½-inch pieces

1 lb kale (preferably *lacinato*), stems
    and center ribs discarded and leaves
    coarsely chopped

Accompaniment: **provolone toasts (recipe follows)**

Cover beans with water by 2 inches in a pot and bring to a boil. Remove from heat and let stand, uncovered, 1 hour. Drain beans in a colander and rinse.

Cook onions in oil in an 8-quart pot over moderately low heat, stirring occasionally, until softened, 4 to 5 minutes. Add garlic and cook, stirring, 1 minute. Add beans, broth, 1 quart water, cheese rind, salt, pepper, bay leaf, and rosemary and simmer, uncovered, until beans are just tender, about 50 minutes.

While soup is simmering, brown sausage (if using) in batches in a heavy skillet over moderate heat, turning, then transfer to paper towels to drain.

Stir carrots into soup and simmer 5 minutes. Stir in kale, sausage, and remaining quart water and simmer, uncovered, stirring occasionally, until kale is tender, 12 to 15 minutes. Season soup with salt and pepper.

Cooks' notes:
• Soup is best if made 1 or 2 days ahead and cooled completely, uncovered, then chilled, covered. Thin with water if necessary.
• *Lacinato* is available at farm stands, specialty produce markets, and natural foods stores. Be aware that it has many aliases: Tuscan kale, black cabbage, *cavolo nero*, dinosaur kale, and flat black cabbage.

PHOTO ON PAGE 47

PROVOLONE TOASTS

Serves 6
Active time: 15 min   Start to finish: 15 min

½ lb sliced provolone
1 loaf Italian bread, cut crosswise into
    ½-inch-thick slices

Preheat broiler.

Cut provolone to fit bread slices and set aside.

Toast bread (without cheese) on a large baking sheet 4 inches from heat until golden, 30 seconds to 1 minute. Turn bread over and arrange provolone on top. Broil until cheese is melted, 1 to 2 minutes.

CELERY-ROOT BISQUE WITH SHIITAKES

Serves 8 to 10 (makes about 10 cups)
Active time: 45 min   Start to finish: 1¾ hr

2 lb celery root (sometimes called celeriac),
    peeled with a knife and cut into
    ½-inch cubes
3 celery ribs, chopped
½ lb shallots, chopped
1 stick (½ cup) unsalted butter
8 cups water
2 teaspoons salt, or to taste
¼ teaspoon black pepper, or to taste
¼ cup heavy cream
1 tablespoon fresh lemon juice, or to taste
6 oz fresh shiitakes, stems discarded and
    caps sliced ¼ inch thick

Cook celery root, chopped celery, and shallots in
½ stick butter in a 5-quart heavy pot over moderate
heat, covered, stirring occasionally, until softened but
not browned, about 15 minutes. Add water, salt, and
pepper and simmer, uncovered, until vegetables are
very tender, about 30 minutes.

Purée soup in batches in a blender until smooth
(use caution when blending hot liquids), then return
to pot.

Stir in cream and reheat bisque over low heat, stirring occasionally, about 5 minutes. Stir in lemon juice.

While bisque is reheating, melt 2 tablespoons butter
in a 12-inch heavy skillet over moderately high heat
until foam subsides, then sauté mushrooms with salt
and pepper to taste, stirring, until golden brown, about
3 minutes. Transfer mushrooms with a slotted spoon to
a plate and add remaining 2 tablespoons butter to skillet. Cook butter over moderate heat, swirling skillet,
until browned, about 2 minutes, then transfer to a
small bowl.

Serve bisque topped with mushrooms and drizzled
with brown butter.

Cooks' note:
• Bisque can be made (without lemon juice, mushrooms,
  and brown butter) 2 days ahead and chilled, covered.
  Reheat over moderate heat, stirring occasionally, then
  add lemon juice and proceed with recipe.

PHOTO ON PAGE 99

MUSSEL CHOWDER

Serves 8 (first course)
Active time: 1 hr   Start to finish: 1¼ hr

4½ lb mussels (preferably cultivated), cleaned
    and steamed (using half white wine and
    half water; procedures on page 121) and
    reserving cooking liquid
2 medium leeks (white and pale green parts
    only), finely chopped
2 medium carrots, finely chopped
2 large orange bell peppers, finely chopped
1 large shallot, finely chopped
½ teaspoon salt
¼ teaspoon black pepper
½ stick (¼ cup) unsalted butter
2 tablespoons olive oil
2 large garlic cloves, minced
½ cup dry white wine
¼ cup heavy cream

Accompaniment: **crusty bread**

Pour reserved mussel cooking liquid through a fine-
mesh sieve lined with a dampened paper towel into a
bowl. Set aside 24 mussels in their shells, then shuck
remainder and halve crosswise.

Wash chopped leeks in a bowl of cold water, then
lift out and drain well.

Cook leeks, carrots, bell peppers, and shallot with
salt and pepper in butter and oil in a 5-quart heavy pot
over moderate heat, covered, stirring occasionally, until
tender, about 7 minutes. Stir in garlic and cook, uncovered, stirring, 1 minute. Add strained mussel cooking
liquid and wine and simmer 10 minutes.

Stir in halved mussels and cream and simmer, stirring, 5 minutes. Add reserved mussels in their shells
and simmer until just heated through, about 1 minute.
Season with salt and pepper.

CHILLED PEA BROTH WITH LEMON CREAM

Serves 6
Active time: 30 min   Start to finish: 8½ hr (includes chilling)

2 medium onions, chopped
3 tablespoons olive oil
2 lb sugar snap peas, trimmed and cut
    crosswise into ½-inch pieces
1 teaspoon sugar
6 cups plus 2½ tablespoons water
2 teaspoons salt, or to taste
3 tablespoons sour cream
1 teaspoon finely grated fresh lemon zest

Garnish: **pea sprouts**

Cook onions in oil in a wide 6-quart heavy pot over moderately low heat, stirring occasionally, until softened, 5 to 7 minutes. Add sugar snaps and cook, stirring occasionally, until crisp-tender and bright green, 6 to 8 minutes. Add sugar and cook, stirring, 1 minute.

Purée pea mixture with 6 cups water in a blender in 6 batches until very smooth, about 30 seconds per batch, then pour through a fine-mesh sieve, discarding solids (do not press on solids). Stir in salt and chill broth, covered, until very cold, about 8 hours. (Do not chill longer or soup will discolor.)

Whisk together sour cream, zest, and remaining 2½ tablespoons water in a bowl, then pour through sieve into another small bowl (to remove air bubbles).

Serve broth topped with lemon cream.

PHOTO ON PAGE 64

SHELLFISH CHOWDER

Serves 4 (main course) or 6 (first course)
Active time: 20 min   Start to finish: 40 min

5 bacon slices, finely chopped
2 boiling potatoes (¾ lb total), cut into
    ¼-inch dice (1½ cups)
½ cup finely chopped shallot
¾ cup bottled clam juice
2½ cups whole milk
⅛ teaspoon cayenne
¼ lb large shrimp in shell (21 to 25 per lb),
    peeled, deveined, and cut into
    ½-inch pieces

½ lb sea scallops, quartered and tough muscle
    removed from side of each if necessary
1 teaspoon salt
½ lb shelled cooked lobster meat, cut into
    ½-inch-thick pieces, or ½ lb lump
    crabmeat, picked over
2 tablespoons chopped fresh cilantro
2 tablespoons chopped fresh chives

Cook bacon in a 5-quart heavy pot over moderate heat, stirring occasionally, until crisp, about 5 minutes. Transfer bacon with a slotted spoon to paper towels to drain. Pour off all but 1 tablespoon fat from pot and stir in potatoes, shallot, and clam juice. Simmer, covered, until potatoes are tender and most of liquid is evaporated, about 8 minutes. Stir in milk and cayenne and return just to a simmer.

Add shrimp, scallops, and salt and simmer, stirring occasionally, until shellfish is just cooked through, 3 to 5 minutes. Stir in lobster and half of herbs and simmer 1 minute. Serve chowder topped with bacon and remaining herbs.

MISO SOUP WITH CARROTS AND TOFU

Serves 6
Active time: 10 min   Start to finish: 20 min

Traditional miso soup begins with dashi, *a Japanese seaweed and fish broth, but we found this simplified version, made with water, very satisfying as well.*

6 cups water
⅛ teaspoon salt, or to taste
1 medium carrot, cut into ¼-inch dice
⅓ cup *shiro miso* (white fermented
    soybean paste)
½ cup diced (¼-inch) silken tofu (3 oz)

Bring 5½ cups water with salt to a boil in a 2-quart saucepan. Add carrot, then reduce heat and simmer, covered, until tender, about 3 minutes. Remove from heat.

Whisk together *shiro miso* and remaining ½ cup water in a small bowl until smooth, then whisk into carrot mixture. Add tofu and serve immediately.

Each serving about 51 calories and 2 grams fat

JERUSALEM ARTICHOKE SOUP WITH PUMPERNICKEL CROUTONS

Serves 4
Active time: 40 min   Start to finish: 40 min

1 (¼-inch-thick) slice pumpernickel bread, crust discarded and bread cut into ¼-inch dice
1½ lb Jerusalem artichokes (sometimes called Sun Chokes)
1½ cups nonfat (skim) milk
½ cup water
½ teaspoon salt
⅛ teaspoon black pepper

Garnish: tablespoons chopped fresh flat-leaf parsley

Preheat oven to 400°F.

Toast bread in a shallow baking pan in middle of oven, stirring once or twice, until crisp, about 7 minutes.

Peel artichokes with a vegetable peeler and cut into 1-inch pieces, then simmer in milk and water in a 3-quart heavy saucepan, partially covered (be careful not to let it boil over), stirring occasionally, until artichokes are very tender, about 15 minutes.

Purée artichokes with cooking liquid, salt, and pepper in 2 batches in a blender until smooth (use caution when blending hot liquids). Transfer purée to same saucepan and thin with additional water if necessary. Heat soup over moderate heat, stirring, until hot. Serve topped with croutons and parsley.

Each serving about 113 calories and less than 1 gram fat

BUTTERNUT SQUASH SOUP WITH STAR ANISE AND GINGER SHRIMP

Serves 8 (first course; makes about 5 cups)
Active time: 20 min   Start to finish: 40 min

24 large shrimp in shell (about 1 lb), peeled, leaving tail and first segment of shell intact, and deveined
1 tablespoon finely grated peeled fresh ginger
⅔ cup chopped shallot
1 garlic clove, thinly sliced
3 whole star anise
2 tablespoons unsalted butter
1¾ lb butternut squash, peeled, seeded, and cut into ½-inch pieces (5 cups)
4 cups chicken stock or broth
2 cups water
¼ teaspoon salt
1 tablespoon vegetable oil

Garnish: **fresh cilantro sprigs**

Toss shrimp with ginger in a bowl and marinate, chilled, 30 minutes (do not marinate any longer or enzymes from ginger will begin to cook shrimp).

Make soup while shrimp marinate:

Cook shallot, garlic, and anise in butter in a 3-quart heavy saucepan over moderate heat, stirring, until shallot is softened, about 5 minutes. Add squash, stock, and water and simmer, uncovered, until squash is very tender, about 20 minutes. Remove star anise.

Purée soup in 2 batches in a blender (use caution when blending hot liquids) until very smooth, about 1 minute per batch, then transfer to cleaned pan and keep warm, covered.

Sprinkle marinated shrimp with salt. Heat oil in a 12-inch nonstick skillet over moderately high heat until hot but not smoking, then sauté shrimp in 2 batches, stirring, until just cooked through, about 3 minutes per batch, transferring to paper towels.

Bring soup to a simmer and season with salt and pepper. Divide among 8 shallow soup bowls and mound 3 shrimp in each bowl.

Cooks' note:
• Soup (without shrimp) can be made 3 days ahead and chilled, covered. If making soup ahead, begin marinating shrimp about 40 minutes before serving.

PHOTO ON PAGE 104

MUSHROOM BARLEY SOUP

Serves 8

Active time: 20 min   Start to finish: 1 hr

⅓ cup quick-cooking barley
7 cups water
¼ oz dried porcini (¼ cup)
1 large leek (white and pale green parts only), halved lengthwise and thinly sliced crosswise
1 tablespoon olive oil
1 large onion, chopped
2 celery ribs, cut into ⅓-inch dice
2 carrots, chopped
½ lb fresh shiitakes, stems discarded and caps thinly sliced
2 tablespoons tomato paste
2 tablespoons medium-dry Sherry
1¾ cups low-sodium fat-free beef broth
1½ teaspoons salt
¼ teaspoon black pepper

Garnish: **chopped fresh flat-leaf parsley**

Simmer barley in 3½ cups water in a 5- to 6-quart heavy pot, uncovered, until almost tender, 10 to 15 minutes. Drain in a colander.

While barley is cooking, soak porcini in ½ cup water in a small bowl until softened, about 20 minutes. Drain in a medium-mesh sieve lined with a dampened paper towel set over a bowl, reserving liquid. Rinse porcini to remove any grit, then coarsely chop. Wash sliced leek in a large bowl of water, then lift out and drain in sieve.

Heat oil in cleaned pot over moderately high heat until hot but not smoking, then sauté onion and celery, stirring occasionally, until golden, 6 to 8 minutes. Add carrots, shiitakes, leek, and porcini and sauté, stirring frequently, until liquid mushrooms give off is evaporated and mushrooms are golden, 4 to 6 minutes.

Stir in tomato paste, Sherry, beef broth, mushroom soaking liquid, barley, salt, pepper, and remaining 3 cups water and bring to a boil. Reduce heat and simmer, uncovered, stirring occasionally, until vegetables and barley are tender, 10 to 15 minutes. Season with salt and pepper.

Cooks' note:
· Soup can be made 3 days ahead and cooled, uncovered, then chilled, covered. Reheat soup and thin with water as necessary.

Each serving about 71 calories and 2 grams fat
PHOTO ON PAGE 44

FISH AND SHELLFISH

fish

HALIBUT WITH GRAPEFRUIT BEURRE BLANC

Serves 4
Active time: 1¼ hr   Start to finish: 1¼ hr

For beurre blanc
  **3 grapefruit (preferably 2 white and
    1 pink or red)**
  ¼ cup dry white wine
  1 shallot, minced
  2 tablespoons white-wine vinegar
  **1¼ sticks (½ cup plus 2 tablespoons) unsalted
    butter, cut into tablespoon pieces**
For fish and vegetables
  **4 (½-inch-thick) halibut steaks with skin
    (1½ lb)**
  3 tablespoons vegetable oil
  **1 lb fresh shiitake mushrooms, stems
    discarded and caps thinly sliced**
  **2 Belgian endives, trimmed and cut crosswise
    into 1-inch-thick slices**

Make beurre blanc:
Finely grate 1 teaspoon zest from a grapefruit.
Squeeze ½ cup juice from a white grapefruit.

Cut peel, including all white pith, from remaining
fruit with a sharp paring knife and cut segments free
from membranes. Chop enough grapefruit segments
(use all colors) to measure ½ cup. Reserve 1 cup of
remaining whole segments.

Boil juice, wine, shallot, and vinegar in a small
heavy saucepan until reduced to about 1 tablespoon.
Reduce heat to low and whisk in butter 1 piece at a
time, lifting pan from heat occasionally to cool sauce
and adding each new piece of butter before previous
one has melted completely (sauce must not get hot
enough to separate).

Stir in chopped grapefruit and season with salt and
pepper. Keep beurre blanc warm in a metal bowl set
over a saucepan of hot water.

Cook fish and vegetables:

Preheat oven to 250°F.

Pat halibut dry and season with salt and pepper.
Heat 1½ tablespoons oil in a large nonstick skillet over
moderately high heat until hot but not smoking, then
sauté fish, in batches if necessary, turning over once,
until golden brown and just cooked through, about
5 minutes total. Transfer fish to a shallow baking pan
and keep warm in oven.

Wipe skillet clean and heat remaining 1½ tablespoons oil over moderately high heat until hot but not
smoking, then sauté mushrooms with salt and pepper to
taste, stirring, until golden brown, 5 to 7 minutes. Add
endives and sauté, stirring, until leaves are slightly wilted, about 1 minute. Stir in reserved whole grapefruit
segments and remove from heat.

Serve fish over mushrooms, topped with beurre
blanc and zest.

GROUPER WITH TOMATO AND BASIL

Serves 2
Active time: 15 min   Start to finish: 25 min

  2 tablespoons extra-virgin olive oil
  **1 (1-lb) piece grouper or red snapper fillet
    (¾ inch thick), skinned and halved
    crosswise**
  ¼ teaspoon salt
  ⅛ teaspoon black pepper
  ½ cup coarsely chopped tomato
  1 small garlic clove, minced (optional)
  2 tablespoons thinly sliced fresh basil

Accompaniment: **fresh corn spoon bread
    (page 132)**

Working off heat, put 1 tablespoon oil in a 10-inch
nonstick skillet and add fish, turning to coat with oil on
both sides. Arrange fish skinned sides down and sprinkle with salt and pepper.

Toss together tomato, garlic (if using), basil,
remaining tablespoon oil, and salt and pepper to taste in
a small bowl, then mound on top of fish. Cover skillet
with a tight-fitting lid and cook fish over moderately
high heat until just cooked through, about 8 minutes.

SAUTÉED HALIBUT WITH PECAN SHALLOT TOPPING

Serves 4
Active time: 20 min   Start to finish: 30 min

4 (1¼-inch-thick) pieces halibut fillet
  (6 oz each), skinned
3 tablespoons olive oil
1 cup chopped shallot (6 oz)
½ cup pecans (2 oz), chopped
½ tablespoon unsalted butter
½ teaspoon finely grated fresh lemon zest
2 tablespoons finely chopped fresh
  flat-leaf parsley

Accompaniment: **lemon wedges**

Pat halibut dry and season with salt and pepper. Heat 2 tablespoons oil in a 12-inch heavy skillet over moderately high heat until hot but not smoking, then sauté fish, turning once, until golden and just cooked through, 4 to 6 minutes total. Transfer to plates and keep warm, loosely covered with foil.

Add remaining tablespoon oil to skillet and cook shallot over moderate heat, stirring occasionally, until pale golden, 3 to 4 minutes. Add pecans and sauté over moderately high heat, stirring, until fragrant and a shade darker, about 3 minutes. Add butter and stir until melted.

Remove skillet from heat and stir in zest, parsley, and salt and pepper to taste. Sprinkle pecan shallot topping over fish.

SAUTÉED COD ON SNOW PEAS AND CABBAGE WITH MISO SESAME VINAIGRETTE

Serves 4
Active time: 1 hr   Start to finish: 1 hr

For vinaigrette
2 tablespoons seasoned rice vinegar
3 tablespoons water
2 tablespoons red or white miso
  (fermented soybean paste)
1 tablespoon sugar
1 tablespoon *mirin* (Japanese sweet rice wine)
2 tablespoons finely grated peeled fresh
  ginger
4 teaspoons *nerigoma* (Japanese sesame paste)
  or well-stirred tahini
3 tablespoons vegetable oil
For cabbage
2 tablespoons vegetable oil
2 garlic cloves, finely chopped
½ lb Savoy cabbage, very thinly sliced
  crosswise
½ lb Napa cabbage, very thinly sliced
  crosswise
¼ lb snow peas, very thinly sliced lengthwise
For fish
2 tablespoons vegetable oil
4 (5-oz) pieces cod fillet (¾ to 1 inch thick)

Make vinaigrette:
Purée all vinaigrette ingredients in a blender until smooth.
Sauté cabbage:
Heat oil in a 12-inch nonstick skillet over moderately high heat until hot but not smoking, then sauté garlic until golden, about 30 seconds. Add cabbages and snow peas and sauté until cabbages are wilted and peas are crisp-tender, about 5 minutes. Season with salt and transfer to a bowl, then wipe skillet clean.
Cook fish:
Heat oil in skillet over high heat until hot but not smoking, then sauté cod, turning once, until golden and just cooked through, about 6 minutes total.

Divide cabbage among 4 plates. Top with fish and drizzle with some dressing. Serve remainder on the side.

Cooks' note:
• Dressing can be made 1 day ahead and chilled, covered. Bring to room temperature before serving.
PHOTO ON PAGE 80

SOLE GOUJONS WITH PAPRIKA SALT

Serves 4 (main course) or 6 (hors d'oeuvre)
Active time: 25 min   Start to finish: 25 min

8 cups vegetable oil
1 tablespoon plus ¾ teaspoon salt
½ teaspoon smoked paprika (sweet or hot) or
   1 teaspoon regular paprika (sweet or hot)
2 lb sole fillets
¾ cup all-purpose flour
¼ teaspoon black pepper
1 cup fresh seltzer or club soda, chilled

Special equipment: **a deep-fat thermometer**

Heat oil in a 4-quart heavy pot over moderate heat until thermometer registers 375°F.

Stir together 1 tablespoon salt and half of paprika in a small bowl.

Pat sole dry, then diagonally cut crosswise into ½-inch-wide strips. Whisk together flour, remaining paprika, remaining ¾ teaspoon salt, and pepper, then whisk in seltzer. Working with 6 pieces at a time, dip fish in batter to coat, shaking off excess, and fry, turning occasionally, until golden brown and fish is just cooked through (cut a piece open to test), 3 to 4 minutes. Transfer with a slotted spoon to paper towels to drain, then sprinkle with some of paprika salt. Skim any bits of fried batter from pot and return oil to 375°F between batches.

Serve remaining paprika salt on the side for dipping.

ROASTED SALMON

Serves 1
Active time: 5 min   Start to finish: 15 min

1 (5-oz) piece salmon fillet with skin
1 teaspoon extra-virgin olive oil plus
   additional for drizzling
½ tablespoon chopped fresh chives
½ tablespoon fresh tarragon leaves (optional)

Preheat oven to 425°F.

Rub salmon all over with 1 teaspoon oil and season with salt and pepper. Roast, skin side down, on a foil-lined baking sheet in upper third of oven until fish is just cooked through, about 12 minutes.

Cut salmon in half crosswise, then lift flesh from skin with a metal spatula and transfer to a plate. Discard skin, then drizzle salmon with additional oil and sprinkle with chives and tarragon (if using).

PHOTO ON PAGE 113

GRILLED BRINED SALMON AND EGGPLANT WITH FENNEL CUCUMBER RELISH

Serves 8
Active time: 1 hr   Start to finish: 3 hr

7½ cups water
3 cups packed light brown sugar
   (from two 1-lb boxes)
1½ cups kosher salt
½ cup plus 2 tablespoons granulated sugar
1 cup chopped fresh dill
8 (6- to 8-oz) pieces salmon fillet with skin
2 lb small eggplants, cut diagonally into
   ⅓-inch-thick slices
2 tablespoons olive oil

Accompaniment: **fennel cucumber relish**
   (recipe follows)
Special equipment: **a 1-lb weight such as a**
   soup can

Bring water, brown sugar, salt, and 6 tablespoons granulated sugar to a boil in a 5-quart heavy pot, stirring until sugar is dissolved. Transfer 6 cups brine to a 13- by 9-inch glass or ceramic baking dish, then stir in dill and cool. Transfer remaining 4 cups brine to a large bowl and add remaining 4 tablespoons granulated sugar, stirring until dissolved, then cool completely.

Marinate salmon, skin sides up, in brine in baking dish, chilled, 1 hour. (Do not turn salmon.) Put eggplant in brine in bowl, then invert a small plate over eggplant and weight it with soup can (to keep eggplant immersed). Marinate eggplant at room temperature 30 minutes. (Do not brine salmon or eggplant longer than indicated or they will be too salty.)

Prepare charcoal or gas grill for cooking. If using charcoal, open vents on bottom of grill.

Remove salmon from brine and pat dry, discarding brine. Remove eggplant from brine, then rinse and pat dry, discarding brine. Toss eggplant with oil and pepper to taste in a bowl.

When fire is moderate (you can hold your hand 5 inches above rack for 3 to 4 seconds), grill eggplant on lightly oiled grill rack, turning once, until golden, about 4 minutes total. Transfer to a platter with tongs and keep warm, covered.

Reduce grill temperature to moderately low. When you can hold your hand 5 inches above rack for 5 to 6 seconds, grill salmon, starting with skin sides up and turning once, until just cooked through and skin is crisp, about 8 minutes total.

Serve salmon over eggplant.

Cooks' note:
• Brine (without dill) can be made 1 day ahead and kept, covered, at room temperature.
PHOTO ON PAGE 74

FENNEL CUCUMBER RELISH

Makes about 4 cups
Active time: 25 min   Start to finish: 40 min

1 lb fennel bulb (sometimes called anise), stalks discarded and bulb finely chopped
1 lb seedless cucumbers (usually plastic-wrapped), halved lengthwise, cored, and cut into ¼-inch dice
6 tablespoons cider vinegar, or to taste
2 tablespoons finely chopped shallot
1½ tablespoons chopped fresh dill
1½ tablespoons vegetable oil
1 tablespoon sugar
¼ teaspoon salt, or to taste

Stir together all ingredients in a bowl and let stand 15 minutes.

Cooks' note:
• Relish can be made 1 day ahead (though color will not be quite as bright) and chilled, covered. Bring to room temperature before serving.

PROSCIUTTO-WRAPPED SALMON

Serves 6
Active time: 15 min   Start to finish: 25 min

6 (6-oz) center-cut pieces of salmon fillet, skinned and halved crosswise
12 very thin slices prosciutto (¼ lb)
2 tablespoons extra-virgin olive oil

Accompaniment: **herbed bean ragout (page 188)**

Preheat oven to 425°F.

Season salmon lightly with salt and wrap each piece in a slice of prosciutto, leaving ends of salmon exposed. Transfer, seam sides down, to an oiled large shallow baking pan. Season with pepper and drizzle each piece with ½ teaspoon oil. Bake in middle of oven until just cooked through, 8 to 9 minutes.

Serve over herbed bean ragout.
PHOTO ON PAGE 56

BACON-WRAPPED TROUT WITH ROSEMARY

Serves 1
Active time: 10 min   Start to finish: 20 min

1 (10- to 12-oz) whole trout, cleaned
2 (4- to 5-inch) fresh rosemary sprigs
3 bacon slices
3 (⅛-inch-thick) lemon slices

Preheat broiler.

Put fish in a shallow baking pan (1 inch deep) or a large heavy ovenproof skillet, then pat dry and season cavity with salt and pepper. Put rosemary inside cavity and season outside of fish with salt and pepper, then wrap bacon slices around fish.

Broil fish 5 to 7 inches from heat until skin of fish and bacon are crisp, about 5 minutes. Turn fish over gently with a spatula and broil 2 minutes more. Add lemon slices to pan in 1 layer alongside fish and continue to broil until fish is just cooked through and rest of bacon is crisp, 2½ to 3 minutes more.

shellfish

LOBSTERS WITH TARRAGON VERMOUTH SAUCE

Serves 4
Active time: 30 min   Start to finish: 1 hr

For lobsters
   6 qt water
   3 tablespoons fine sea salt
   4 (1¼- to 1½-lb) live lobsters
For sauce
   1 stick (½ cup) unsalted butter
   3 tablespoons dry vermouth
   1 tablespoon tarragon white-wine vinegar
   3 large egg yolks
   ¼ teaspoon salt
   ¼ teaspoon black pepper
   ½ teaspoon fresh lemon juice
   1½ teaspoons chopped fresh tarragon

Special equipment: **an instant-read thermometer**

Cook lobsters:
   Bring water and sea salt to a boil in an 8- to 10-quart pot. Plunge 2 lobsters headfirst into water and cook, covered, over high heat 7 minutes from time lobsters enter water, then transfer with tongs to sink to drain. Return water to a boil and cook remaining 2 lobsters in same manner.
   Make sauce while lobsters cook and drain:
   Melt butter and cool until just warm.
   Whisk together vermouth, vinegar, and yolks in a metal bowl, then set bowl over a small saucepan of boiling water and heat mixture, whisking, until warm. Add melted butter in a slow stream, whisking, then whisk in salt and pepper. Cook sauce, whisking, until thickened and registers 160°F on thermometer, about 5 minutes. Remove pan from heat and keep bowl in saucepan. Just before serving, stir in lemon juice and tarragon.
   Working from belly side, halve each lobster lengthwise with a sharp heavy knife or kitchen shears. Serve lobsters with sauce.

PHOTO ON PAGE 86

MUSSEL GRATIN

Serves 6 (main course)
Active time: 1 hr   Start to finish: 1¼ hr

   4 lb mussels (preferably cultivated), cleaned and steamed (procedure on page 121), then shucked
   2 lb plum tomatoes, halved lengthwise, seeded, and halves cut into sixths
   ½ cup chopped fresh basil
   ½ cup crème fraîche
   ½ cup finely grated Parmigiano-Reggiano (1 oz)
   2 large garlic cloves, 1 minced and 1 halved
   ½ teaspoon salt
   ¼ teaspoon black pepper
   15 (⅓-inch-thick) baguette slices
   2 tablespoons extra-virgin olive oil

   Preheat oven to 450°F.
   Toss together mussels, tomatoes, basil, crème fraîche, cheese, minced garlic, salt, and pepper in an oiled 3-quart (about 13- by 9½- by 2-inch) baking dish.
   Rub 1 side of each bread slice with halved garlic and arrange bread, garlic side up, over mussel mixture in baking dish. Brush tops of bread with oil.
   Bake gratin in middle of oven until bread is golden brown on top, about 15 minutes.
   Serve mussels spooned over garlic toasts.

SCALLOP AND SHRIMP FRITTERS WITH CHIPOTLE MAYONNAISE

Serves 4 (main course)
Active time: 25 min   Start to finish: 35 min

For chipotle *mayonnaise*
  ½ cup mayonnaise
  1 tablespoon finely chopped canned *chipotle* chiles in *adobo* plus 2 teaspoons *adobo* sauce
  ¼ teaspoon fresh lemon juice
For fritters
  ½ lb sea scallops, tough muscle removed from side of each if necessary
  1 large egg white
  1 tablespoon chopped shallot
  ½ teaspoon salt
  ⅛ teaspoon black pepper
  ⅓ cup chilled heavy cream
  ½ lb large shrimp in shell (21 to 25 per lb), peeled, deveined, and cut into ¼-inch pieces
  1 cup plain fine dry bread crumbs
  About ½ cup vegetable oil

Accompaniment: **lemon wedges**

Make chipotle *mayonnaise:*
  Stir together mayonnaise, chiles, *adobo* sauce, and lemon juice in a small bowl, then season with salt.
  Make fritters:
  Purée scallops, egg white, shallot, salt, and pepper in a food processor. Add cream and pulse until just combined. Transfer mixture to a bowl and stir in shrimp. Chill, covered, 10 minutes.
  Put bread crumbs in a pie plate. Drop 6 (2-tablespoon) mounds of scallop mixture onto crumbs, then gently coat with crumbs and shape mounds into 3-inch patties. Transfer as coated to a wax-paper-lined tray. Make 6 more patties in same manner with remaining scallop mixture and crumbs.
  Heat ¼ inch oil in a 12-inch heavy skillet over moderately high heat until hot but not smoking, then fry patties in 2 batches, turning once, until golden and firm to the touch, about 4 minutes total. Drain on paper towels.
  Serve fritters with *chipotle* mayonnaise.

SEA SCALLOPS WITH CILANTRO GREMOLATA AND GINGER LIME BEURRE BLANC

Serves 4 (main course) or 6 (first course)
Active time: 30 min   Start to finish: 30 min

For gremolata
  1½ tablespoons finely chopped fresh cilantro
  1 small garlic clove, minced
  Finely grated zest of 1 small lime (¾ teaspoon)
For beurre blanc
  2 tablespoons minced shallot
  1 tablespoon finely grated peeled fresh ginger
  3 tablespoons fresh lime juice
  ¼ cup dry white wine
  1 stick (½ cup) cold unsalted butter, cut into tablespoon pieces
  White pepper
For scallops
  24 sea scallops (1½ lb), tough muscle removed from side of each if necessary
  1 tablespoon olive oil

Make gremolata:
  Stir together cilantro, garlic, and lime zest in a small bowl.
  Make beurre blanc:
  Simmer shallot and ginger in lime juice and wine in a small heavy saucepan until liquid is reduced to about 2 tablespoons.
  Whisk in butter 1 tablespoon at a time, adding each new piece before previous one has completely melted and occasionally lifting pan from heat to cool mixture. (Sauce must not get too hot or it will separate.) Pour sauce through a fine-mesh sieve into a bowl, discarding solids, then return to cleaned pan. Season with salt and white pepper and keep warm while cooking scallops.
  Sauté scallops:
  Pat scallops dry and season with salt and pepper. Heat oil in a 12-inch nonstick skillet over moderately high heat until hot but not smoking, then sauté scallops, turning once, until golden and just cooked through, 4 to 5 minutes total.
  Sprinkle scallops with *gremolata* and serve with sauce.

SEARED SCALLOPS
WITH TOMATO BEURRE BLANC

Serves 6
Active time: 45 min   Start to finish: 2¼ hr

For beurre blanc
  ¼ cup packed soft dried tomatoes
    (not packed in oil; 1¼ oz)
  1½ sticks (¾ cup) unsalted butter, softened
  ⅛ teaspoon salt
  ⅓ cup minced shallot
  ⅔ cup dry white wine
  3 tablespoons water
  1 teaspoon fresh lemon juice
For scallops
  2 lb large sea scallops (30), tough muscle
    removed from side of each if necessary
  About 2 tablespoons vegetable oil

Make beurre blanc:
Soak tomatoes in warm water to cover until softened, 20 to 25 minutes. Drain and pat dry, then mince.
Stir together tomatoes, butter, and salt, then form into
an 8-inch log on a sheet of plastic wrap and chill,
wrapped in plastic wrap, until firm, about 1 hour. Cut
tomato butter into 12 equal pieces.

Cook shallot in 1 piece of tomato butter (keep
remaining butter chilled) in a small heavy saucepan
over moderately low heat, stirring, until softened, about
3 minutes. Add wine and boil until liquid is reduced to
about ⅓ cup, about 10 minutes.

Reduce heat to low and whisk in remaining cold
tomato butter 1 piece at a time, adding each piece
before previous one has completely melted and lifting
pan from heat occasionally to cool mixture (sauce
should not get hot enough to separate). Whisk in water
and lemon juice, then season with salt and pepper.

Transfer beurre blanc to a bowl and keep warm,
covered, in a larger bowl of warm water.
Sauté scallops:
Pat scallops dry and season with salt and pepper.
Heat 1 teaspoon oil in a 12-inch nonstick skillet over
moderately high heat until hot but not smoking, then
sear 6 to 8 scallops, turning once, until golden brown
and just cooked through, 2 to 4 minutes total. Transfer

to a platter as cooked and keep warm, loosely covered
with foil. Sear remaining scallops in same manner,
wiping out skillet and adding about 1 teaspoon oil
between batches.

Spoon 3 tablespoons beurre blanc onto each of
6 plates, then top with scallops.
PHOTO ON PAGE 64

SOY CITRUS MARINATED SCALLOPS

Serves 6
Active time: 15 min   Start to finish: 25 min

  ⅔ cup soy sauce
  ¼ cup fresh lemon juice
  ¼ cup fresh lime juice
  3 tablespoons plus 1 teaspoon sugar
  2 teaspoons finely grated peeled fresh ginger
  2 teaspoons Asian sesame oil
  2 lb large sea scallops (30), tough muscle
    removed from side of each if necessary
  2 teaspoons vegetable oil

Garnish: sesame seeds (preferably black), toasted
  (see Tips, page 8)
Accompaniment: **soba** salad (page 215)

Whisk together soy sauce, lemon and lime juices,
sugar, ginger, and sesame oil in a wide shallow nonreactive bowl. Add scallops and marinate, covered, at
room temperature, 5 minutes on each side (do not
marinate any longer, or scallops will become mushy
once cooked). Transfer scallops to a plate and
reserve marinade.

Heat ½ teaspoon vegetable oil in a 12-inch nonstick
skillet over moderately high heat until hot but not
smoking, then sauté scallops, 6 to 8 at a time, turning
once, until golden brown and just cooked through, 4 to
6 minutes total, transferring to a plate as cooked. Wipe
out skillet and add ½ teaspoon oil between batches.

Wipe out skillet again, then add marinade and boil
until reduced to about ⅓ cup, about 2 minutes. Drizzle
scallops with sauce.

Each serving about 198 calories and 5 grams fat

MEATS

beef

GRILLED NEW YORK STRIP STEAK WITH SALSA VERDE

Serves 1
Active time: 15 min   Start to finish: 35 min

1½ tablespoons coarsely crumbled firm white
    sandwich bread
1½ teaspoons red-wine vinegar
1½ teaspoons drained bottled capers, finely
    chopped
¼ teaspoon minced garlic
⅛ teaspoon anchovy paste
⅛ teaspoon Dijon mustard
2 tablespoons finely chopped fresh
    flat-leaf parsley
1½ tablespoons extra-virgin olive oil
2 teaspoons water
1 (12-oz) boneless beef top loin steak
    (New York strip; 1 inch thick)

Prepare grill for cooking. If using a charcoal grill, open vents on bottom of grill.

Mash together bread crumbs, vinegar, capers, garlic, anchovy paste, and mustard using a mortar and pestle (or see cooks' note, below). Add parsley, oil, and salt and pepper to taste and stir until combined well. Stir in water.

Pat steak dry and season on both sides with salt and pepper. When fire is hot (you can hold your hand 5 inches above rack for 1 to 2 seconds), grill steak on lightly oiled grill rack, uncovered, turning once, about 10 minutes total for medium-rare. Let stand 10 minutes.

Stir sauce and serve with steak.

Cooks' note:
• Sauce can also be whisked together in a small bowl. Mince and mash garlic to a paste with a pinch of salt before adding to bowl.

PHOTO ON PAGE 112

SPICED FILLET OF BEEF WITH MIZUNA SALAD

Serves 6
Active time: 15 min   Start to finish: 1 hr

For beef
2 teaspoons whole black peppercorns
2½ teaspoons cumin seeds
2½ teaspoons coriander seeds
2 teaspoons dried hot red pepper flakes
4 teaspoons kosher salt
3½ lb center-cut beef tenderloin roast (fillet
    of beef), trimmed and, if necessary, tied
2 tablespoons vegetable oil
For salad
1 tablespoon extra-virgin olive oil
1½ teaspoons fresh lemon juice
1 teaspoon minced shallot
¼ teaspoon salt
4 oz *mizuna* or baby arugula, trimmed

Special equipment: **an instant-read thermometer**

For beef:
Preheat oven to 425°F.

Toast peppercorns, cumin, and coriander (see Tips, page 8), then cool completely. Grind spices with red pepper flakes in an electric coffee/spice grinder or with a mortar and pestle. Stir in kosher salt.

Pat beef dry and sprinkle with spices on all sides, pressing to adhere. Heat oil in a large flameproof roasting pan set across 2 burners over high heat until just smoking, then brown beef on all sides, about 2 minutes.

Roast beef in middle of oven until thermometer inserted diagonally 2 inches into center registers 120°F, about 25 minutes. Let beef stand in pan 25 minutes. Beef will continue to cook as it stands, reaching 130°F (medium-rare).

Make salad and slice beef:
Whisk together oil, lemon juice, shallot, and salt in a bowl, then add pepper to taste.

Untie beef if necessary, then slice. Toss *mizuna* with dressing and serve beef topped with salad.

PHOTO ON PAGE 95

GRILLED MATAMBRE

Spinach and Carrot Stuffed Flank Steak

Serves 6
Active time: 2½ hr   Start to finish: 3 hr

Matambre *(literally, "kill the hunger") is a classic South American meat dish. Every family has its own favorite combination of ingredients for the filling— some use vegetables, eggs, and nuts; others use ground pork, calves' brains, and spinach. We kept it simple and went with spinach and carrots.*

Traditionally, this dish is poached, but we decided to grill ours. After testing this recipe on both gas and charcoal grills, we found that we prefer the flavor that charcoal imparts to the dish. We used a 22½-inch kettle grill, a large chimney starter, and a 10-pound bag of hardwood charcoal.

4 medium carrots, cut crosswise into thirds
**6 bacon slices, cut crosswise into
    ½-inch pieces**
1 cup fine fresh bread crumbs
¼ cup finely chopped fresh flat-leaf parsley
2 garlic cloves, minced
1 teaspoon finely chopped fresh oregano
2 teaspoons kosher salt
½ teaspoon black pepper
⅛ teaspoon ground clove
⅛ teaspoon freshly grated nutmeg
1 (2½-lb) flank steak, trimmed
½ lb spinach, stems discarded

Special equipment: **kitchen string; an instant-read
    thermometer**

Cook carrots in a saucepan of boiling salted water (see Tips, page 8) until barely tender, 6 to 8 minutes, then drain (carrots will continue to cook as they cool). When cool, cut each section lengthwise into 3 pieces.

Cook bacon in a skillet over moderate heat, stirring, until crisp, then transfer with a slotted spoon to paper towels to drain, reserving fat. Stir together bacon, bread crumbs, parsley, garlic, oregano, kosher salt, pepper, clove, nutmeg, and 2 tablespoons fat in a bowl until combined well.

Put steak on 2 overlapping sheets of plastic wrap (each about 2 feet long) with a short side of steak nearest you. Holding a sharp knife parallel to work surface and beginning on a long side, butterfly steak by cutting it almost in half horizontally (not all the way through), then open it like a book.

Turn steak so a long side is nearest you, then arrange spinach evenly over steak, leaving a 1-inch border along edge farthest from you. Top spinach with carrot pieces, arranging them parallel to long side and spacing them evenly, then sprinkle evenly with bread crumb mixture.

Beginning with side nearest you and using plastic wrap as an aid, roll up steak, gently pressing on filling (do not roll too tightly or filling will slip out from ends), then tie steak crosswise with string at ¾-inch intervals. Season with salt and pepper.

To cook steak using a charcoal grill:
Open vents on bottom of grill and on lid. Light a heaping chimneyful of charcoal and pour it evenly over 1 side of bottom rack (you will have a double or triple layer of charcoal).

When charcoal turns grayish white (15 to 20 minutes from lighting) and you can hold your hand 5 inches above top rack for 3 to 4 seconds, sear steak on all sides on lightly oiled rack over coals until well browned, 8 to 10 minutes.

Move steak to side of grill with no coals underneath and cook, covered with lid, turning once, until thermometer inserted diagonally 2 inches into thickest part of steak registers 125°F, 15 to 20 minutes total.

To cook steak using a gas grill:
Preheat all burners on high, then adjust heat to moderately high. Sear steak on all sides on lightly oiled rack over flames until well browned, 8 to 10 minutes.

Turn off burner directly below steak and cook, covered with lid, turning once, until thermometer inserted diagonally 2 inches into thickest part of steak registers 125°F, 25 to 30 minutes total.

Carve steak:
Transfer steak to a cutting board and let stand, covered loosely with foil, 20 minutes. Beef will continue to cook as it stands, reaching 130°F (medium-rare). Discard string, being careful not to unroll steak, and cut steak into ½-inch-thick slices with a sharp knife.

Cooks' notes:
• Steak can be rolled and tied 1 day ahead and chilled, wrapped in plastic wrap.
• If you aren't able to grill, steak can be seared in a 12-inch heavy skillet (ends of roll will come up side) in remaining bacon fat or 1 tablespoon oil, turning, 8 to 10 minutes, then transferred to a roasting pan and roasted in middle of a 350°F oven 20 to 25 minutes.

PHOTO ON PAGE 70

SKIRT STEAK FAJITAS
WITH LIME AND BLACK PEPPER

Serves 6
Active time: 40 min   Start to finish: 40 min

2 large onions, peeled and cut lengthwise into
   6 wedges, leaving root ends intact
2½ tablespoons olive oil
2½ teaspoons balsamic vinegar
1½ teaspoons salt
¼ cup fresh lime juice
2 lb skirt steak, halved crosswise
2½ teaspoons coarsely ground black pepper
18 flour tortillas
1 cup loosely packed fresh cilantro leaves

Accompaniment: **tomatillo or tomato salsa;
   lime wedges**
Special equipment: **metal skewers or a grill basket**

Prepare charcoal or gas grill for cooking. If using
charcoal, open vents on bottom of grill.

Thread onions onto skewers (or put in grill basket),
then brush with ½ tablespoon oil and season with salt
and pepper. When fire is medium-hot (you can hold
your hand 5 inches above rack for 3 to 4 seconds), grill
onions on lightly oiled grill rack, turning occasionally,
until tender, 16 to 20 minutes. Transfer to a cutting
board. When just cool enough to handle, cut onions
into 1-inch pieces and toss with vinegar and
½ teaspoon salt.

While onions are grilling, stir together lime juice
and remaining teaspoon salt and remaining 2 tablespoons oil in a shallow dish, then add steak and marinate at room temperature, turning once, 10 minutes.

Pat steak dry, then rub with pepper. Grill steak on
lightly oiled grill rack, turning once, 6 to 10 minutes
total for medium-rare. Transfer to cutting board, then
let stand 5 minutes before cutting diagonally into
thin slices.

While steak is standing, toast tortillas directly on
grill rack, turning once, until puffed slightly and
browned in spots, about 1 minute total. Serve steak,
onions, cilantro, and salsa all wrapped in tortillas.

Cooks' note:
• If you aren't able to grill, onions (no need to skewer)
  and steak can be cooked in a lightly oiled well-
  seasoned ridged grill pan over moderately high heat
  and tortillas can be toasted over gas (hold with tongs)
  or directly on top of electric burners. Cut skirt steak
  into pieces to fit in grill pan and grill in batches
  without crowding.

MIXED-PEPPER STEAK WITH ONIONS

Serves 4
Active time: 30 min   Start to finish: 30 min

1 tablespoon soy sauce
1 teaspoon cornstarch
⅓ cup plus 2 tablespoons cold water
1½ lb beef loin sirloin steak, cut crosswise into
   3- by ¼- by ¼-inch strips
½ teaspoon salt
¼ teaspoon black pepper
¼ cup olive oil or vegetable oil
4 bell peppers in assorted colors, cut into
   ¼-inch-thick strips
1 large onion, halved lengthwise and cut
   crosswise into ¼-inch-thick slices
3 garlic cloves, sliced

Accompaniment: **cooked white rice**

Stir together soy sauce, cornstarch, and ⅓ cup water
in a cup.

Pat steak dry and sprinkle with salt and pepper.
Heat 2 tablespoons oil in a 12-inch heavy skillet over
moderately high heat until hot but not smoking, then
stir-fry half of steak until browned but still pink inside,
about 4 minutes. Transfer to a bowl with a slotted
spoon and repeat with remaining steak, adding 1 tablespoon oil to skillet.

Add remaining tablespoon oil to skillet and stir-fry
bell peppers, onion, and garlic until onion is golden,
6 to 7 minutes. Stir in remaining 2 tablespoons water
and cook, covered, 3 minutes. Return steak to skillet,
then stir in cornstarch mixture. Bring to a boil and
cook, stirring, 2 minutes.

RED WINE–BRAISED SHORT RIBS WITH VEGETABLES

Serves 6
Active time: 45 min   Start to finish: 3½ hr

   1 (750-ml) bottle dry red wine
   5 cups beef stock or broth
   2 fresh thyme sprigs
  12 small shallots (1 lb), peeled and trimmed
1½ tablespoons vegetable oil
   5 large garlic cloves, peeled
   4 lb beef short ribs, cut into 1-rib pieces
        if necessary
   1 tablespoon red-currant jelly
   1 lb carrots
   1 lb zucchini
1½ lb small (1½-inch) boiling potatoes
   3 tablespoons all-purpose flour

Boil wine, beef broth, and thyme in a 6- to 7-quart wide heavy pot until reduced to about 5 cups, about 30 minutes, then pour through a fine-mesh sieve into a heatproof bowl.

Cook whole shallots in oil in cleaned pot over moderate heat, stirring frequently, until golden, about 6 minutes. Add garlic and cook, stirring frequently, until garlic is golden and shallots are golden brown, about 2 minutes. Transfer with a slotted spoon to a plate, reserving fat in pot.

Pat ribs dry and season well with salt and pepper. Heat fat in pot over high heat, then sear ribs in 3 batches until browned on all sides, about 4 minutes per batch, transferring with tongs to a bowl. Pour off any fat in pot.

Return ribs, shallots, garlic, and reduced wine to pot with jelly and salt to taste, then simmer, covered, without stirring, 1¾ hours.

After meat has been simmering 1¼ hours, peel carrots, then cut carrots and zucchini diagonally into ½-inch-thick slices. Peel potatoes.

Add potatoes and carrots to pot (don't stir) and simmer, covered, until ribs are tender and potatoes and carrots are just tender, about 30 minutes.

Add zucchini to pot (don't stir) and simmer, covered, until just tender, about 6 minutes.

Transfer meat and vegetables with a slotted spoon to a large serving dish. Discard any loose bones and keep meat and vegetables warm, covered.

Skim fat from sauce and reserve 1 tablespoon fat.

Stir together reserved fat and flour in a small bowl to make a dry paste. Thin paste with 2 tablespoons warm sauce. Bring sauce to a boil and whisk in half of flour paste until thickened. (If necessary, whisk more paste into boiling sauce until thickened to desired consistency.) Simmer sauce, whisking occasionally, about 3 minutes. Pour over meat and vegetables.

Cooks' note:
• Ribs can be cooked (without zucchini) 1 day ahead and cooled in pot, uncovered, then chilled, covered. Reheat in sauce, then add zucchini. Simmer, covered, until tender.

PHOTO ON PAGE 110

MEATBALLS IN TOMATO SAUCE

Serves 4
Active time: 40 min   Start to finish: 45 min

Often local supermarkets offer a "meatloaf mix" that consists of equal parts ground beef chuck, ground pork, and ground veal. If this is not available, you can buy the beef, pork, and veal threesome on your own. Serve these hearty meatballs over noodles or mashed potatoes.

   1 (28- to 32-oz) can whole plum tomatoes
   2 garlic cloves, chopped
   1 teaspoon dried oregano, crumbled
1½ teaspoons salt
   ½ cup fine fresh bread crumbs
   ½ cup whole milk
   ½ lb ground beef chuck
   ½ lb ground pork
   ½ lb ground veal
   1 medium onion, coarsely grated
   5 tablespoons chopped fresh flat-leaf parsley
   ¼ teaspoon dried hot red pepper flakes
1½ tablespoons vegetable oil

Pulse tomatoes with their juice in a food processor until chopped. Simmer tomatoes with garlic, oregano, and ½ teaspoon salt in a 3-quart heavy saucepan, uncovered, stirring occasionally, until thickened, about 20 minutes.

While sauce is simmering, stir together bread crumbs and milk in a large bowl and let stand 5 minutes. Add all meat, onion, 3 tablespoons parsley, red pepper flakes, and remaining teaspoon salt and blend with your hands until just combined (do not overmix). Form 2-tablespoon amounts into meatballs (about 20).

Heat oil in a 12-inch heavy skillet over high heat until hot but not smoking, then sauté meatballs in 2 batches, turning occasionally, until well browned, about 5 minutes. Transfer with a slotted spoon to tomato sauce.

Simmer meatballs, covered, stirring occasionally, until cooked through, about 5 minutes. Serve sprinkled with remaining 2 tablespoons parsley.

veal

PAN-ROASTED VEAL CHOPS WITH ARUGULA

Serves 4
Active time: 30 min Start to finish: 40 min

4 (1- to 1¼-inch-thick) veal rib chops (10 to 12 oz each), bones frenched if desired
2½ tablespoons unsalted butter
1½ tablespoons olive oil
1 garlic clove
¼ teaspoon salt
1½ tablespoons balsamic vinegar
3 tablespoons minced shallot
½ cup dry white wine
1 cup low-sodium chicken broth
¾ teaspoon minced fresh rosemary or ¼ teaspoon dried, crumbled
2 small bunches arugula, trimmed

Special equipment: **an instant-read thermometer**

Preheat oven to 425°F.

Pat veal chops dry and season with salt and pepper. Heat ½ tablespoon butter and ½ tablespoon oil in a 12-inch ovenproof skillet (wrap plastic skillet handle in a triple layer of foil) over moderately high heat until hot but not smoking, then sear chops, turning once, until golden brown, about 6 minutes total.

Transfer skillet to middle of oven and roast chops until thermometer inserted horizontally into a chop registers 155°F (do not touch bone), 10 to 15 minutes (depending on thickness).

While chops are roasting, mash garlic to a paste with salt using a mortar and pestle (or mince and mash with a large heavy knife), then transfer half of paste to a bowl and whisk in ½ tablespoon vinegar, remaining tablespoon oil, and salt and pepper to taste.

Transfer chops to a plate and keep warm, loosely covered with foil. Add shallot and remaining garlic paste to skillet and cook over moderate heat, stirring, until shallot is softened, about 1 minute. Add wine and remaining tablespoon vinegar and boil, stirring and scraping up brown bits, until reduced to about 2 tablespoons, about 4 minutes. Add broth and rosemary and boil until reduced by half, about 4 minutes. Remove from heat and add remaining 2 tablespoons butter, swirling skillet to incorporate, then stir in any veal juices accumulated on plate. Season with salt and black pepper.

Add arugula to dressing in bowl and toss to coat. Serve chops with sauce and arugula.

VEAL PICCATA

Serves 8
Active time: 20 min   Start to finish: 30 min

For sauce
1¼ cups low-fat chicken stock or low-sodium fat-free chicken broth
⅓ cup dry white wine
1 tablespoon all-purpose flour
2 tablespoons water
1 tablespoon unsalted butter
1 tablespoon fresh lemon juice
2 tablespoons chopped fresh flat-leaf parsley

For veal
2 lb veal cutlets (also called scallopini; ¼ inch thick)
¾ teaspoon salt
½ teaspoon black pepper
1 lemon, thinly sliced

Special equipment: **a well-seasoned ridged grill pan**
Accompaniment: **buttered noodles with chives (page 179)**

Make sauce:
Boil stock and wine in a 2- to 3-quart heavy saucepan until reduced by about half (to about ¾ cup), about 3 minutes. Whisk together flour and water in a cup, then whisk into stock. Boil, stirring, 1 minute, then remove from heat and stir in butter, lemon juice, and salt and pepper to taste. Keep sauce warm.

Prepare veal:
Cut veal into 3-inch pieces, then pat dry with paper towels. Lightly oil grill pan and heat over high heat until just smoking.

While pan is heating, sprinkle veal with salt and pepper. Grill veal in batches, without crowding, turning once, until browned, about 1 minute total, transferring with tongs to a platter. Grill lemon slices, in batches if necessary, until lightly browned, about 1 minute per side, transferring to platter with veal.

Stir parsley into warm sauce and pour over veal.

Cooks' note:
• If uncooked cutlets are more than ¼ inch thick, pound to ¼ inch thick between 2 sheets of plastic wrap with a rolling pin.

Each serving (not including noodles) about 143 calories and 2 grams fat
PHOTO ON PAGE 45

pork

ROAST PORK WITH APRICOT AND SHALLOT STUFFING

Serves 8
Active time: 30 min   Start to finish: 1½ hr

4 slices firm white sandwich bread
½ cup chopped shallot
2 tablespoons unsalted butter
½ lb firm-ripe apricots (3 large), cut into ⅓-inch pieces
2 tablespoons chopped fresh flat-leaf parsley
½ teaspoon salt
¼ teaspoon black pepper
1 (3- to 3½-lb) center-cut boneless pork loin roast (3½ inches in diameter), not tied
2 tablespoons vegetable oil
½ cup water

Special equipment: **an instant-read thermometer**

Preheat oven to 375°F.
Make stuffing:
Cut just enough bread into ⅓-inch pieces to measure 1 cup and spread evenly in a shallow baking pan. Toast bread in middle of oven, stirring occasionally, until golden, about 10 minutes, then transfer to a bowl. Leave oven on (for pork).

Cook shallot in butter in a large nonstick skillet over moderately low heat, stirring occasionally, until softened, about 10 minutes. Add apricots and cook, stirring, until slightly softened, about 3 minutes. Remove from heat and stir in bread, parsley, salt, and pepper.

Stuff and roast pork:
Make a hole for stuffing that runs lengthwise through pork loin: Beginning in middle of 1 end of roast, insert a sharp long thin knife lengthwise toward center of loin, then repeat at opposite end of loin to complete incision running through middle.

Open up incision with your fingers, working from both ends, to create a 1½-inch-wide opening, then pack with all of stuffing, pushing from both ends toward center.

Pat pork dry and and season well with salt and pepper. Heat oil in a 12-inch heavy skillet over high heat until very hot and just smoking, then brown pork on all sides, about 2 minutes.

Transfer to a roasting pan and roast in middle of oven until thermometer inserted diagonally 2 inches into meat (avoid stuffing) registers 160°F, 45 to 50 minutes. Transfer to a cutting board and let stand 20 minutes.

While loin is standing, straddle roasting pan across 2 burners. Add water and deglaze pan by boiling over moderate heat, stirring and scraping up brown bits, 1 minute.

Slice meat and serve with sauce.

apple

ROAST PORK TENDERLOIN WITH APPLES AND CIDER SAUCE

Serves 6
Active time: 20 min   Start to finish: 45 min

2 (¾-lb) pork tenderloins
1 tablespoon vegetable oil
2 teaspoons unsalted butter
2 (½-lb) Granny Smith apples, peeled, cored, and each cut into 16 wedges
1 cup low-sodium fat-free chicken broth
⅔ cup unfiltered apple cider
½ teaspoon arrowroot
1 tablespoon water
2 teaspoons cider vinegar
½ teaspoon salt
¼ teaspoon black pepper

Special equipment: **an instant-read thermometer**

Preheat oven to 425°F.

Pat tenderloins dry and season with salt and pepper. Heat oil in a 12-inch nonstick skillet over moderately high heat until hot but not smoking, then brown tenderloins on all sides, turning with tongs, about 5 minutes total. (If the handle of your skillet is not ovenproof, wrap handle in a triple layer of foil, shiny side out.)

Transfer skillet to upper third of oven and roast until thermometer inserted diagonally into center of meat registers 155°F, 12 to 15 minutes. Transfer to a platter

and let stand, loosely covered with foil, 15 minutes before slicing.

While meat is standing, heat butter in same skillet (handle will be hot) over moderately high heat until foam subsides, then sauté apple wedges, turning occasionally, until tender and golden brown, 5 to 7 minutes. Transfer apples to a plate, then add chicken broth and cider to skillet and bring to a boil over high heat. Meanwhile, whisk together arrowroot and water in a small bowl. Whisk arrowroot mixture into sauce and boil until thickened and reduced to about 1 cup, about 5 minutes. Remove from heat and stir in vinegar, salt, pepper, and any juices that have accumulated on platter.

Cut meat into ½-inch-thick slices and serve topped with apples and sauce.

Each serving about 200 calories and 7 grams fat
PHOTO ON PAGE 109

SAUTÉED PORK CHOPS WITH MUSHROOMS, DILL, AND SOUR CREAM

Serves 2
Active time: 20 min   Start to finish: 20 min

4 (¼- to ⅓-inch-thick) boneless pork chops (⅔ lb total)
2 tablespoons unsalted butter
1 small onion, halved lengthwise and thinly sliced lengthwise
¼ lb mushrooms, cut into ¼-inch-thick slices
⅓ cup sour cream
¼ cup water
2 tablespoons chopped fresh dill

Pat pork chops dry and season with salt and pepper. Heat 1 tablespoon butter in a 10-inch heavy skillet over high heat until foam subsides, then sauté chops, turning once, until browned and just cooked through, about 3 minutes total. Transfer chops to a platter and keep warm, covered.

Reduce heat to moderate and add remaining tablespoon butter to skillet. When foam subsides, cook onion and mushrooms, stirring, until tender, about 6 minutes. Reduce heat to low and stir in sour cream, water, any meat juices that have accumulated on platter, dill, and salt and pepper to taste and cook, stirring, until heated through. (Do not let boil.) Spoon sauce over chops.

SMOKED PORK CHOPS WITH PINEAPPLE ROSEMARY SAUCE

Serves 2
Active time: 35 min   Start to finish: 1¼ hr

We don't recommend doubling the sauce ingredients if you're cooking for more than two people—the sauce will lose its intensity. Instead, you may want to make two batches.

1 pineapple (labeled "extra sweet"), peeled (reserving rind), quartered, and cored
1 (4-inch) fresh rosemary sprig
1 large garlic clove, smashed
¼ cup olive oil
2 teaspoons fresh lemon juice
⅛ teaspoon salt
2 (6- to 8-oz) fully cooked smoked pork chops
Rounded ¼ teaspoon black pepper

Special equipment: **cheesecloth**

Set aside one fourth of pineapple for another use. Cut enough of remainder into ¼-inch dice to measure ½ cup and reserve remainder. Squeeze juice from reserved rind with your hands into a blender. Cut reserved pineapple into 1-inch chunks and purée with juice in blender at high speed until very smooth, about 1 minute.

Pour purée into a dampened-cheesecloth-lined medium-mesh sieve set over a bowl. Drain until there is 1 cup juice, about 30 minutes.

Boil juice in a small skillet over moderately high heat until reduced to about ¼ cup, 10 to 14 minutes.

Meanwhile, cook rosemary sprig and garlic in oil in a small heavy saucepan over moderately low heat, stirring, until garlic is golden, 2 to 3 minutes. Discard rosemary and garlic and transfer 1 tablespoon oil to a 10-inch heavy skillet. Whisk remaining oil into reduced juice and stir in diced pineapple, lemon juice, and salt.

Pat chops dry and sprinkle with pepper. Heat oil in skillet over moderately high heat until hot but not smoking, then sauté chops, turning once, until browned and heated through, about 5 minutes. Transfer to a platter and keep warm.

Discard fat from skillet, then add pineapple sauce and deglaze skillet by boiling over moderate heat, stirring and scraping up any brown bits, 1 minute. Pour sauce over chops.

BRINED PORK CHOPS

Serves 6
Active time: 20 min   Start to finish: 2 days (includes brining)

2 qt water
¼ cup kosher salt
¼ cup mustard seeds
¼ cup sugar
2 tablespoons pickling spices
6 garlic cloves, smashed with side of a large knife
6 (1½-inch-thick) rib pork chops
4 to 6 tablespoons olive oil
½ cup dry Riesling
½ cup chicken broth

Special equipment: **an instant-read thermometer**

Brine pork chops:
Bring water to a boil with kosher salt, mustard seeds, sugar, pickling spices, and garlic and simmer 15 minutes. Cool brine completely, then add chops and chill, covered, 1 to 2 days.

Roast chops:
Preheat oven to 425°F.

Remove chops from brine and pat dry. Heat 2 tablespoons oil in a 12-inch heavy skillet over moderately high heat until hot but not smoking, then brown chops in batches, without crowding, turning once, 3 to 4 minutes on each side. (Add oil 1 to 2 tablespoons at a time as needed between batches.)

Transfer chops to a roasting pan and roast in middle of oven until thermometer inserted horizontally 2 inches into center of meat (do not touch bone) registers 155°F, 15 to 20 minutes. Transfer chops to a platter and let stand, loosely covered, 5 minutes before serving (do not clean pan).

Straddle pan across 2 burners and add any meat juices accumulated on platter along with wine and broth and deglaze by boiling over moderately high heat, stirring and scraping up brown bits, until reduced to about ½ cup, about 4 minutes. Season pan juices with salt and pepper and serve with chops.

PHOTO ON PAGE 51

rosemary

PORK CHOPS WITH PECAN CORN BREAD DRESSING AND CIDER GRAVY

Serves 6
Active time: 45 min   Start to finish: 2 hr
(includes making corn bread)

If you don't happen to have any day-old corn bread on hand, just follow our recipe (this page)—fresh regular corn bread may be too moist.

4½ cups coarsely crumbled (½-inch pieces) corn
      bread (recipe follows)
  1 celery rib, coarsely chopped
  1 medium onion, coarsely chopped
  1 medium green bell pepper, coarsely
      chopped
  2 tablespoons unsalted butter
  ¼ lb fresh shiitakes, stems discarded and caps
      coarsely chopped
  2 cups chicken broth
  1 cup pecans (4 oz), coarsely chopped and
      toasted (see Tips, page 8)
1½ teaspoons finely chopped fresh sage
  3 tablespoons finely chopped fresh flat-leaf
      parsley
  ¼ teaspoon salt, or to taste
  ⅛ teaspoon black pepper
  2 to 3 tablespoons olive oil
  6 (1-inch-thick) rib pork chops
  ⅔ cup unfiltered apple cider
  1 tablespoon cornstarch mixed with
      3 tablespoons cold water

Preheat oven to 325°F.

Lightly toast corn bread in a shallow baking pan in middle of oven until dry and pale golden, 15 to 20 minutes. Remove from oven.

Increase oven temperature to 375°F.

Sauté celery, onion, and bell pepper in butter in a 12-inch heavy skillet over moderately high heat, stirring occasionally, until softened and beginning to brown, about 5 minutes. Stir in shiitakes and sauté, stirring, until tender, 2 to 3 minutes. Add 1 cup broth and deglaze skillet by boiling, stirring and scraping up brown bits. Add corn bread, pecans, sage, parsley, salt, and pepper and toss well, then transfer to a buttered 3-quart gratin dish or large baking pan.

Heat 1½ tablespoons oil in cleaned skillet over moderately high heat until hot but not smoking. While oil is heating, pat dry 3 pork chops and season with salt and pepper. Brown chops, turning once, about 6 minutes total, then arrange on corn bread. Brown remaining 3 chops in same manner, adding more oil if necessary. Reserve skillet.

Roast chops on corn bread in middle of oven until pork is just cooked through, 18 to 22 minutes. After pork has roasted 10 minutes, pour off fat from skillet and heat skillet over moderately high heat until hot. Add cider and deglaze skillet by boiling, stirring and scraping up brown bits, then add remaining cup broth. Stir cornstarch mixture and add to hot cider mixture. Bring sauce to a boil, whisking constantly, then boil, whisking, 1 minute and season with salt and pepper. Serve chops and dressing with sauce on the side.

CORN BREAD FOR DRESSING

Makes about 4½ cups crumbled
Active time: 15 min   Start to finish: 30 min

This corn bread is on the dry side—ideal for our dressing (recipe precedes) but not for eating on its own.

½ cup yellow cornmeal (not coarse)
½ cup all-purpose flour
1 teaspoon baking powder
½ teaspoon sugar
½ teaspoon salt
1 large egg
½ cup whole milk
2 tablespoons olive oil

Preheat oven to 400°F.

Whisk together cornmeal, flour, baking powder, sugar, and salt in a bowl. Whisk together egg, milk, and oil in another bowl, then add to cornmeal mixture and stir until just combined.

Pour batter into a greased 8- or 9-inch square baking pan and bake in middle of oven until a tester comes out clean, 12 to 15 minutes. Cool 5 minutes in pan on a rack, then turn bread out onto rack to cool completely.

Cooks' note:
• Corn bread can be made 2 days ahead and chilled, wrapped in plastic wrap.

PORK CHOPS WITH GOLDEN ONION AND WILTED TOMATOES

Serves 4
Active time: 40 min   Start to finish: 40 min

  3 tablespoons olive oil
  1 large onion, halved lengthwise, then thinly
    sliced lengthwise
  ½ teaspoon salt
  4 (1-inch-thick) pork loin chops
  1 pt red grape tomatoes or cherry tomatoes,
    halved lengthwise
  ½ pt yellow grape tomatoes or cherry
    tomatoes, halved lengthwise
  2½ teaspoons balsamic vinegar

Heat 2 tablespoons oil in a 12-inch heavy skillet over moderately high heat until hot but not smoking, then sauté onion with salt, stirring occasionally, until golden brown, about 8 minutes. Transfer to a bowl.

Pat pork chops dry and season with salt and pepper. Heat remaining tablespoon oil in skillet over high heat until just smoking, then sauté chops, turning once, until browned and just cooked through, about 6 minutes total. Transfer chops to a platter and keep warm, covered.

Return onion to skillet and add tomatoes, then sauté over moderately high heat, stirring, until tomatoes are slightly wilted, about 2 minutes. Remove from heat and stir in vinegar and salt and pepper to taste.

Serve chops topped with onion and tomato.

PANFRIED PORK CHOPS WITH POMEGRANATE AND FENNEL SALSA

Serves 4
Active time: 40 min   Start to finish: 40 min

  1 lb fennel bulb (sometimes called anise),
    stalks cut off and discarded
  3 tablespoons vegetable oil
  1 cup pomegranate seeds (from 1 large
    pomegranate)
  2 scallions, finely chopped
  ¼ cup chopped fresh cilantro
  1 teaspoon seasoned rice vinegar
  2 teaspoons honey
  ¼ teaspoon salt
  4 (½- to ¾-inch-thick) pork chops

Halve fennel bulb lengthwise and core it, then cut into ¼-inch dice. Cook fennel in 2 tablespoons oil in a 12-inch heavy skillet over moderate heat, stirring, until tender, about 15 minutes. Transfer fennel to a bowl and stir in pomegranate seeds, scallions, cilantro, vinegar, honey, and salt.

Pat pork chops dry and season with salt and pepper. Heat remaining tablespoon oil in skillet over moderately high heat until hot but not smoking, then sauté chops, turning once, until deep golden and just cooked through, 8 to 10 minutes total. Transfer chops to plates and let stand, loosely covered, 5 minutes.

Serve chops topped with salsa.

Cooks' note:
• To extract pomegranate seeds, quarter the fruit, then, over a large bowl, break the seeds away from the pith using your fingertips.

lamb

GRILLED MARINATED LAMB CHOPS WITH BALSAMIC CHERRY TOMATOES

Serves 4
Active time: 30 min   Start to finish: 2¼ hr

If you are using cherry tomatoes on the vine and get 1 large cluster, simply cut the vines into 4 clusters before grilling and serving with the lamb.

  2 tablespoons honey
  2 tablespoons red-wine vinegar
  2 garlic cloves, finely chopped
  ½ teaspoon salt
  ¼ teaspoon black pepper
  8 rib lamb chops (1½ lb total), bones
    frenched and all fat trimmed
  1½ lb cherry tomatoes (preferably on the vine)
  1½ tablespoons balsamic vinegar

Accompaniment: **barley with toasted cumin
    and mint (page 182)**
Special equipment: **a 12- by 8- by 2-inch
    disposable aluminum roasting pan**

Stir together honey, red-wine vinegar, garlic, salt, and pepper and transfer to a sealable plastic bag. Add lamb, then seal bag, pressing out excess air and turning to distribute marinade. Marinate lamb, chilled, turning occasionally, 1 hour. Bring lamb to room temperature.

Prepare gas or charcoal grill for cooking. If using a charcoal grill, open vents on bottom of grill and on lid.

Remove lamb from marinade, reserving marinade. When fire is medium-hot (you can hold your hand 5 inches above rack for 3 to 4 seconds), grill lamb on lightly oiled grill rack, turning once, about 4 minutes total for medium-rare. Transfer to a platter and keep warm, covered.

Cook tomatoes (still on vine, if using) in disposable roasting pan, covered with grill lid, carefully turning, until softened and just beginning to split, about 8 minutes. Drizzle balsamic vinegar over tomatoes, turning to coat, then cook, uncovered, until vinegar is reduced by about half, about 2 minutes. Remove from grill.

Bring reserved marinade with any lamb juices that have accumulated on platter to a boil in a small heavy saucepan, covered.

Drizzle lamb with marinade and serve with roasted tomatoes.

Cooks' note:
• Lamb and tomatoes can also be grilled in batches in a lightly oiled well-seasoned ridged grill pan over moderately high heat (tomatoes will take less time to soften, about 3 minutes).

Each serving (including barley) about 429 calories and 14 grams fat

LAMB AND FETA PATTIES WITH PEPPER RELISH

Serves 4
Active time: 30 min   Start to finish: 45 min

For relish
  ¾ cup cider vinegar
  ¼ cup sugar
  ⅔ cup water
  2 orange or red bell peppers, cut into ½-inch pieces
  ⅓ cup golden raisins
  1 Golden Delicious apple, peeled, cored, and cut into ½-inch cubes
  1 teaspoon mustard seeds
  ⅛ teaspoon cayenne
  ½ teaspoon salt
For patties
  1 slice firm white sandwich bread, torn into pieces
  1 scallion, coarsely chopped
  1 garlic clove
  ⅓ cup coarsely chopped fresh mint
  1¼ lb ground lamb
  1 large egg, lightly beaten
  ¼ lb feta, crumbled (¾ cup)
  ¾ teaspoon salt
  ¼ teaspoon black pepper

Make relish:
Bring vinegar and sugar to a boil in a 2-quart nonreactive heavy saucepan, stirring until sugar is dissolved, then boil, uncovered, 1 minute. Add remaining relish ingredients and simmer briskly, uncovered, stirring occasionally, until peppers and apple are tender, about 25 minutes.

Make patties while relish simmers:
Preheat broiler.

Pulse bread, scallion, garlic, and mint in a food processor until finely chopped, then transfer to a bowl with lamb, egg, feta, salt, and pepper. Blend with your hands until just combined (do not overwork mixture, or patties will be tough). Form into 4½-inch patties (about ½ inch thick).

Broil patties on oiled rack of a broiler pan about 5 inches from heat until browned but still slightly pink in center, about 4 minutes on each side. Serve patties with relish.

NAVARIN D'AGNEAU
Lamb Stew with Spring Vegetables

Serves 6
Active time: 1 hr   Start to finish: 2 hr

6 fresh parsley sprigs
2 fresh thyme sprigs
2 fresh rosemary sprigs
2 Turkish bay leaves or 1 California
6 whole black peppercorns
3 lb boneless lamb shoulder, trimmed
     of excess fat
3 tablespoons olive oil
1 large onion, finely chopped
4 garlic cloves, finely chopped
1½ cups dry white wine
2½ cups beef stock or broth
1 teaspoon salt
¼ teaspoon black pepper
10 oz pearl onions
½ lb baby turnips, trimmed and halved
     lengthwise if large
½ lb baby carrots, peeled, trimmed, and
     halved lengthwise if large
½ lb baby zucchini, trimmed and halved
     lengthwise
½ lb sugar snap peas, trimmed
2 tablespoons unsalted butter, softened
3 tablespoons all-purpose flour

Special equipment: **cheesecloth; kitchen string**

Preheat oven to 325°F.

Wrap herb sprigs, bay leaves, and peppercorns in a square of cheesecloth and tie into a bundle with string to make a *bouquet garni.*

Pat lamb dry, then cut into 1½-inch pieces and season with salt and pepper. Heat 2 tablespoons oil in a 6- to 7-quart wide heavy pot over moderately high heat until hot but not smoking, then brown lamb in 3 batches, turning occasionally, about 4 minutes per batch, transferring with a slotted spoon to a bowl.

Add remaining tablespoon oil to pot and sauté chopped onion and garlic over moderately high heat, stirring, until onion is golden, about 6 minutes. Add wine and stock and deglaze pot by boiling, stirring and scraping up brown bits, 1 minute.

Return lamb to pot along with any juices that have accumulated in bowl and add *bouquet garni.* Braise lamb, covered, in middle of oven until tender, about 1½ hours. Stir in salt and pepper.

While lamb is braising, cook pearl onions in a 5- to 6-quart pot of boiling salted water (see Tips, page 8) until tender, about 10 minutes, then transfer with a slotted spoon to a large bowl of ice and cold water to stop cooking (reserve cooking water). Peel onions.

Boil turnips, carrots, zucchini, and sugar snaps separately in reserved cooking water until just tender, about 5 minutes for turnips, 4 to 6 minutes for carrots, 2 minutes for zucchini, and 1½ minutes for sugar snaps. Transfer vegetables as cooked with a slotted spoon to ice water and, when all are cooked, drain vegetables in a colander.

Make a *beurre manié* by stirring together butter and flour in a small bowl to form a paste. Bring lamb stew to a simmer on stovetop and whisk in enough *beurre manié,* bit by bit, to thicken to desired consistency, then simmer about 2 minutes. Add vegetables and simmer, stirring occasionally, until heated through, about 2 minutes. Season with salt and pepper.

Cooks' notes:
· Lamb can be braised 2 days ahead and cooled, uncovered, then chilled, covered. Reheat before adding *beurre manié* and vegetables.
· Vegetables can be cooked 1 day ahead and chilled, wrapped in paper towels in a sealed plastic bag.

LAMB CHOPS WITH CUMIN, CARDAMOM, AND LIME

Serves 4
Active time: 20 min   Start to finish: 40 min

3 garlic cloves, finely chopped
¼ teaspoon ground cumin
¼ teaspoon ground cardamom
2 tablespoons fresh lime juice
¾ teaspoon salt
½ teaspoon black pepper
2 tablespoons plus 2 teaspoons olive oil
8 (½- to ¾-inch-thick) rib lamb chops (2 lb)

Whisk together garlic, cumin, cardamom, lime juice, salt, pepper, and 2 teaspoons oil and transfer to a sealable plastic bag just large enough to hold lamb. Add lamb and seal bag, forcing out excess air, then massage lamb until evenly coated. Marinate at room temperature, turning bag occasionally, 15 minutes.

Heat 1 tablespoon oil in a 12-inch nonstick skillet over moderately high heat until hot but not smoking, then cook half of lamb, turning once, about 6 minutes total (for medium-rare). Transfer cooked lamb to a platter. Wipe out skillet, then heat remaining tablespoon oil and cook remaining lamb in same manner. Transfer to platter and let stand 5 minutes.

other meats

BUFFALO PRIME RIB

Serves 8
Active time: 40 min   Start to finish: 5¼ hr (4¾ hr for beef)

Buffalo meat can be very red, even when cooked to medium-rare. Don't be alarmed—this is a naturally occurring phenomenon that has to do with the animal's diet and how little fat is marbled through the muscle.

Before you begin roasting your buffalo, roughly calculate the total roasting time: Plan on about 16 minutes per pound once the oven temperature is reduced to 350°F (20 minutes per pound for beef), but start checking the temperature of either type of roast about 30 minutes before you think it will be done.

1 (7- to 8-lb) bone-in buffalo prime rib roast or bone-in beef prime rib roast (sometimes called standing rib roast; 3 or 4 ribs), brought to room temperature (allow 1 hour)
4½ to 5 cups water
Orange balsamic glaze (page 160)
For jus
⅔ cup dry red wine
¼ cup Madeira (preferably Sercial)
1½ cups beef broth

Special equipment: **a V-rack for roasting; a meat or instant-read thermometer**

Cook roast:
Preheat oven to 450°F.

If using beef, trim all but a thin layer of fat from roast. Generously season buffalo or beef with salt and pepper. Roast buffalo, fat side up, on V-rack in a 17- by 12- by 2-inch flameproof roasting pan in middle of oven 15 minutes (use a 13- by 9- by 2-inch flameproof roasting pan for beef, which is taller and narrower than buffalo).

Reduce oven temperature to 350°F and add ½ cup water to roasting pan, then continue to roast meat 30 minutes more. Brush meat with some of glaze and add ½ cup water to pan, then continue to roast, brushing with glaze and adding ½ cup water to pan every 15 minutes, until thermometer inserted into center of roast (do not touch bone) registers 125°F, 2 to 2¼ hours more (115°F for beef, 1¾ to 2 hours more). Transfer meat to a large platter and let stand, uncovered, 25 minutes. (Meat will continue to cook as it stands, reaching about 135°F for medium-rare buffalo or 130°F for medium-rare beef.)

Make jus while meat stands:
If using buffalo, straddle roasting pan across 2 burners, then add red wine and Madeira and deglaze pan by boiling over moderately high heat, stirring and scraping up brown bits, 2 minutes. Add broth and boil until reduced to about 1½ cups, about 3 minutes. (If using beef, pour pan juices into a 1-quart fat-separator pitcher or glass measure and skim off fat, then pour juices back into pan. Straddle roasting pan across 2 burners and deglaze pan by boiling juices over moderately high heat, stirring and scraping up brown bits, until reduced to about ⅔ cup, about 8 minutes. Add red wine and Madeira and boil until reduced to about ⅔ cup, 3 to 4 minutes. Add broth and boil until reduced to about 2 cups, about 6 minutes.)

Stir in any buffalo or beef juices accumulated on platter and season *jus* with salt, if necessary. Pour *jus* through a fine-mesh sieve into a gravy boat and keep warm, covered.

Carve roast and serve with *jus*.

PHOTO ON PAGE 106

ORANGE BALSAMIC GLAZE

Makes about 2¼ cups
Active time: 20 min   Start to finish: 45 min

1½ tablespoons unsalted butter
1 cup finely chopped shallot
1 cup thawed frozen orange juice
   concentrate (8 oz)
½ cup water
½ cup sweet orange preserves
½ cup balsamic vinegar
1 tablespoon salt
½ tablespoon cracked black peppercorns
1½ teaspoons finely grated fresh orange zest

Heat butter in a 3-quart heavy saucepan over moderate heat until foam subsides, then cook shallot, stirring, until golden brown, about 5 minutes. Stir in remaining ingredients and simmer briskly, uncovered, stirring occasionally, until thickened and reduced to about 2¼ cups, about 25 minutes.

Cooks' note:
• Glaze can be made 3 days ahead and chilled, covered. Bring to room temperature before using.

POULTRY

chicken

PANFRIED PRESSED POUSSINS

Serves 4
Active time: 15 min   Start to finish: 50 min

In this recipe, based on a dish from the Republic of Georgia called tabaka, *small chickens are flattened and weighted so they cook evenly and quickly. We call for* poussins *or Cornish hens, but the same technique works well with a frying chicken.*

  2 (1¼- to 1½-lb) *poussins* or Cornish hens
  1 teaspoon fine sea salt
  ½ teaspoon black pepper
  3 tablespoons unsalted butter
  ¾ cup chicken stock or broth

Accompaniment: **fresh tomato and onion chutney (page 222)**
Special equipment: **kitchen shears; 2 (10-inch) heavy skillets (one preferably well-seasoned cast-iron or heavy nonstick); a 10-inch round of parchment paper; 5 to 6 lb of weights such as 3 (28- to 32-oz) cans of tomatoes**

Cut out backbones from birds with kitchen shears. Pat birds dry, then spread flat, skin sides up, on a cutting board. Cut a ½-inch slit on each side of each bird in center of triangle of skin between thighs and breasts (near drumstick), then tuck bottom knob of drumstick through each slit. Tuck wing tips under breasts. Sprinkle birds on both sides with sea salt and pepper.

Heat butter in 10-inch cast-iron or heavy nonstick skillet over moderate heat until foam subsides. Add birds, skin sides down, and cover with parchment round and second skillet, then top with weights. Cook birds until skin is browned, about 15 minutes. Turn birds over, cover with parchment round, skillet, and weights, then cook until just cooked through, 10 to 15 minutes more.

Transfer birds to a platter, discarding parchment, and cover loosely with foil. Add stock to skillet and deglaze by boiling over high heat, stirring and scraping up brown bits, until reduced to about ½ cup, about 5 minutes. Skim fat from surface.

Halve birds lengthwise and serve each half drizzled with pan juices.

PHOTO ON PAGE 97

ROAST CHICKEN WITH LEMON TARRAGON BUTTER

Serves 4
Active time: 15 min   Start to finish: 45 min

  ½ stick (¼ cup) unsalted butter, softened
  1 teaspoon finely grated fresh lemon zest
  ½ teaspoon dried tarragon, crumbled
  ½ teaspoon salt
  ½ teaspoon black pepper
  1 (3- to 4-lb) quartered chicken

Special equipment: **an instant-read thermometer**

Preheat oven to 500°F.

Stir together butter, zest, tarragon, salt, and pepper.

Pat chicken dry and arrange, skin sides up, in a shallow roasting pan (1 inch deep). Loosen skin on chicken by gently working your fingers between skin and meat, keeping skin attached on 1 side and being careful not to tear skin. Rub butter mixture evenly under skin of each piece of chicken, then rub top of chicken with butter remaining on your hands. Season with salt and pepper.

Bake chicken in middle of oven until thermometer inserted 2 inches into fleshy part of chicken (do not touch bone) registers 170°F, about 30 minutes.

BRAISED CHICKEN AND VEGETABLES IN PEANUT SAUCE

Serves 6
Active time: 1 hr   Start to finish: 2¼ hr

It's believed that this stew—called mafé *or* maafe—
originated among the Bambara people of Mali.

1½ cups unsalted roasted peanuts (½ lb) or
    1 cup "all natural" creamy peanut butter
3 cups water
4½ to 5½ lb chicken pieces such as drumsticks,
    thighs, and breast halves
2 tablespoons vegetable oil
1 medium onion, chopped
1 red bell pepper, chopped
3 garlic cloves, finely chopped
1 (14- to 16-oz) can diced tomatoes
    including juice
1 to 1½ teaspoons cayenne
2 teaspoons salt
1½ lb sweet potatoes (2 medium), peeled and
    cut into 1-inch pieces
4 medium turnips (1 lb), peeled if desired,
    halved horizontally, and cut into
    ¾-inch wedges
1 lb spinach, coarse stems discarded

Accompaniment: **white rice (page 183)**

Preheat oven to 325°F.

If using peanuts, blend in a food processor until they form a butter, 2 to 3 minutes. Put fresh or jarred peanut butter in a bowl and gradually whisk in 1½ cups water.

Pat chicken dry and season with salt. Heat oil in an ovenproof 4- to 5-quart heavy pot (with a tight-fitting lid, for use later) over moderately high heat until hot but not smoking, then brown chicken, uncovered, in 3 or 4 batches, without crowding, about 6 minutes. Transfer chicken to a bowl as browned. Pour off all but about 2 tablespoons fat from pot, then add onion and bell pepper and sauté, stirring occasionally, until onion begins to brown, about 4 minutes. Add garlic and sauté, stirring, 1 minute. Stir in peanut butter mixture, remaining 1½ cups water, tomatoes with juice, cayenne (to taste), salt, and chicken with any juices accumulated in bowl and bring to a simmer. Cover pot with lid, then braise chicken in middle of oven until tender, 45 minutes to 1 hour.

Transfer chicken with tongs to a large (4-quart) serving dish and keep warm, covered. Stir potatoes and turnips into sauce and simmer on top of stove, uncovered, until vegetables are tender, 15 to 20 minutes. Transfer cooked vegetables with a slotted spoon to serving dish.

Simmer sauce, uncovered, stirring, until reduced to about 4 cups, about 5 minutes. Remove from heat and stir in spinach, then let stand, partially covered, until spinach is wilted, 2 to 3 minutes. Season with salt if necessary, then spoon over chicken.

   Cooks' note:
- Chicken can be braised in sauce (without vegetables) 1 day ahead. Cool, uncovered, then chill, covered. Reheat chicken in sauce, then transfer chicken to serving dish before proceeding.

PHOTO ON PAGE 41

SPICY FRIED CHICKEN CUTLETS

Serves 4
Active time: 20 min   Start to finish: 35 min

Fans of Buffalo wings will want to serve these chicken cutlets with a crisp green salad with blue cheese dressing.

4 skinless boneless chicken breast halves
    (1½ lb)
1 cup well-shaken buttermilk
1 teaspoon bottled hot sauce plus additional
    for serving
1 teaspoon salt
½ teaspoon black pepper
3 cups fresh bread crumbs (from 6 slices firm
    white sandwich bread)
½ teaspoon cayenne
1 cup vegetable oil for frying

Gently pound chicken breasts between sheets of plastic wrap to ⅓ inch thickness with a flat meat pounder or a rolling pin.

Whisk together buttermilk, hot sauce, ½ teaspoon salt, and black pepper in a shallow dish, then add chicken, turning to coat, and let stand 15 minutes.

Stir together bread crumbs, cayenne, and remaining ½ teaspoon salt in another shallow dish. Remove chicken from buttermilk 1 piece at a time, letting excess drip off, then dredge in bread crumbs, pressing gently to help them adhere. Transfer chicken as coated to a sheet of wax paper.

Heat oil in a 10-inch heavy skillet over moderately high heat until hot but not smoking, then fry chicken 2 pieces at a time, turning once, until golden brown and cooked through, about 6 minutes total. Transfer chicken with tongs to paper towels to drain.

Serve with hot sauce on the side.

CHICKEN AND SAUSAGE JAMBALAYA

Serves 6 to 8
Active time: 1½ hr   Start to finish: 2½ hr

5½ lb chicken pieces (drumsticks, thighs, and
    breast halves with skin and bones)
4 tablespoons vegetable oil
1½ lb andouille or other spicy smoked
    pork sausage, cut crosswise into
    ¼-inch-thick slices
3 medium onions, chopped
2 celery ribs, chopped
1 green bell pepper, chopped
4 large garlic cloves, finely chopped
2 cups chicken broth
1½ cups water
1 (14- to 16-oz) can whole tomatoes
    in juice, drained and chopped
¼ teaspoon cayenne (optional)
2½ cups long-grain white rice, rinsed
    and drained well
1 cup thinly sliced scallion greens

Pat chicken dry and season with salt. Heat 2 tablespoons oil in a 10- to 12-inch heavy skillet over moderately high heat until hot but not smoking, then brown chicken in batches, without crowding, turning once, 6 to 8 minutes total (add remaining 2 tablespoons oil as needed between batches). Transfer to a bowl as browned.

Reduce heat to moderate and brown sausage in 4 batches in fat remaining in skillet, turning, 3 to 4 minutes. Transfer to a paper-towel-lined bowl as browned.

Pour off all but about 1 tablespoon fat from skillet, then cook onions, celery, and bell pepper in skillet over moderate heat, stirring occasionally, until onions are golden brown and softened, about 8 minutes. Add garlic and cook, stirring, 1 minute. Add 1 cup stock and cook, stirring, 1 minute. Transfer mixture to a wide 8-quart heavy pot and add chicken, water, tomatoes, cayenne (if using), and remaining cup stock. Simmer, partially covered, until chicken is tender, about 30 minutes.

Preheat oven to 325°F.

Transfer chicken with tongs to a clean bowl and measure cooking liquid with vegetables, adding additional water as necessary to measure 7 cups. If over 7 cups, boil to reduce.

Stir rice into cooking liquid (in pot). Arrange chicken over rice (do not stir), then bring to a boil over high heat, uncovered, without stirring.

Cover pot and transfer to middle of oven. Bake jambalaya until rice is tender and most of liquid is absorbed, about 30 minutes.

Remove from oven and let jambalaya stand, covered, 10 minutes. Gently stir in scallion greens, sausage, and salt to taste.

APPLE, CURRANT, AND CARAWAY STUFFED CHICKEN BREASTS

Serves 6
Active time: 1 hr   Start to finish: 1 hr

For stuffing
    1 Granny Smith apple
    3 tablespoons unsalted butter
    1 teaspoon caraway seeds
    1 medium onion, chopped
 1½ celery ribs, sliced crosswise
        ⅛ inch thick
    ½ cup coarse fresh rye bread crumbs
        (with or without seeds)
    ¼ cup chopped fresh flat-leaf parsley
    3 tablespoons dried currants
    ½ teaspoon salt
    ¼ teaspoon black pepper
For chicken and pan sauce
    6 skinless boneless chicken breast
        halves (2 lb)
 1½ tablespoons vegetable oil
    2 teaspoons all-purpose flour
    1 cup unfiltered apple cider
    1 cup chicken broth

Make stuffing:
Peel and core apple and cut into ¼-inch dice. Melt butter in a 12-inch heavy skillet over moderately high heat until foam subsides, then sauté caraway seeds, stirring, 1 minute. Add onion and sauté, stirring, until softened, about 6 minutes. Add apple and celery and sauté, stirring occasionally, until crisp-tender, about 4 minutes. Remove from heat and stir in remaining stuffing ingredients. Cool completely.

Stuff chicken:
Preheat oven to 425°F.

Arrange chicken, skinned sides down, on a work surface. Remove tender (fillet strip on side where breast bone was) from each breast half if attached and reserve for another use.

Cut a pocket in each breast half: Beginning at center of thicker end of breast, insert a small knife horizontally, stopping about 1 inch from opposite end. Open incision with your fingers to create a 1-inch-wide pocket. Pack one sixth of stuffing into each pocket.

Cook chicken:
Pat chicken dry and season with salt. Heat oil in a 12-inch heavy skillet over moderately high heat until hot but not smoking, then brown chicken in 2 batches,
turning once, about 4 minutes total, transferring to a small roasting pan as browned (reserve skillet).

Roast chicken in middle of oven until just cooked through, 14 to 16 minutes.

While chicken is roasting, stir flour into fat remaining in skillet and cook roux over moderately low heat, stirring, 1 minute. Whisk in cider and broth and bring to a boil, whisking, then boil, whisking occasionally, until thickened and reduced to about 1 cup, about 8 minutes.

Let chicken stand 5 minutes, then cut each breast half diagonally into thirds. Add any juices from roasting pan and salt and pepper to taste to sauce and spoon over chicken.

Cooks' notes:
• Chicken can be stuffed 1 day ahead and chilled, covered.
• We prefer unfiltered apple cider in this recipe because it gives the sauce a better color.
PHOTO ON PAGE 60

GRILLED JERK CHICKEN

Serves 8
Active time: 45 min   Start to finish: 26½ hr (includes marinating)

Jerk seasoning—here a spicy blend of garlic, onion, chiles, thyme, allspice, nutmeg, and cinnamon, though recipes vary—originated in Jamaica and is traditionally used on pork and chicken. Because the marinade can burn easily, the chicken requires slow cooking on the grill, which also helps keep the meat moist.

For jerk marinade
    3 scallions, chopped
    4 large garlic cloves, chopped
    1 small onion, chopped
    4 to 5 fresh Scotch bonnet or *habanero* chiles,
        stemmed and seeded
    ¼ cup fresh lime juice
    2 tablespoons soy sauce
    3 tablespoons olive oil
 1½ tablespoons salt
    1 tablespoon packed brown sugar
    1 tablespoon fresh loosely packed
        thyme leaves
    2 teaspoons ground allspice
    2 teaspoons black pepper
    ¾ teaspoon freshly grated nutmeg
    ½ teaspoon cinnamon

For chicken
**4 chicken breast halves with skin and bones
   (3 lb), halved crosswise
2½ to 3 lb chicken thighs and drumsticks**

Accompaniment: **papaya salsa (page 220)**

Make marinade:
Blend all marinade ingredients in a blender
until smooth.

Marinate and grill chicken:
Divide chicken pieces and marinade between
2 sealable plastic bags. Seal bags, pressing out excess
air, then turn bags over several times to distribute
marinade. Put bags of chicken in a shallow pan and
marinate, chilled, turning once or twice, 1 day.

Let chicken stand at room temperature 1 hour
before cooking.

To cook chicken using a charcoal grill:
Open vents on bottom of grill and on lid. Light a
large chimney of charcoal briquettes (about 100) and
pour them evenly over 1 side of bottom rack (you will
have a double or triple layer of charcoal).

When charcoal turns grayish white (15 to 20 minutes) and you can hold your hand 5 inches above rack
for 3 to 4 seconds, sear chicken in batches on lightly
oiled rack over coals until well browned on all sides,
about 3 minutes per batch. Move chicken as seared to
side of grill with no coals underneath. Cook, covered
with lid, until cooked through, 25 to 30 minutes more.

To cook chicken using a gas grill:
Preheat burners on high, then adjust heat to moderate. Brown chicken well on all sides on lightly oiled
grill rack, 15 to 20 minutes. Adjust heat to low and
cook chicken, covered with lid, until cooked through,
about 25 minutes more.

Serve chicken with salsa.

PHOTO ON PAGE 67

ASIAN CHICKEN AND WATER CHESTNUT PATTIES

Serves 6
Active time: 20 min   Start to finish: 20 min

**1½ lb skinless boneless chicken breasts, cut
   into 1½-inch pieces
1 (8-oz) can whole water chestnuts, rinsed
   and drained
1 bunch scallions, chopped (1 cup)
1 teaspoon minced fresh jalapeño chile
   (including seeds)
2 tablespoons chopped fresh cilantro
1¼ teaspoons salt
2 teaspoons vegetable oil**

Special equipment: **6 (8-inch) wooden skewers**
Accompaniment: **gingered noodle salad (page 215)**

Pulse chicken in a food processor until coarsely
chopped and transfer to a large bowl. Add water chestnuts, scallions, and jalapeño to processor and pulse
until finely chopped, then add to chicken along with
cilantro and salt. Stir together with your hands until
just combined.

Form mixture into 18 (2-inch-diameter) patties on a
baking sheet, then thread 3 patties horizontally through
their sides onto each skewer.

Heat 1 teaspoon oil in a 12-inch nonstick skillet
over moderate heat until hot but not smoking, then
transfer 3 skewers of patties using a large metal spatula
to skillet and cook, turning once, until golden and just
cooked through, about 6 minutes total. Transfer to a
platter and keep warm, covered with foil. Add remaining teaspoon oil to skillet and cook remaining patties in
same manner.

Each serving (not including salad) about 159 calories and 3 grams fat
PHOTO ON PAGE 108

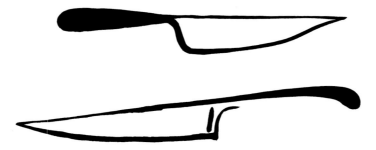

SESAME CHICKEN AND SHIITAKE STIR-FRY

Serves 4
Active time: 30 min   Start to finish: 30 min

1½ lb skinless boneless chicken breasts
    (4 halves), cut crosswise into
    ¼-inch-thick slices
  2 tablespoons water
  2 tablespoons rice vinegar (not seasoned)
  2 tablespoons soy sauce
  2 teaspoons sugar
  ½ teaspoon dried hot red pepper flakes
  3 tablespoons vegetable oil
  1 large onion, halved lengthwise, then thinly
    sliced lengthwise
  ¾ lb fresh shiitake mushrooms, stems
    discarded and caps quartered
1¼ cups frozen peas, thawed
  2 tablespoons sesame seeds, toasted
    (see Tips, page 8)

Accompaniment: **steamed rice**

Pat chicken dry and season with salt.

Stir together water, rice vinegar, soy sauce, sugar, and red pepper flakes in a small bowl until sugar is dissolved.

Heat a wok or 12-inch skillet over high heat until a bead of water dropped onto cooking surface evaporates immediately. Add 1 tablespoon oil, swirling wok to coat evenly, and heat until hot and just smoking. Add onion and stir-fry until golden and crisp-tender, about 2 minutes. Transfer onion to a large bowl.

Add ½ tablespoon oil to wok and heat until just smoking, then stir-fry half of chicken until just cooked through, about 1½ minutes. Transfer to bowl with onion and stir-fry remaining chicken in ½ tablespoon oil in same manner, transferring to bowl.

Add remaining tablespoon oil to wok and heat until just smoking, then stir-fry mushrooms until just tender, 3 to 4 minutes. Add peas and stir-fry until heated through, about 1 minute, then transfer to bowl.

Add vinegar mixture and sesame seeds to wok and, when liquid just reaches a boil, add chicken mixture and stir-fry until heated through, about 1 minute. Season with salt and pepper and serve over rice.

GRILLED CHICKEN WITH LEMON, GARLIC, AND OREGANO

Serves 16
Active time: 1 hr   Start to finish: 1¼ hr

  ¼ cup fresh lemon juice
  ¼ cup finely chopped fresh oregano
  2 tablespoons minced garlic
  2 tablespoons kosher salt
  2 teaspoons black pepper
  ⅓ cup olive oil
 12 whole chicken legs (7 lb)
  8 chicken breast halves with skin
    and bones (8 lb)
  5 lemons, cut crosswise into
    ⅓-inch-thick slices

Whisk together lemon juice, oregano, garlic, ½ tablespoon kosher salt, and ½ teaspoon pepper in a large bowl, then add oil in a slow stream, whisking.

Discard excess fat from chicken and season with remaining 1½ tablespoons salt and 1½ teaspoons black pepper.

To cook chicken using a charcoal grill:

Open vents on bottom of grill and on lid. Light a large chimney starter of charcoal briquettes (80 to 100) and pour them evenly over 1 side of bottom rack (you will have a double or triple layer of briquettes).

When charcoal turns grayish white (15 to 20 minutes) and you can hold your hand 5 inches above rack for 3 to 4 seconds, sear chicken legs in 3 batches on lightly oiled grill rack over coals, uncovered, turning once, until well browned, 6 to 8 minutes total, then transfer to a tray.

Put all browned legs on side of grill with no coals underneath and cook, covered with lid, turning occasionally, until just cooked through (flesh will no longer be pink when cut near joint), 15 to 25 minutes more. Transfer legs to bowl with lemon dressing and turn to coat, then transfer to a serving platter and keep warm, loosely covered with foil, while cooking breasts.

Add 15 briquettes evenly to coals and wait until they just light, about 5 minutes. (They will not be grayish white yet but will give off enough heat with other briquettes to maintain correct cooking temperature.)

Sear chicken breasts, starting with skin sides down, in 2 batches on rack over coals, uncovered, turning once, until well browned, 6 to 8 minutes total, then transfer to tray.

Put all browned chicken breasts on side of grill with no coals underneath and cook, covered with lid, turning occasionally, until just cooked through (the meat next to the tender, when opened slightly, will be moist but no longer pink), 12 to 15 minutes more. Transfer breasts to bowl with lemon dressing and turn to coat, then transfer to platter with legs.

Grill lemon slices on rack over coals, uncovered, until grill marks appear, about 3 minutes on each side, and transfer to platter with chicken.

To cook chicken using a gas grill:

Preheat all burners on high, then adjust heat to moderately high. Turn off 1 burner and arrange chicken legs on lightly oiled rack above it. Cook, covered with lid, turning legs once, until cooked through, about 40 minutes total. Transfer legs to bowl with lemon dressing and turn to coat, then transfer to a serving platter and keep warm, loosely covered with foil, while cooking breasts.

Cook chicken breasts on rack above unlit burner, covered with lid, turning once, until just cooked through (the meat next to the tender, when opened slightly, will be moist but no longer pink), about 30 minutes total. Transfer breasts to bowl with lemon dressing and turn to coat, then transfer to platter with legs.

Grill lemon slices on rack over flames, uncovered, until grill marks appear, about 3 minutes on each side, and transfer to platter with chicken.

Cooks' note:
· If you aren't able to grill, chicken can be roasted, skin sides up, in 2 shallow baking pans in upper and lower thirds of a 500°F oven, switching position of pans halfway through baking, until skin is crisp and chicken is cooked through, about 40 minutes total. Lemon slices can be grilled in a well-seasoned ridged grill pan.

PHOTO ON PAGE 78

garlic

assorted fowl

PARMESAN-COATED TURKEY CUTLETS

Serves 4
Active time: 20 min   Start to finish: 20 min

1¼ lb turkey breast cutlets, halved
    crosswise if large
2 large eggs
1 tablespoon water
¼ teaspoon salt
¼ teaspoon black pepper
¾ cup finely grated Parmigiano-
    Reggiano (1½ oz)
2 tablespoons chopped fresh flat-leaf
    parsley or basil
2 tablespoons unsalted butter, cut
    into pieces
2 tablespoons olive oil

Accompaniment: **lemon wedges**

Gently pound cutlets between 2 sheets of plastic wrap with a flat meat pounder or a rolling pin until ¼ inch thick.

Whisk together eggs, water, salt, pepper, cheese, and parsley in a shallow bowl (batter will be thick).

Heat 1 tablespoon butter and 1 tablespoon oil in a 12-inch nonstick skillet over moderately high heat until foam subsides. Working quickly, dip 1 cutlet in batter, letting excess drip off, and add to skillet. Repeat with about 3 more cutlets (do not crowd in skillet) and cook, turning over once, until golden and just cooked through, about 4 minutes total. Repeat with remaining butter, oil, and cutlets.

MOROCCAN-STYLE ROAST CORNISH HENS WITH VEGETABLES

Serves 8
Active time: 45 min   Start to finish: 2¼ hr

This dish is delicious over couscous, which will absorb the flavorful broth.

  1 teaspoon caraway seeds
1½ tablespoons salt
  4 garlic cloves
 ¼ cup mild honey
 ¼ cup fresh lemon juice
  2 tablespoons olive oil
  2 tablespoons paprika
  4 teaspoons ground cumin
  2 teaspoons ground ginger
1½ teaspoons ground cinnamon
 ½ teaspoon cayenne
  1 teaspoon black pepper
  2 large zucchini (1¼ lb total), halved
     lengthwise and cut into 1½-inch pieces
  2 medium turnips (½ lb total), peeled, halved
     lengthwise, and cut crosswise into
     1-inch-thick pieces
  2 red bell peppers, quartered and
     cut into 1½-inch pieces
1½ lb butternut squash, peeled, seeded,
     and cut into 1½-inch chunks
  2 medium onions, cut into
     1-inch-thick wedges
  1 (28-oz) can whole tomatoes, drained
     and chopped
 ½ cup chicken broth
  4 (1¼- to 1½-lb) Cornish hens, halved
     lengthwise
  6 tablespoons chopped mixed fresh parsley,
     cilantro, and mint

Preheat oven to 425°F.

Coarsely grind caraway seeds with salt in an electric coffee/spice grinder or crush with a rolling pin. Mince and mash garlic to a paste with salt mixture using a large heavy knife. Transfer paste to a large bowl and whisk in honey, lemon juice, oil, spices, and pepper.

Toss zucchini, turnips, bell peppers, butternut squash, and onions with half of spice mixture in an oiled large roasting pan. Stir tomatoes and broth into vegetables. Add hens to large bowl with remaining spice mixture and toss to coat, then arrange hens, breast sides up, over vegetables in pan.

Cover pan tightly with foil and roast in middle of oven 1 hour. Uncover and roast until hens are browned and vegetables are tender, 20 to 30 minutes more.

Divide vegetables among 8 plates and top each with a piece of hen. Skim fat from cooking liquid. Sprinkle herbs on top of hens and vegetables and spoon some cooking liquid over hens.

PHOTO ON PAGE 110

PLUM-GLAZED ROAST TURKEY WITH SPINACH, BACON, AND CASHEW STUFFING AND PLUM GRAVY

Serves 8 to 10
Active time: 2 hr   Start to finish: 7¼ hr (includes making stuffing (page 194) and giblet stock (recipe follows) and roasting turkey)

We think all turkeys are improved by brining (soaking in salt water), but it's a cumbersome task that few holiday schedules can accommodate. We find kosher turkeys, which are salted during the koshering process, to be just as flavorful and succulent as brined ones, without all the fuss. However, if you'd like to try brining, stir together 8 quarts water with 2 cups kosher salt in a 5-gallon bucket lined with a large heavy-duty plastic garbage bag and soak your raw turkey, covered and chilled, 10 hours.

For glazed turkey
 ½ cup plum jam (preferably damson plum) or
     red currant jelly (6 oz)
  2 teaspoons Chinese five-spice powder
  2 tablespoons whole black peppercorns
  2 tablespoons water
1½ teaspoons salt
  1 (12- to 14-lb) turkey (preferably kosher),
     any feathers and quills removed with
     tweezers or needlenose pliers, and neck
     and giblets (excluding liver) reserved for
     making stock
  5 to 7 cups spinach, bacon, and cashew
     stuffing (see stuffed onions, page 194)
 ½ stick (¼ cup) unsalted butter, melted
For plum gravy
   Pan juices from roast turkey
   About 3½ cups turkey giblet stock
   (recipe follows)
 ½ cup dry red wine

¼ **cup plum jam (preferably damson plum) or red currant jelly (3 oz)**
⅓ **cup all-purpose flour**

Special equipment: **kitchen string; 2 small metal skewers or wooden toothpicks; an instant-read thermometer**

Make glaze and roast turkey:
Preheat oven to 425°F.

Simmer jam, five-spice powder, peppercorns, water, and ½ teaspoon salt in a small saucepan, stirring, until jam is melted, about 3 minutes. Pour glaze through a fine-mesh sieve into a small bowl, pressing on and discarding solids, then cool.

Rinse turkey inside and out and pat dry. Season inside and out with remaining teaspoon salt. Loosely fill large body cavity (and neck cavity if desired) with stuffing and tie drumsticks together with string. Fold neck skin under body and secure with skewers, then tuck wings under.

Put turkey on a rack set in a large flameproof roasting pan and roast in middle of oven 30 minutes.

Reduce oven temperature to 350°F.

Brush melted butter over turkey and roast, basting every 30 minutes (add a little water to pan if juices get too dark), 1½ hours.

Brush turkey with plum glaze and continue to roast until thermometer inserted in center of body cavity (stuffing) registers 165°F (fleshy part of thigh will be about 180°F; do not touch bone), 1 to 1¾ hours more. If glaze starts browning too much, tent turkey with foil. (Total roasting time: 3 to 3¾ hours.) Transfer turkey to a platter (do not clean roasting pan), then remove skewers and discard string. Transfer stuffing from cavity to a serving dish and keep warm, covered. Let turkey stand 30 minutes.

Make gravy while turkey stands:
Transfer pan juices to a 2-quart glass measure, then skim fat, reserving 3 tablespoons of it. Add enough turkey stock to pan juices to total 4½ cups. Straddle roasting pan across 2 burners, then add wine and deglaze pan by boiling over moderately high heat, stirring and scraping up brown bits, until wine is reduced by half, about 5 minutes. Add stock mixture and jam and boil, stirring, until jam is melted. Pour through fine-mesh sieve into glass measure.

Whisk together reserved fat and flour in a large heavy saucepan (it will be about the thickness of peanut butter) and cook roux over moderately low heat, stir-ring, 3 minutes. Add hot stock mixture in a fast stream, whisking constantly to prevent lumps, and simmer, whisking occasionally, until thickened, about 5 minutes. Stir in turkey juices accumulated on platter and simmer 1 minute. Season with salt and pepper.

Serve turkey with gravy.

Cooks' note:
• **If you choose not to cook your stuffing inside the bird, your turkey will take less time to roast (thigh should register at least 170°F).**
PHOTO ON PAGE 100

TURKEY GIBLET STOCK

Makes about 6 cups
Active time: 15 min   Start to finish: 1 hr

Neck and giblets (excluding liver) from turkey (recipe precedes)
1 tablespoon vegetable oil
1 celery rib, coarsely chopped
1 carrot, coarsely chopped
1 red onion, coarsely chopped
1 cup dry white wine
5 cups water
1¾ cups chicken broth
1 Turkish or ½ California bay leaf
4 whole black peppercorns

Pat neck and giblets dry. Heat oil in a 4-quart heavy saucepan over moderately high heat until hot but not smoking, then brown neck and giblets, turning occasionally, about 5 minutes. Add vegetables and sauté, stirring occasionally, until golden, about 5 minutes. Add wine and boil 1 minute. Add remaining ingredients and simmer briskly, uncovered, until liquid is reduced to about 6 cups, about 30 minutes.

Pour stock through a large fine-mesh sieve into a large bowl and discard solids. Skim off and discard any fat.

Cooks' note:
• **Stock can be made 2 days ahead and cooled completely, uncovered, then chilled, covered. Discard solidified fat before reheating.**

SPICE-RUBBED QUAIL

Serves 4
Active time: 20 min   Start to finish: 1½ hr

8 (4- to 5-oz) semiboneless quail
1 teaspoon salt
¾ teaspoon black pepper
   Scant ½ teaspoon cayenne
   Scant ½ teaspoon ground allspice
½ cup chicken broth
¼ cup fresh lime juice
3 tablespoons molasses (not robust)
2 tablespoons finely chopped scallion
1 tablespoon unsalted butter
3 tablespoons olive oil

Marinate quail:
   Wash quail and pat dry. Stir together salt, black pepper, cayenne, and allspice and rub all over quail.

Arrange quail in 1 layer in a baking pan and marinate, covered and chilled, at least 1 hour.
   Make sauce:
   Simmer broth, lime juice, molasses, and scallion in a small heavy saucepan, uncovered, stirring occasionally, until slightly thickened, 8 to 10 minutes. Remove from heat and whisk in butter until incorporated. Season sauce with salt and pepper and keep warm.
   Broil quail:
   Arrange oven rack so that top of quail (on top of broiler pan) will be 2 inches from heat, then preheat broiler.
   Lightly oil broiler pan and heat under broiler until hot. Brush quail (on both sides) with olive oil and broil 2 inches from heat, turning once, until just cooked through, 6 to 10 minutes total.
   Serve quail drizzled with sauce.

Cooks' note:
• Quail can marinate up to 1 day.

BREAKFAST, BRUNCH, AND SANDWICHES

breakfast and brunch dishes

SAUSAGE AND EGG SANDWICH

Serves 2
Active time: 15 min   Start to finish: 15 min

If you can't get premade patties, buy bulk pork sausage meat and form your own.

1½ tablespoons unsalted butter, softened
4 (½-inch-thick) slices country-style bread
    (4 to 5½ inches wide)
1 tablespoon vegetable oil
4 (⅓-inch-thick) breakfast pork sausage
    patties (6 oz), thawed if frozen
6 tablespoons coarsely grated Swiss cheese
    (2 oz)
4 large eggs

Butter bread slices and arrange 2, buttered sides down, on a large plate.

Heat oil in a 12-inch nonstick skillet over moderately high heat until hot but not smoking, then cook patties, pressing with a spatula to flatten and turning once, until golden brown and cooked through, about 4 minutes total. Transfer to paper towels to drain briefly, then arrange 2 patties side by side on each plated bread slice. Top with cheese.

Fry eggs in fat remaining in skillet over moderate heat, seasoning with salt and pepper, until whites are barely set, about 1½ minutes. Flip eggs with spatula and cook until whites are set and yolks are just set but still soft, 45 seconds to 1 minute more.

Carefully transfer eggs to sandwiches, topping each patty with an egg. Cover with remaining 2 bread slices, buttered sides up. Wipe out skillet.

Carefully transfer sandwiches to skillet and cook over moderate heat, turning carefully once, until golden, 2 to 4 minutes total. Halve sandwiches.

Cooks' note:
• The yolks in this recipe are not fully cooked, which may be of concern if salmonella is a problem in your area.

BAKED EGGS AND MUSHROOMS IN HAM CRISPS

Serves 6
Active time: 45 min   Start to finish: 1¼ hr

¾ lb mushrooms, finely chopped
¼ cup finely chopped shallot
2 tablespoons unsalted butter
½ teaspoon salt
¼ teaspoon black pepper
2 tablespoons crème fraîche or sour cream
1 tablespoon finely chopped fresh tarragon
12 slices Black Forest or Virginia ham
    (without holes; 10 oz)
12 large eggs

Garnish: **fresh tarragon leaves**
Accompaniment: **buttered brioche or challah toast**
Special equipment: **a muffin tin with**
    12 (½-cup) muffin cups

Preheat oven to 400°F.
Prepare mushrooms:
Cook mushrooms and shallot in butter with salt and pepper in a large heavy skillet over moderately high heat, stirring, until mushrooms are tender and liquid they give off is evaporated, about 10 minutes. Remove from heat and stir in crème fraîche and tarragon.

Assemble and bake:
Fit 1 slice of ham into each of 12 lightly oiled muffin cups (ends will stick up and hang over edges of cups). Divide mushrooms among cups and crack 1 egg into each. Bake in middle of oven until whites are cooked but yolks are still runny, about 15 minutes. Season eggs with salt and pepper and remove (with ham) from muffin cups carefully, using 2 spoons or small spatulas.

Cooks' note:
• The eggs in this recipe are not fully cooked, which may be of concern if salmonella is a problem in your area.

PHOTO ON PAGE 49

CHEDDAR SHORTCAKES WITH CORNED BEEF HASH

Serves 6
Active time: 1¼ hr   Start to finish: 3 hr (includes making salsa)

For biscuits
> 1 cup sour cream
> ¾ cup water
> 3 cups all-purpose flour
> 1½ teaspoons baking powder
> 1 teaspoon baking soda
> 1½ teaspoons salt
> 3 tablespoons cold unsalted butter,
>   cut into bits
> 6 oz sharp Cheddar, coarsely grated

For hash
> 2 lb yellow-fleshed potatoes such as
>   Yukon Gold
> 2 onions, coarsely chopped
> ¾ stick (6 tablespoons) unsalted butter
> 2 red bell peppers, coarsely chopped
> 1 lb sliced (⅛ inch thick) cooked corned beef,
>   cut crosswise into ⅛-inch-wide strips
> 1 teaspoon salt
> ½ teaspoon black pepper
> ½ cup minced fresh flat-leaf parsley

Accompaniment: **tomatillo salsa (page 220)**

Make biscuits:
Preheat oven to 425°F.

Stir together sour cream and water until smooth. Sift together flour, baking powder, baking soda, and salt into a bowl, then blend in butter with your fingertips or a pastry blender until there are no longer any lumps. Add Cheddar and toss, then stir in thinned sour cream with a fork until just combined.

Drop dough in 6 evenly spaced mounds on a buttered baking sheet and bake in middle of oven until pale golden and cooked through, 15 to 20 minutes. Transfer biscuits to a rack to cool slightly.

Make hash while biscuits bake:
Peel potatoes and cut into ⅓-inch dice. Cook in a pot of boiling salted water (see Tips, page 8) until just tender, 8 to 10 minutes, then drain in a colander.

While potatoes are boiling, cook onions in butter in a deep 12-inch nonstick skillet over moderate heat, stirring occasionally, until softened and beginning to brown, about 5 minutes. Add bell peppers and cook, stirring, until crisp-tender, about 5 minutes.

Add potatoes, corned beef, salt, and pepper and cook over high heat, stirring occasionally, until hash is browned and crisp, about 15 minutes. Stir in parsley.

Split biscuits and spoon hash and salsa onto bottom halves. Put tops on biscuits.

PHOTO ON PAGE 52

ZUCCHINI FRITTATA WITH BLOSSOMS

Serves 6 to 8 (lunch or brunch)
Active time: 15 min   Start to finish: 25 min

> 7 whole large eggs
> 3 large egg whites
> ½ cup whole milk
> 5 oz *ricotta salata*, finely crumbled (1 cup)
> ¾ teaspoon salt
> ½ teaspoon black pepper
> 2 medium zucchini (1 to 1¼ lb total),
>   quartered lengthwise and cut crosswise
>   into ½-inch-thick pieces
> 1 tablespoon olive oil
> 1 garlic clove, finely chopped
> 1½ teaspoons chopped fresh oregano
> ¼ cup finely grated Parmigiano-Reggiano
>   (1 oz)
> 6 large zucchini blossoms (optional), tough
>   ends removed

Whisk together whole eggs, whites, milk, *ricotta salata*, ¼ teaspoon salt, and ¼ teaspoon pepper in a large bowl.

Preheat broiler.

Cook zucchini in oil in a 12-inch ovenproof nonstick skillet (or wrap plastic handle in a double layer of foil) over moderate heat, stirring, until just tender, about 8 minutes. Add garlic, oregano, remaining ½ teaspoon salt, and remaining ¼ teaspoon pepper and cook, stirring, 1 minute. Pour egg mixture over zucchini and cook over moderately high heat, lifting up cooked egg around edges to let uncooked egg flow underneath, 3 to 5 minutes (top will still be moist).

Sprinkle top with Parmigiano-Reggiano and arrange blossoms (if using) evenly on top, pressing them in lightly.

Broil frittata about 6 inches from heat until set, puffed, and golden brown, about 3 minutes.

Cool 5 minutes, then loosen edges with a spatula and slide onto a platter. Cut into wedges and serve warm or at room temperature.

FRIED EGGS WITH VEGETABLE CONFETTI

Serves 4
Active time: 45 min   Start to finish: 45 min

> 3 tablespoons plus 1 teaspoon olive oil
> 1 yellow bell pepper, cut into ¼-inch dice
> 1 medium onion, cut into ¼-inch dice
> 1 tablespoon minced garlic
> ½ teaspoon salt
> 1 medium zucchini, cut into ¼-inch dice
> 1 pt grape tomatoes, quartered
> ½ cup coarsely chopped fresh cilantro
> 8 large eggs

Heat 2 tablespoons oil in a 12-inch nonstick skillet over moderately high heat until hot but not smoking, then sauté bell pepper, onion, and garlic with salt, stirring, until softened, about 5 minutes. Add zucchini and tomatoes and sauté, stirring, until zucchini is tender, about 5 minutes. Stir in cilantro and salt and pepper to taste, then transfer vegetable confetti to a bowl and keep warm.

Fry eggs and serve:
Heat 2 teaspoons oil in cleaned skillet over moderately low heat and crack 4 eggs into skillet. Cook, uncovered, over low heat until whites are cooked, about 3 minutes, then transfer eggs with a spatula to 2 plates. Season eggs with salt and pepper and scatter one fourth of vegetable confetti on each plate. Repeat with remaining 2 teaspoons oil, 4 eggs, and confetti.

Cooks' note:
· The eggs in this recipe are not fully cooked, which may be of concern if salmonella is a problem in your area.

sandwiches

STEAK SANDWICHES WITH HORSERADISH MUSTARD BUTTER AND WATERCRESS

Serves 4
Active time: 20 min   Start to finish: 25 min

> ¾ stick (6 tablespoons) unsalted butter, softened
> 3 tablespoons drained bottled horseradish
> 3 tablespoons Dijon mustard
> 1½ tablespoons minced shallot
> 1 (1-lb) piece flank steak (¾ to 1 inch thick)
> 1 (20- to 22-inch) baguette
> 1 large bunch watercress, tough stems discarded

Preheat broiler.

Blend together butter, horseradish, mustard, shallot, and salt and pepper to taste in a bowl with a fork until combined well.

Pat steak dry, then season both sides well with salt and pepper and put on rack of a broiler pan. Spread top of steak with 1 tablespoon mustard butter, then broil 2 to 3 inches from heat 5 minutes. Turn over and spread other side with 1 tablespoon mustard butter, then broil 4 to 5 minutes more for medium-rare. Transfer meat to a cutting board and let stand 5 minutes. (Leave broiler on.)

Cut baguette crosswise into 4 equal sections, then halve sections horizontally. Broil bread, cut sides up, about 3 inches from heat, rotating pan once, until golden, 30 seconds to 1 minute.

Holding knife at a 45-degree angle, very thinly slice steak across the grain. Spread cut sides of bread with mustard butter and mound steak on half of bread. Top with watercress and remaining bread.

MOROCCAN CARROT AND GOAT CHEESE SANDWICHES WITH GREEN OLIVE TAPENADE

Makes 6 sandwiches
Active time: 30 min   Start to finish: 4½ hr (includes marinating)

The inspiration for this recipe came from a tea sandwich one of our food editors discovered at Alice's Tea Cup, in Manhattan. It's surprisingly substantial—a bit like an overstuffed deli sandwich, but not as heavy.

For carrots
    2 tablespoons sugar
    1 tablespoon fresh lemon juice
    2 teaspoons sweet paprika
    1 teaspoon ground cumin
    ½ teaspoon cinnamon
    ¼ teaspoon cayenne
    1 teaspoon salt
    ¼ cup olive oil
    1½ lb medium carrots (8)
For tapenade
    1¼ cups green olives (6 to 7 oz) such as Cerignola or *picholine*, pitted
    3 tablespoons drained bottled capers, rinsed
    ¼ cup chopped fresh flat-leaf parsley
    1 flat anchovy fillet, chopped
    1 teaspoon finely grated fresh lemon zest
    1½ tablespoons fresh lemon juice
    ½ teaspoon black pepper
    ¼ cup olive oil
For sandwiches
    12 slices good-quality pumpernickel sandwich bread
    6 oz soft mild goat cheese (¾ cup) at room temperature

Special equipment: **a Japanese Benriner or other adjustable-blade slicer**

Prepare carrots:
Whisk together sugar, lemon juice, spices, salt, and oil in a large bowl until sugar is dissolved.

Halve carrots crosswise on a long diagonal, then, starting from diagonal ends, cut into ¹⁄₁₆-inch-thick slices using slicer. Cook carrots in a 4- to 5-quart pot of boiling salted water (see Tips, page 8) until crisp-tender, about 45 seconds. Drain well in a colander and immediately toss with dressing. Cool to room temperature, stirring occasionally, then marinate, covered and chilled, at least 4 hours.

Make tapenade and assemble sandwiches:
Pulse olives with capers, parsley, anchovy, zest, lemon juice, and pepper in a food processor until coarsely chopped, then scrape down side of bowl with a rubber spatula. Pulsing motor, add oil in a slow stream and continue to pulse until mixture is finely chopped (do not pulse to a paste).

Spread tapenade on 6 slices of bread and goat cheese on remaining 6 slices, then make sandwiches with carrots.

Cooks' notes:
• Carrots can marinate up to 2 days.
• Tapenade can be made 1 week ahead and chilled, covered.
PHOTO ON PAGE 89

HAM AND SWEET ONION SANDWICHES WITH PARSLEY BUTTER

Makes 2 sandwiches
Active time: 10 min   Start to finish: 10 min

    ¾ cup coarsely chopped fresh flat-leaf parsley
    2 tablespoons unsalted butter, softened
    ½ teaspoon salt
    1 large sweet onion such as Vidalia or Walla Walla
    4 slices good-quality whole-wheat sandwich bread
    ¼ lb thinly sliced cooked ham (preferably Black Forest)

Finely chop parsley in a food processor, then add butter and salt and blend to a paste.

Cut 4 (⅛-inch-thick) slices crosswise from center of onion, reserving remainder for another use.

Spread 1½ teaspoons parsley butter on 1 side of each slice of bread. Arrange 1 onion slice on each of 2 bread slices and spread each with 1½ teaspoons parsley butter, then top each with one fourth of ham. Make another layer in same manner, then cover with remaining bread slices, buttered sides down.

CHICKEN AND ROASTED PEPPER SANDWICHES WITH CILANTRO ALMOND RELISH

Makes 6 sandwiches
Active time: 40 min   Start to finish: 1 hr

Pack these sandwiches next to an ice pack to keep them cool and fresh as you travel to a picnic.

  10 cups water
   6 skinless boneless chicken breast halves
     (2½ lb)
   4 large yellow bell peppers
  ⅔ cup blanched slivered almonds, toasted
     (see Tips, page 8)
   1 garlic clove
1½ tablespoons chopped fresh jalapeño chile
     (including seeds)
   1 cup chopped fresh cilantro
  ¼ cup mayonnaise
   3 tablespoons fresh lime juice
   3 tablespoons sour cream
   1 teaspoon salt
  12 slices good-quality whole-wheat
     sandwich bread

Poach chicken:

Bring water to a simmer in a 4- to 5-quart pot, then add chicken and simmer, uncovered, 6 minutes. Remove pan from heat and let stand, covered, until chicken is cooked through, about 15 minutes. Transfer chicken to a plate and cool completely, then cut diagonally into thin slices.

Roast bell peppers:

Roast bell peppers on racks of gas burners over high heat, turning with tongs, until skins are blackened, 10 to 12 minutes. (Or broil peppers on rack of a broiler pan about 5 inches from heat, turning occasionally, about 15 minutes.) Transfer to a large bowl and cover tightly with plastic wrap, then let stand 20 minutes.

When cool enough to handle, peel peppers, then discard stems and seeds, and cut lengthwise into 1½-inch-wide strips.

While peppers are standing, pulse almonds, garlic, and jalapeño in a food processor until finely chopped. Add cilantro, mayonnaise, lime juice, sour cream, and salt and blend to a paste.

Spread cilantro relish on each slice of bread, then make sandwiches with chicken and roasted peppers, seasoning with salt and pepper.

Cooks' notes:
· Chicken can be poached (but not sliced) 1 day ahead and chilled, covered.
· Bell peppers can be roasted, peeled, and sliced 1 day ahead and chilled, covered.
· Relish can be made 1 day ahead and chilled, its surface covered with plastic wrap.
PHOTO ON PAGE 90

STROMBOLI
Salami and Cheese Rolls

Serves 4 (main course)
Active time: 15 min   Start to finish: 45 min

  1 lb pizza dough, thawed if frozen
¼ cup finely grated Parmigiano-Reggiano
    (½ oz)
  3 oz thinly sliced salami (12 slices)
  4 oz thinly sliced provolone (12 slices)
⅔ cup jarred roasted bell peppers, rinsed and
    chopped
  1 large egg, lightly beaten

Preheat oven to 400°F.

Quarter dough. Roll out 1 piece into a 10-inch round on a lightly floured surface and sprinkle evenly with 1 tablespoon parmesan and black pepper to taste. Arrange one fourth each of salami, provolone, and roasted peppers in an even layer over dough. Roll up dough round, then tuck ends under and pinch edges to seal.

Make 3 more rolls in same manner and arrange 2 inches apart on a lightly greased baking sheet. Brush lightly with egg and cut 3 (½-inch) steam vents in each roll. Bake in middle of oven until golden, 30 to 35 minutes.

TUNA AND ARTICHOKE PANINI

Makes 4 sandwiches
Active time: 15 min   Start to finish: 15 min

½ cup brine-cured black olives, rinsed,
      drained, and pitted
2 teaspoons drained bottled capers
1 small garlic clove, chopped
½ teaspoon finely grated fresh lemon zest
2 (6½-oz) jars marinated artichokes, drained,
      reserving marinade, and chopped
⅓ cup mayonnaise
2 (6-oz) cans tuna in olive oil, drained
      and any large chunks broken into
      smaller pieces

4 (7-inch-long) *ciabatta* rolls or other
      crusty rolls with soft, chewy crumb
¾ cup loosely packed fresh flat-leaf
      parsley leaves

Blend olives, capers, garlic, zest, and 3 tablespoons artichoke marinade in a blender, scraping down sides frequently, until as smooth as possible, 1 to 2 minutes. Transfer to a bowl and stir in mayonnaise. Stir together chopped artichokes and tuna in another bowl.

Split each roll horizontally and remove inner crumb from top half. Spread olive mayonnaise on cut sides of rolls and make sandwiches with tuna and artichokes, seasoning filling with pepper and topping with parsley.

PASTA AND GRAINS

pasta

PEARL COUSCOUS WITH OLIVES AND ROASTED TOMATOES

Serves 6
Active time: 30 min   Start to finish: 2½ hr

For roasted tomatoes and dressing
  2 pt red grape or cherry tomatoes (1½ lb), halved lengthwise
  3 large garlic cloves, left unpeeled
  ¼ cup extra-virgin olive oil
  ¼ cup warm water
  1 teaspoon fresh lemon juice
  1 teaspoon salt
  ¼ teaspoon black pepper

For couscous
  2¾ cups chicken broth
  2¼ cups pearl (Israeli) couscous
  1 tablespoon olive oil
  ½ cup Kalamata or other brine-cured black olives, pitted and chopped
  ⅓ cup chopped fresh flat-leaf parsley
  ¼ cup chopped fresh mint
  1 teaspoon chopped fresh thyme

Roast tomatoes and make dressing:
Preheat oven to 250°F.

Arrange tomatoes, cut sides up, in 1 layer in a large shallow baking pan (1 inch deep). Add garlic to pan and roast in middle of oven until tomatoes are slightly shriveled around edges, about 1 hour. Cool in pan on a rack 30 minutes.

Peel garlic and purée with oil, water, lemon juice, salt, pepper, and ½ cup roasted tomatoes in a blender until dressing is very smooth.

Make couscous:
Bring broth to a boil in a 3-quart heavy saucepan and stir in couscous, then simmer, uncovered, 6 minutes. Cover pan and remove from heat. Let stand 10 minutes.

Spread couscous in 1 layer on a baking sheet and cool 15 minutes.

Transfer couscous to a bowl and stir in remaining ingredients, dressing, roasted tomatoes, and salt and pepper to taste.

Cooks' note:
• **Roasted tomatoes, dressing, and couscous can be made 1 day ahead and kept separately, covered and chilled. Bring to room temperature before proceeding.**
PHOTO ON PAGE 95

PASTA WITH MUSSELS AND CHORIZO

Serves 6 (main course)
Active time: 1 hr   Start to finish: 1¼ hr

  ½ cup extra-virgin olive oil
  2 Spanish chorizo links (spicy cured pork sausage; ½ lb total), finely chopped
  2 shallots, finely chopped
  1 tablespoon minced garlic
  ½ cup dry white wine
  1 lb dried pasta such as *campanelli* (bellflower)
  4 lb mussels (preferably cultivated), cleaned and steamed (procedures on page 121), then shucked
  ¼ cup finely chopped fresh flat-leaf parsley
  ½ cup finely chopped fresh cilantro
  2 tablespoons fresh lemon juice, or to taste

Heat oil in a 12-inch heavy skillet over moderately high heat until hot but not smoking, then sauté chorizo and shallots, stirring, until chorizo is golden brown on edges, about 4 minutes. Add garlic and sauté, stirring, 1 minute. Add wine and simmer until liquid is reduced by half, about 5 minutes. Keep sauce warm, covered.

Cook pasta in a large pot of boiling salted water (see Tips, page 8) until al dente, then reserve 1 cup pasta cooking water and drain pasta in a colander.

Return pasta to pot and add sauce, mussels, parsley, cilantro, and ½ cup pasta cooking water. Cook over low heat, stirring, until mussels are heated through. Add more cooking water if pasta seems dry.

Toss pasta with lemon juice and salt and pepper to taste.

EGGPLANT AND SPINACH LASAGNE SPIRALS

Serves 4

Active time: 1½ hr   Start to finish: 2 hr

For tomato sauce

  3 lb plum tomatoes, halved lengthwise
  5 tablespoons olive oil
  ¾ teaspoon salt
  ½ teaspoon black pepper
  1 small onion, finely chopped
  2 garlic cloves, minced
  ½ cup water
  ¼ cup chopped fresh basil

For lasagne

  2 lb Asian or baby Italian eggplants (4 to 6), halved crosswise, then cut lengthwise into slices slightly less than ¼ inch thick
  3 tablespoons olive oil
  1 large garlic clove, finely chopped
  1¼ teaspoons salt
  ½ teaspoon black pepper
  10 oz baby spinach
  1 lb ricotta (preferably fresh)
  1 large egg yolk, lightly beaten
  ½ cup finely grated Parmigiano-Reggiano (1 oz)
  8 dried lasagne noodles (not no-boil; 8 oz)

Roast tomatoes for sauce:
Preheat oven to 450°F.

Toss tomatoes with 3 tablespoons oil, ½ teaspoon salt, and ¼ teaspoon pepper and arrange, cut sides up, in 1 layer in 2 oiled glass or ceramic shallow baking dishes. Roast tomatoes in upper and lower thirds of oven, switching position of dishes halfway through baking, until skins are wrinkled and beginning to brown, 35 to 40 minutes. Cool slightly in baking dishes on racks.

Roast eggplant for lasagne:
Toss eggplant slices with oil, garlic, ½ teaspoon salt, and ¼ teaspoon pepper and arrange in 1 layer on 2 oiled baking sheets. Bake in upper and lower thirds of oven, switching position of sheets halfway through baking and turning slices over once, until tender, 12 to 14 minutes.

Reduce oven temperature to 350°F.

Finish tomato sauce:
When tomatoes are cool enough to handle, peel off skin and discard. Purée tomatoes with their juices in a blender, pulsing until almost smooth.

Cook onion and garlic in remaining 2 tablespoons oil in a 3- to 4-quart heavy saucepan over moderate heat, stirring, until golden, about 10 minutes. Stir in tomato purée, water, remaining ¼ teaspoon salt, and remaining ¼ teaspoon pepper and simmer, partially covered, stirring occasionally, until slightly thickened and reduced to about 4 cups, about 15 minutes. Stir in basil.

Make filling and assemble lasagne:
While sauce is simmering, cook spinach in a 3- to 4-quart pot of boiling salted water (see Tips, page 8), uncovered, 1 minute, then drain in a colander. When cool enough to handle, squeeze any excess water from spinach and coarsely chop, then stir together with ricotta, yolk, parmesan, remaining ¾ teaspoon salt, and remaining ¼ teaspoon pepper until combined well.

Cook lasagne noodles in a 6- to 8-quart pot of boiling salted water (see Tips, page 8), stirring occasionally, until tender. Drain noodles in a colander and rinse under cold running water.

Spoon 2 cups tomato sauce into a 13- by 9-inch glass baking dish (or other 3-quart shallow baking dish). Lay 4 lasagne noodles on a work surface, then spread ⅓ cup filling evenly over each noodle and cover with eggplant slices in 1 layer. Roll up each noodle and arrange spirals, seam sides down and without touching, over sauce in dish, then make 4 more rolls and arrange in dish. Brush noodles with some water, then spoon some sauce down middle of rolls and cover dish tightly with foil.

Bake in middle of oven until heated through, about 20 minutes. Heat remaining tomato sauce and serve on the side.

PHOTO ON PAGE 110

LINGUINE WITH PECAN ARUGULA PESTO

Serves 4 to 6 (main course)
Active time: 30 min   Start to finish: 45 min

¾ **cup pecans (3 oz), toasted (see Tips, page 8)**
 1 **large garlic clove**
 ½ **teaspoon salt**
 10 **oz arugula, coarse stems discarded**
 ½ **cup finely grated Parmigiano-Reggiano**
    (1½ oz)
 ½ **cup olive oil**
 ½ **teaspoon black pepper**
 1 **lb dried linguine**

Finely chop ¼ cup pecans (preferably with a knife).
Mash garlic to a paste with salt using a mortar and
pestle (or mince and mash with a large heavy knife).
Blend remaining ½ cup pecans, arugula, cheese, oil,
pepper, and garlic paste in a food processor until
smooth, about 1 minute.

Cook pasta in a 6- to 8-quart pot of boiling salted
water (see Tips, page 8) until al dente, 10 to 12
minutes. Ladle out and reserve 1½ cups cooking water.
Drain pasta in a colander, then return to pot and toss
with pesto, ½ cup cooking water, and chopped pecans,
adding more cooking water as necessary if pasta
seems dry.

Cooks' note:
• You can substitute 2 cups fresh flat-leaf parsley for the
  arugula, but then you should use only ⅓ cup olive oil
  (instead of ½ cup) in the pesto.

FUSILLI WITH ASPARAGUS AND BACON

Serves 4
Active time: 30 min   Start to finish: 30 min

 4 **oz sliced bacon, cut crosswise into**
    ½-inch pieces
 2 **tablespoons extra-virgin olive oil**
 1 **medium onion, finely chopped**
 1½ **lb asparagus, trimmed and cut**
    on a long diagonal into
    ½-inch-thick slices
 1 **lb fusilli (short corkscrew pasta)**
 ½ **cup finely grated Parmigiano-Reggiano**
    (1½ oz) plus additional for serving

Cook bacon in a 12-inch heavy skillet over moderately high heat, stirring occasionally, until browned and
crisp, about 6 minutes. Transfer bacon with a slotted
spoon to paper towels to drain. Pour off all but 2 tablespoons fat from skillet, then add oil and onion to skillet
and cook, stirring occasionally, until onion is golden,
about 4 minutes. Add asparagus and sauté, stirring,
until crisp-tender, 4 to 5 minutes. Season with salt
and pepper.

While onion and asparagus are cooking, cook pasta
in a 6- to 8-quart pot of boiling salted water (see Tips,
page 8) until al dente. Reserve 1 cup pasta cooking
water and drain pasta in a colander.

Return pasta to pot along with asparagus mixture,
½ cup pasta cooking water, and cheese. Add remaining
½ cup cooking water to skillet and deglaze by boiling,
stirring and scraping up brown bits, 1 minute. Add to
pasta and toss over moderately low heat until combined
well, about 30 seconds.

Serve pasta sprinkled with bacon and with additional cheese on the side.

BUTTERED NOODLES WITH CHIVES

Serves 8
Active time: 5 min   Start to finish: 10 min

 10 **oz no-yolk egg noodles**
 2 **tablespoons unsalted butter,**
    cut into bits
 ½ **cup low-fat chicken stock or**
    low-sodium fat-free chicken
    broth, heated
 ¼ **cup chopped fresh chives**
 ¾ **teaspoon salt**
 ¼ **teaspoon black pepper**

Cook noodles in a large pot of boiling salted water
(see Tips, page 8), stirring occasionally, until tender,
10 to 12 minutes. Drain in a colander and immediately
toss with remaining ingredients in a large bowl.

Each serving about 161 calories and 2 grams fat
PHOTO ON PAGE 45

PEANUT SESAME NOODLES

Serves 6 (side dish) or 4 (vegetarian main course)
Active time: 30 min   Start to finish: 30 min

The secret to this Chinese favorite is not to let the noodles sit in the sauce very long—toss them together a few seconds before serving.

For peanut dressing
    ½ cup smooth peanut butter
    ¼ cup soy sauce
    ⅓ cup warm water
    2 tablespoons chopped peeled fresh ginger
    1 medium garlic clove, chopped
    2 tablespoons red-wine vinegar
    1½ tablespoons Asian sesame oil
    2 teaspoons honey
    1 teaspoon dried hot red pepper flakes
For noodle salad
    ¾ lb dried *linguine fini* or spaghetti
    4 scallions, thinly sliced
    1 red bell pepper, cut into ⅛-inch-thick strips
    1 yellow bell pepper, cut into ⅛-inch-thick strips
    3 tablespoons sesame seeds, toasted (see Tips, page 8)

Make dressing:
Purée all dressing ingredients in a blender until smooth, about 2 minutes, then transfer to a large bowl.
Make salad:
Cook pasta in a 6- to 8-quart pot of boiling salted water (see Tips, page 8) until tender. Drain in a colander, then rinse well under cold water.
    Add pasta, scallions, bell peppers, and sesame seeds to dressing, tossing to combine, and serve immediately.

ORECCHIETTE WITH SAVOY CABBAGE, PEAS, AND LEMON CREAM

Serves 4 (main course)
Active time: 35 min   Start to finish: 35 min

    1 lb *orecchiette* (ear-shaped pasta) or pasta shells
    2 tablespoons unsalted butter
    ½ lb Savoy cabbage, quartered lengthwise, core discarded, and leaves very thinly sliced crosswise
    1 bunch scallions, thinly sliced (1 cup)
    ½ cup chicken broth
    ½ cup heavy cream
    1 cup thawed frozen peas
    2 teaspoons finely grated fresh lemon zest
    ¼ cup chopped fresh dill
    ¾ teaspoon salt
    ¼ teaspoon black pepper

Cook pasta in a 6- to 8-quart pot of boiling salted water (see Tips, page 8) until al dente.
    While pasta is cooking, heat butter in a 12-inch nonstick skillet over moderately high heat until foam subsides, then sauté cabbage, stirring, until pale golden, about 6 minutes. Add scallions, chicken broth, and cream and bring to a boil, then reduce heat and simmer, uncovered, stirring occasionally, until cabbage is tender, about 2 minutes.
    Remove from heat and stir in peas, zest, dill, salt, and pepper. Ladle out 1 cup pasta cooking water and reserve, then drain pasta in a colander. Stir together pasta, cabbage mixture, and ¾ cup reserved pasta water in a large bowl (or in pot). If pasta looks dry, moisten with some of remaining water.

ORZO WITH TOMATOES AND ARUGULA

Serves 1
Active time: 10 min   Start to finish: 25 min

    ¼ cup orzo
    1½ teaspoons extra-virgin olive oil
    ½ teaspoon balsamic vinegar plus additional to taste
    1 small tomato, seeded and cut into ¼-inch dice
    ½ cup coarsely chopped arugula
    1 tablespoon thinly sliced fresh basil
    1 tablespoon pine nuts (optional), lightly toasted (see Tips, page 8)

Cook orzo in a 2- to 3-quart saucepan of boiling salted water (see Tips, page 8) until al dente, then drain well and transfer to a small bowl. Toss with oil and ½ teaspoon vinegar and cool to room temperature.
    Stir in tomato, arugula, basil, pine nuts (if using), and additional vinegar and salt and pepper to taste.
    PHOTO ON PAGE 112

SICILIAN-STYLE PASTA WITH SARDINES

Serves 4 (main course)
Active time: 30 min   Start to finish: 45 min

⅛ teaspoon crumbled saffron threads
½ cup raisins
½ cup dry white wine
1 large fennel bulb (sometimes called anise;
   1¼ lb), any fronds chopped and stalks
   cut off and discarded
1 medium onion, finely chopped
1 tablespoon fennel seeds,
   crushed
½ cup extra-virgin olive oil
2 (3¾- to 4⅜-oz) cans sardines in
   oil, drained
1 lb *perciatelli* or spaghetti
½ cup pine nuts, toasted (see Tips, page 8)
⅓ cup plain dry bread crumbs, toasted and
   tossed with 2 tablespoons extra-virgin
   olive oil and salt to taste

Stir together saffron, raisins, and wine in a bowl.
Finely chop fennel bulb. Cook fennel bulb, onion, and fennel seeds in oil with salt to taste in a 12-inch heavy skillet over moderate heat, stirring, until fennel is tender, about 15 minutes.

Add wine mixture and half of sardines, breaking sardines up with a fork, and simmer 1 minute.

While sauce is cooking, cook *perciatelli* or spaghetti in a 6- to 8-quart pot of boiling salted water (see Tips, page 8) until al dente, then drain in a colander.

Toss hot pasta in a bowl with fennel sauce, remaining sardines, fennel fronds, pine nuts, and salt and pepper to taste. Add bread crumbs and toss again.

TAGLIATELLE WITH ZUCCHINI AND SHRIMP

Serves 2 (main course)
Active time: 25 min   Start to finish: 25 min

10 large shrimp in shell (21 to 25 per lb),
   peeled and deveined
⅛ teaspoon black pepper
½ teaspoon salt
2½ tablespoons extra-virgin olive oil
½ lb zucchini (1 medium), cut lengthwise into
   2- by ¼-inch sticks
4 teaspoons minced garlic
5 oz dried egg tagliatelle or egg fettuccine
½ teaspoon finely grated fresh lemon zest
⅓ cup finely chopped fresh basil

Pat shrimp dry and sprinkle with pepper and ¼ teaspoon salt.

Heat 1 tablespoon oil in a 12-inch heavy skillet over moderately high heat until hot but not smoking, then sauté shrimp, stirring frequently, until lightly browned and just cooked through, about 2 minutes. Transfer to a bowl.

Heat remaining 1½ tablespoons oil in skillet over moderately high heat until hot but not smoking, then sauté zucchini, stirring frequently, until lightly browned, 2 to 3 minutes. Add garlic and sauté, stirring, until zucchini is just tender, 2 to 3 minutes. Season with pepper and remaining ¼ teaspoon salt.

Boil pasta while zucchini cooks:

Cook pasta in a large pot of boiling salted water (see Tips, page 8) until al dente, then drain well in a colander.

Add pasta to zucchini along with shrimp, zest, and basil. Cook over moderately high heat, tossing, until shrimp are heated through, about 1 minute.

HERBED ORZO AND SUGAR SNAP PEAS

Serves 6 (side dish)
Active time: 10 min   Start to finish: 15 min

10 cups water
2 cups low-sodium fat-free chicken broth
1½ teaspoons salt
½ lb sugar snap peas, trimmed and cut
    diagonally into ½-inch pieces
3 scallions, chopped
2 tablespoons chopped fresh dill
1⅓ cups orzo (½ lb)
¼ teaspoon black pepper

Bring water, broth, and 1 teaspoon salt to a boil and blanch sugar snaps 1 minute. Transfer sugar snaps with a slotted spoon to a bowl of cold water to stop cooking, reserving broth, then drain sugar snaps in a colander. Put sugar snaps, scallions, and dill in a bowl.

Return broth to a boil and cook orzo, stirring occasionally, until tender. Reserve ½ cup broth, then drain orzo in a medium-mesh sieve. Add hot orzo to vegetables along with pepper and remaining ½ teaspoon salt and toss, adding some of reserved broth if pasta seems dry.

Each serving about 161 calories and 1 gram fat

grains

BARLEY WITH TOASTED CUMIN AND MINT

Serves 4
Active time: 15 min   Start to finish: 30 min

2 cups water
1 cup quick-cooking barley
½ teaspoon salt
⅛ teaspoon turmeric
¼ cup finely chopped fresh mint
2 to 3 tablespoons finely chopped red onion
1½ tablespoons fresh lemon juice
¾ teaspoon cumin seeds, toasted (see Tips,
    page 8)
1 teaspoon extra-virgin olive oil

Bring water, barley, salt, and turmeric to a boil in a 2-quart heavy saucepan, then simmer, covered, until

barley is tender, about 10 minutes. Remove from heat and let stand, covered, 5 minutes. Drain barley in a colander and transfer to a bowl. Stir in mint, onion (to taste), lemon juice, cumin, oil, and salt and pepper to taste.

Each serving about 144 calories and 2 grams fat

HERBED QUINOA

Serves 6
Active time: 35 min   Start to finish: 35 min

1½ cups quinoa (½ lb)
2½ tablespoons extra-virgin olive oil
½ cup thinly sliced scallion greens
1 teaspoon fresh thyme leaves

Rinse quinoa in 5 changes of water in a bowl, rubbing grains and letting them settle before pouring off water (if quinoa does not settle, drain in a large fine-mesh sieve after each rinse).

Cook quinoa in a large saucepan of boiling salted water (see Tips, page 8) 10 minutes. Drain in sieve and rinse under cold water.

Set sieve with quinoa over saucepan filled with 1½ inches boiling water (sieve should not touch water) and steam quinoa, covered with a kitchen towel and lid, until fluffy and dry, 10 to 12 minutes. (Check water level in pan occasionally, adding water if necessary.)

Toss quinoa with oil and salt and pepper to taste in a large bowl. Cool, then toss with scallion and thyme.

Cooks' note:
• Quinoa (without scallion and thyme) can be made 1 day ahead and chilled, covered. Bring to room temperature and toss with scallion greens and thyme just before serving.
PHOTO ON PAGE 70

SPICED BASMATI RICE

Serves 4
Active time: 5 min   Start to finish: 25 min

1⅓ cups water
½ teaspoon salt
1 (4- by 1-inch) strip fresh lemon zest,
    removed with a vegetable peeler
1 (2-inch) piece cinnamon stick
⅛ teaspoon cardamom seeds (from 4 pods)
¾ cup white basmati rice

Bring water, salt, zest, cinnamon stick, and cardamom to a boil in a 2-quart heavy saucepan. Stir in rice and return to a boil, then cover tightly and reduce heat to low. Cook until water is absorbed, about 15 minutes.

Remove from heat and fluff rice with a fork, then cover pan and let stand 5 minutes. Discard zest and cinnamon stick.

Each serving about 150 calories and less than 1 gram fat

RICE WITH JULIENNED CARROTS

Serves 2
Active time: 20 min   Start to finish: 35 min

½ cup finely chopped onion
1 tablespoon unsalted butter
1 cup long-grain white rice
1½ cups water
½ teaspoon salt
1 medium carrot, cut into ⅛-inch-thick
    matchsticks

Cook onion in butter in a 2-quart heavy saucepan over moderately low heat, stirring, until softened, about 3 minutes. Add rice and cook, stirring, 1 minute. Stir in water and salt and bring to a boil over high heat. Reduce heat to low and cook, covered, 10 minutes.

Sprinkle carrot over partially cooked rice and continue to cook, covered, until rice is cooked through and carrots are tender, about 6 minutes more.

Remove pan from heat (do not lift lid) and let stand, covered, 5 minutes. Fluff rice with a fork.

APRICOT AND PISTACHIO BAKED RICE

Serves 8
Active time: 15 min   Start to finish: 35 min

1½ cups basmati rice
6 cups water
2 tablespoons kosher salt
2 tablespoons vegetable oil
¾ lb firm-ripe apricots (4 large), cut into
    ½-inch pieces
⅓ cup shelled pistachios (not dyed red)
⅓ cup dried cherries or cranberries
3 tablespoons dried currants

Preheat oven to 350°F.

Wash rice in 6 changes of cold water in a large bowl until water is almost clear. Drain in a large medium-mesh sieve.

Bring 6 cups water and kosher salt to a boil in a 4-quart heavy ovenproof pot with a tight-fitting lid, then stir in rice and cook, uncovered, 6 minutes (rice will still be firm). Drain in sieve.

Heat oil in dried pot over moderate heat until hot but not smoking, then add rice, stirring until well coated, and remove from heat. Stir in remaining ingredients.

Bake, tightly covered, in middle of oven until rice is tender, about 18 minutes, then fluff with a fork.

WHITE RICE

Serves 6 generously
Active time: 5 min   Start to finish: 30 min

4½ cups water
1 teaspoon salt
3 cups long-grain white rice

Bring water with salt to a boil in a 4-quart heavy saucepan with a tight-fitting lid. Add rice and stir once, then reduce heat to low and cook, covered, 20 minutes.

Remove pan from heat (do not lift lid) and let stand, covered, 5 minutes. Fluff rice gently with a fork.

PHOTO ON PAGE 41

CURRIED RICE

Serves 8
Active time: 15 min   Start to finish: 45 min

    1 medium onion, finely chopped
    3 garlic cloves, finely chopped
    3 tablespoons olive oil
    4 teaspoons curry powder
    2 cups long-grain white rice
3¼ cups water
    2 teaspoons salt

Cook onion and garlic in oil in a 3- to 4-quart heavy saucepan over moderately low heat, stirring, until softened. Add curry powder and rice and cook, stirring, 1 minute. Add water and salt and boil, uncovered, without stirring, until surface of rice is covered with steam holes and grains on top appear dry, about 8 minutes.

Reduce heat to as low as possible, then cover pan with a tight-fitting lid and cook 15 minutes more.

Remove pan from heat and let rice stand, covered, 5 minutes, then fluff with a fork.

RISOTTO WITH TUSCAN KALE AND TOASTED PUMPKIN SEEDS

Serves 4 (main course)
Active time: 50 min   Start to finish: 1 hr

3½ cups low-sodium fat-free chicken broth
3½ cups water
    1 teaspoon fine sea salt
    ¾ lb Tuscan kale (also called *cavolo nero*
       or *lacinato* kale), stems and center
       ribs discarded
1¼ cups finely chopped onion
    1 tablespoon olive oil
    2 tablespoons unsalted butter
    3 garlic cloves, minced
1½ cups Arborio rice (10 oz)
    ⅓ cup dry white wine
    ½ cup grated Parmigiano-Reggiano (¾ oz)

Accompaniment: **toasted pumpkin seeds
       (recipe follows)**

Bring broth and water to a boil with ¾ teaspoon sea salt in a 3- to 4-quart saucepan. Stir kale into broth in

batches and simmer (all of kale), stirring occasionally, until tender, 5 to 10 minutes. Transfer kale with tongs to a large medium-mesh sieve set over a bowl and gently press on greens to extract more liquid. Add liquid in bowl to simmering broth and keep at a bare simmer, covered. Chop kale.

Cook onion in oil and 1 tablespoon butter with remaining ¼ teaspoon sea salt in a wide 4-quart heavy pot, covered, over low heat, stirring occasionally, until softened, about 5 minutes. Increase heat to moderate, then add garlic and cook, uncovered, stirring, 1 minute. Add rice and cook, stirring, 1 minute.

Add wine and simmer briskly, stirring constantly, until absorbed. Stir in ½ cup simmering broth and simmer briskly, stirring constantly, until broth is absorbed. Continue simmering and adding broth, about ½ cup at a time, stirring constantly and letting each addition be absorbed before adding next, until rice is creamy-looking but still al dente (it should be the consistency of thick soup), 17 to 18 minutes. (There will be leftover broth.)

Stir in kale, cheese, and remaining tablespoon butter and cook, stirring, until heated through and butter is incorporated, about 1 minute. Season risotto with sea salt and pepper and, if desired, thin with some of remaining broth. Serve sprinkled with toasted pumpkin seeds.

TOASTED PUMPKIN SEEDS

Makes about 1 cup
Active time: 5 min   Start to finish: 5 min

Don't think of toasted pumpkin seeds merely as a topping for the risotto—they also make a terrific hors d'oeuvre or snack.

    1 cup green (hulled) pumpkin seeds
       (not roasted; 5 oz)
    1 teaspoon olive oil
       Fine sea salt to taste

Cook pumpkin seeds in a dry 9- to 10-inch heavy skillet (preferably cast-iron) over moderate heat, stirring constantly, until puffed and golden, 4 to 5 minutes. Transfer to a bowl and stir in oil and sea salt.

RISOTTO WITH PEAS AND PROSCIUTTO

Serves 4 (main course) or 6 to 8 (side dish)
Active time: 35 min   Start to finish: 35 min

5 cups low-sodium chicken broth
½ cup finely chopped onion
½ stick (¼ cup) unsalted butter
1½ cups Arborio rice (12 oz)
½ cup dry white wine
1 cup frozen baby peas, thawed
2 oz thinly sliced prosciutto, cut crosswise
    into ¼-inch-wide strips
½ teaspoon finely grated fresh lemon zest
1 cup finely grated Parmigiano-Reggiano
    (2 oz)
3 tablespoons finely chopped fresh flat-leaf
    parsley

Bring broth to a simmer in a saucepan and keep at a bare simmer, covered.

Cook onion in 2 tablespoons butter in a 3- to 4-quart heavy saucepan over moderate heat, stirring occasionally, until softened, 3 to 4 minutes. Add rice and cook, stirring, 1 minute. Add wine and simmer, stirring, until absorbed.

Stir in 1 cup simmering broth and cook at a strong simmer, stirring constantly, until broth is absorbed. Continue simmering risotto and adding broth, about ½ cup at a time, stirring constantly and letting each addition become absorbed before adding next, until rice is just tender and creamy but still al dente, 18 to 20 minutes (there will be leftover broth).

Stir in baby peas, prosciutto, zest, ⅔ cup cheese, parsley, remaining 2 tablespoons butter, and salt and pepper to taste. If necessary, thin risotto with some of remaining broth. Serve immediately, with remaining ⅓ cup cheese.

WHEAT BERRIES WITH PECANS

Serves 6
Active time: 15 min   Start to finish: 1¼ hr

There are generally two kinds of wheat berries available at natural foods stores and Middle Eastern markets: hard (high-protein) and soft (low-protein). Though either will work fine, we prefer the chewiness of the hard variety for this particular recipe. If you can find only soft wheat berries, subtract 10 minutes from the cooking time.

2 cups hard wheat berries (12 oz)
1 medium onion, chopped
2 tablespoons unsalted butter
1½ teaspoons vegetable oil
1 large garlic clove, finely chopped
1 teaspoon kosher salt
¼ teaspoon black pepper
1 cup pecans (4 oz), toasted (see Tips, page 8)
    and chopped

Cook wheat berries in a 4-quart pot of boiling water (unsalted), uncovered, until tender, about 1 hour, then drain in a medium-mesh large sieve.

After wheat berries have been cooking 45 minutes, cook onion in butter and oil in a heavy skillet over moderate heat, stirring, until softened, about 6 minutes. Add garlic and cook, stirring, until fragrant, about 1 minute. Stir in wheat berries, kosher salt, pepper, and pecans.

Cooks' note:
• Wheat berries (without pecans) can be made 1 day ahead and chilled, covered. Reheat in a baking dish, covered, in a 350°F oven 30 minutes, then stir in pecans.

PHOTO ON PAGE 59

SCALLION WILD RICE CRÊPES WITH MUSHROOM FILLING AND RED PEPPER SAUCE

Serves 6 (main course)
Active time: 1¾ hr   Start to finish: 3½ hr

If you are making the whole vegetarian Thanksgiving menu, The Peaceable Feast *(page 103), in one oven, the crêpes can bake in the upper third of the oven while the Brussels sprouts are in the lower third.*

For crêpes
　　4 cups water
　　1 cup wild rice (5 oz)
　　1½ teaspoons salt
　　1¾ cups whole milk
　　4 large eggs
　　1 stick (½ cup) unsalted butter, melted
　　　　and cooled slightly
　　1 cup all-purpose flour
　　¼ teaspoon black pepper
　　¾ cup thinly sliced scallions
For sauce
　　3 red bell peppers (18 oz)
　　½ cup water
　　2 tablespoons olive oil
　　1½ teaspoons balsamic vinegar
　　¾ teaspoon salt
For filling
　　1½ oz dried porcini mushrooms
　　¾ cup boiling-hot water
　　2 tablespoons olive oil
　　2 tablespoons unsalted butter
　　1½ lb fresh cremini mushrooms, trimmed
　　　　and thinly sliced
　　3 large garlic cloves, minced
　　¾ teaspoon minced fresh rosemary
　　¾ teaspoon minced fresh thyme
　　¾ teaspoon salt

Garnish: **thinly sliced scallions**
Special equipment: **16 (5-inch) squares of wax paper; a well-seasoned 6- to 7-inch crêpe pan or nonstick skillet**

Make crêpe batter:
Bring 4 cups water to a boil in a 2-quart heavy saucepan, then add rice and ½ teaspoon salt. Reduce heat and cook, covered, over low heat until rice is tender and grains are split open, 1 to 1¼ hours (not all liquid will be absorbed). Drain well in a colander and cool to warm.

Blend together milk, eggs, 3 tablespoons butter, flour, pepper, remaining teaspoon salt, and 1 cup cooked wild rice in a blender until smooth, about 1 minute. Transfer to a large bowl and stir in scallions and 1½ cups cooked wild rice (reserve remainder for another use). Let batter stand, covered, at room temperature 1 hour.

Make sauce while rice cooks:
Roast bell peppers on racks of gas burners over high heat, turning with tongs, until skins are blackened, 10 to 12 minutes. (Or broil peppers on a broiler pan about 5 inches from heat, turning occasionally, about 15 minutes.) Transfer to a large bowl and cover tightly with plastic wrap, then let stand 20 minutes.

When cool enough to handle, peel peppers, discarding stems and seeds, and coarsely chop.

Purée peppers with water, oil, vinegar, and salt in cleaned blender until smooth. Season with pepper and pour into a small heavy saucepan.

Make filling while batter stands:
Soak porcini in boiling-hot water in a small bowl until softened, about 20 minutes. Lift porcini out, squeezing liquid back into bowl, then rinse porcini (to remove any grit) and finely chop. Pour soaking liquid through a sieve lined with a dampened paper towel into another small bowl.

Heat oil and 1 tablespoon butter in a 12- to 13-inch nonstick skillet over moderately high heat until foam subsides, then sauté porcini and cremini mushrooms, tossing with 2 wooden spatulas or spoons, until wilted and any liquid mushrooms give off is evaporated, 3 to 5 minutes. Add garlic, rosemary, thyme, salt, and remaining tablespoon butter and sauté, stirring, 1 minute. Add porcini soaking liquid and boil until most of liquid is evaporated and mushrooms are tender, 3 to 5 minutes. Season with salt and pepper.

Cook and assemble crêpes:
Line a plate with 1 square of wax paper. Heat crêpe pan over moderate heat until hot, then brush lightly with some remaining melted butter. Spoon about 3 tablespoons batter into pan, tilting and rotating to coat bottom. (If batter sets before skillet is coated, reduce heat slightly for next crêpe.) Cook until underside is lightly browned, about 1 minute, then loosen crêpe with a heatproof plastic spatula and flip over with your fingers. Cook crêpe until other side is lightly browned, about 1 minute, and transfer to wax-paper-lined plate. Top crêpe with another square of wax

paper. Make more crêpes with remaining batter, brushing pan lightly with butter as needed. (You will have extra crêpes.)

Preheat oven to 400°F.

Brush some melted butter on bottom of a large shallow baking pan (1 inch deep). Spread ¼ cup filling over half of 1 crêpe, then fold other half over filling to form a half-moon. Fold half-moon in thirds, overlapping outer sections (see photo, page 102), and transfer to baking pan. Repeat procedure with 11 more crêpes, arranging in 1 layer in baking pan.

Brush crêpes generously with remaining melted butter and bake in upper third of oven until outsides are crisp and filling is heated through, about 15 minutes.

While crêpes are baking, heat sauce over low heat until hot, about 5 minutes.

Put 2 crêpes on each of 6 plates and serve with red pepper sauce.

Cooks' notes:
· **Wild rice can be cooked 2 days ahead and cooled, uncovered, then chilled, covered.**
· **Red pepper sauce can be made 2 days ahead and chilled, covered.**
· **Filling can be made 1 day ahead and cooled, uncovered, then chilled, covered.**
· **Crêpes can be made and filled 1 day ahead and chilled, wrapped in foil. Brush with melted butter just before baking.**

PHOTO ON PAGE 102

VEGETABLES

Cook *haricots verts* in a large pot of boiling salted water (see Tips, page 8) until just tender, 3 to 4 minutes. Transfer with a slotted spoon to a bowl of ice and cold water, then drain.

Add *edamame* to boiling water and cook 4 minutes. Drain in a colander, then rinse under cold water. If using *edamame* in pods, shell them and discard pods.

Cook onion, garlic, bay leaf, rosemary, salt, and pepper in oil in a 2- to 4-quart heavy saucepan over moderately low heat, stirring, until softened, about 3 minutes. Add carrot and celery and cook, stirring, until softened, about 3 minutes.

Add white beans and stock and simmer, covered, stirring occasionally, 10 minutes. Add *haricots verts* and *edamame* and simmer, uncovered, until heated through, 2 to 3 minutes. Add butter, parsley, and chervil (if using) and stir gently until butter is melted. Discard bay leaf and rosemary sprigs.

PHOTO ON PAGE 56

HERBED BEAN RAGOUT

Serves 6 (side dish)
Active time: 40 min   Start to finish: 1 hr

6 oz *haricots verts* (French thin green beans), trimmed and halved crosswise
1 (1-lb) bag frozen *edamame* (soybeans in the pod) or 1¼ cups frozen shelled *edamame*, not thawed
⅔ cup finely chopped onion
2 garlic cloves, minced
1 Turkish or ½ California bay leaf
2 (3-inch) fresh rosemary sprigs
½ teaspoon salt
¼ teaspoon black pepper
1 tablespoon olive oil
1 medium carrot, cut into ⅛-inch dice
1 medium celery rib, cut into ⅛-inch dice
1 (15- to 16-oz) can small white beans, rinsed and drained
1½ cups chicken stock or low-sodium broth
2 tablespoons unsalted butter
2 tablespoons finely chopped fresh flat-leaf parsley
1 tablespoon finely chopped fresh chervil (optional)

Garnish: **fresh chervil sprigs**

HARICOTS VERTS WITH LEMON BROWN BUTTER

Serves 1
Active time: 5 min   Start to finish: 10 min

¼ lb *haricots verts* or other thin green beans, trimmed
1⅛ teaspoons salt
2 teaspoons unsalted butter
2 teaspoons fresh lemon juice

Cook beans in a 2-quart heavy saucepan of boiling water seasoned with 1 teaspoon salt until crisp-tender, about 3 minutes, then drain in a colander.

Wipe out pan and cook butter over moderate heat until deep golden, about 2 minutes. Stir in lemon juice and remaining ⅛ teaspoon salt and remove pan from heat. Add beans and toss well.

HARICOTS VERTS WITH ALEPPO CHILE OIL

Serves 4
Active time: 30 min   Start to finish: 30 min

¾ lb *haricots verts* or other thin green beans,
    trimmed, leaving tails intact
3 tablespoons olive oil
1 small garlic clove, minced
½ teaspoon dried Aleppo chile flakes
¼ teaspoon ground coriander
¼ teaspoon fine sea salt

Cook beans in a large pot of boiling salted water (see Tips, page 8) until crisp-tender, about 4 minutes. Transfer with tongs to a bowl of ice and cold water to stop cooking. Drain well and pat dry with paper towels.

Heat oil, garlic, chile flakes, coriander, and sea salt in a small skillet over moderate heat, stirring, until fragrant, about 30 seconds. Cool oil and toss with beans.

Cooks' notes:
• Beans can be boiled (but not tossed with oil) 1 day ahead and chilled, wrapped in paper towels in a sealed plastic bag.
• Flavored oil can be made 1 day ahead and chilled, covered. Warm oil slightly before tossing with beans.
PHOTO ON PAGE 96

GREEN BEANS AND ROASTED SQUASH WITH SHERRY SOY BUTTER

Serves 8 to 10
Active time: 50 min   Start to finish: 1½ hr

2 lb green beans (preferably *haricots verts*),
    trimmed
4 lb butternut squash, halved lengthwise,
    seeded, and diagonally cut crosswise into
    1½-inch-thick triangular pieces
3 tablespoons olive oil
¼ teaspoon salt
¼ teaspoon black pepper
1 stick (½ cup) plus 1 tablespoon unsalted
    butter, stick cut into tablespoon pieces
    and other tablespoon melted
1½ tablespoons Sherry vinegar
1½ tablespoons soy sauce

Preheat oven to 425°F.

Cook beans in 2 batches in a 4-quart saucepan of boiling salted water (see Tips, page 8) until just tender, 3 to 4 minutes, transferring with a slotted spoon to a bowl of ice and cold water to stop cooking. When cool, drain beans and pat dry.

Toss squash with oil, salt, and pepper in a large bowl, then roast in a large shallow baking pan (1 inch deep) in middle of oven, turning occasionally, until golden brown and tender, about 40 minutes.

While squash is roasting, melt 1 stick butter with vinegar and soy sauce over moderately low heat, whisking until emulsified, about 4 minutes. Season with salt and pepper.

Reduce oven temperature to 350°F.

Push roasted squash to 1 side of roasting pan and add beans to other side. Drizzle beans with tablespoon melted butter and heat in middle of oven, uncovered, stirring occasionally, about 20 minutes.

Transfer roasted vegetables to a dish. Just before serving, drizzle with Sherry soy butter and gently toss.

Cooks' notes:
• Squash can be roasted 1 day ahead and chilled, covered. Bring to room temperature before reheating with beans.
• If you are making the entire *Thanksgiving with a Twist* menu (page 98) in a single oven, reheat beans and squash in lower third of oven (with stuffed onions and stuffing in dish in upper third) while turkey is standing.
PHOTO ON PAGE 100

HONEY-GLAZED WAX BEANS

Serves 6
Active time: 15 min   Start to finish: 25 min

1¼ lb wax (yellow) or green beans, trimmed
1 tablespoon mild honey
¾ teaspoon finely grated fresh lemon zest
¼ teaspoon salt

Cook beans in a 4-quart pot of boiling salted water (see Tips, page 8) until just tender, 6 to 8 minutes. Drain in a colander, then immediately toss with honey, zest, and salt in a large bowl.
PHOTO ON PAGE 59

ROASTED BEETS AND CARROTS

Serves 6
Active time: 35 min   Start to finish: 2½ hr

6 medium beets (2½ lb with greens), trimmed, leaving 1 inch of stems attached
2½ lb carrots, cut diagonally into ¾-inch-thick slices
2 tablespoons olive oil

Preheat oven to 425°F.

Wrap beets tightly in foil, making 2 packages, and roast in middle of oven until tender, about 1¼ hours.

Toss carrots with oil and salt and pepper to taste in a shallow baking pan.

Remove beets from oven and roast carrots in middle of oven until tender, about 20 minutes.

While carrots are roasting, unwrap beets and, when just cool enough to handle, slip off skins and remove stems. Cut each beet into 6 wedges.

Add beets to carrots, tossing to combine, and roast until beets are hot and carrots are very tender, about 15 minutes more.

Cooks' note:
• Beets can be roasted and peeled 2 days ahead and chilled, covered.

PHOTO ON PAGE 51

BROCCOFLOWER WITH ANCHOVIES AND GARLIC

Serves 4
Active time: 20 min   Start to finish: 30 min

Broccoflower is a cross between broccoli and cauliflower; it looks like green cauliflower and has a milder flavor than broccoli.

1 head broccoflower or cauliflower (1½ lb), cut into 2-inch-wide florets
¼ cup olive oil
3 garlic cloves, thinly sliced
2½ teaspoons chopped canned anchovies, or to taste
¼ teaspoon dried hot red pepper flakes
¼ cup pine nuts, toasted (see Tips, page 8)
¼ cup golden raisins
2 tablespoons chopped fresh parsley

Cook broccoflower in 2 batches in a 5- to 6-quart pot of boiling salted water (see Tips, page 8) until crisp-tender, about 5 minutes, then transfer with a slotted spoon to a large bowl of ice and cold water to stop cooking. Drain florets and pat dry with paper towels.

Heat oil in a 12-inch nonstick skillet over moderately high heat until hot but not smoking, then sauté garlic, stirring, until golden, about 1 minute. Add anchovies and red pepper flakes and sauté, stirring, until anchovies are dissolved, about 1 minute, then add florets and toss to coat. Add pine nuts, raisins, and salt to taste and sauté, stirring, until heated through, about 2 minutes. Remove from heat and stir in parsley.

SPICY SAUTÉED BROCCOLINI WITH GARLIC

Serves 8
Active time: 20 min   Start to finish: 30 min

2 lb Broccolini (sometimes called baby broccoli) or broccoli rabe, ends trimmed
1 tablespoon olive oil
2 garlic cloves, minced
½ teaspoon dried hot red pepper flakes
¼ cup low-fat chicken stock or low-sodium fat-free chicken broth

Cook Broccolini in a 6- to 8-quart pot of boiling salted water (see Tips, page 8) until stems are crisp-tender, about 5 minutes. Drain in a colander, then plunge into a large bowl of ice and cold water to stop cooking. Drain again and pat dry with paper towels.

Heat 1½ teaspoons oil in a 12-inch nonstick skillet over moderately high heat until hot but not smoking. Add half of garlic and ¼ teaspoon red pepper flakes and sauté, stirring, until garlic is golden, about 1 minute. Add half of Broccolini and 2 tablespoons stock and cook, stirring, 2 minutes. Transfer to a serving dish, then repeat with remaining 1½ teaspoons oil, garlic, ¼ teaspoon red pepper flakes, Broccolini, and 2 table-spoons stock. Season with salt.

Each serving about 32 calories and 1 gram fat

PHOTO ON PAGE 42

ROASTED CARROTS AND PARSNIPS

Serves 8
Active time: 15 min   Start to finish: 1¼ hr

- **2 lb parsnips**
- **2 lb carrots, peeled and cut diagonally into ¾-inch-thick slices**
- **⅓ cup extra-virgin olive oil**
- **2 teaspoons salt**
- **2 teaspoons black pepper**
- **2 teaspoons chopped fresh rosemary**
- **2 teaspoons chopped fresh sage**
- **¼ cup water**

Preheat oven to 350°F.

Peel parsnips and halve each crosswise where it becomes narrow. Diagonally cut narrow portions into ¾-inch-thick slices. Quarter wider portions lengthwise and core. Diagonally cut flesh into ¾-inch-thick slices.

Toss parsnips and carrots with oil, salt, pepper, rosemary, and sage in a large bowl. Spread in a large shallow baking pan (1 inch deep) and pour in water. Roast vegetables in lower third of oven until tender, 50 to 55 minutes.

Cooks' notes:
- Vegetables can be peeled and sliced 1 day ahead and chilled in sealed plastic bags.
- If you're making the entire *Feast of Fancy* menu (page 104) in a single oven, roast vegetables in lower third of oven during last 30 minutes of roasting meat, then continue to roast vegetables while meat is standing.

PHOTO ON PAGE 106

BALSAMIC ROASTED CARROTS

Serves 4
Active time: 10 min   Start to finish: 40 min

- **2 lb carrots, cut into 3½- by ½-inch sticks**
- **2 tablespoons olive oil**
- **¼ teaspoon salt**
- **2 tablespoons balsamic vinegar**

Preheat oven to 425°F.

Toss carrots with oil and salt in a shallow roasting pan (1 inch deep). Roast carrots in middle of oven, stirring occasionally, until golden and tender, 25 to 30 minutes. Drizzle vinegar over carrots and shake pan a few times. Roast carrots until most of vinegar is evaporated, about 2 minutes more.

CUMIN GLAZED CARROTS

Serves 4
Active time: 20 min   Start to finish: 40 min

- **1 lb carrots, cut diagonally into ½-inch-thick slices**
- **2 tablespoons olive oil**
- **¾ teaspoon ground cumin**
- **1 cup water**
- **1 tablespoon fresh lemon juice**
- **1 teaspoon honey**
- **½ teaspoon fine sea salt**
- **⅛ teaspoon black pepper**

Cook carrots with oil and cumin in a 3-quart heavy saucepan over moderate heat, stirring, until well coated, about 1 minute. Add remaining ingredients and simmer, uncovered, shaking pan occasionally, until liquid is evaporated and carrots are tender and glazed, about 20 minutes. Serve warm or at room temperature.

Cooks' note:
- Carrots can be cooked 3 hours ahead and chilled, covered.

PHOTO ON PAGE 96

CAULIFLOWER PURÉE

Serves 1
Active time: 10 min   Start to finish: 20 min

½ lb cauliflower florets, chopped
  (2⅔ cups)
1 garlic clove, smashed
⅓ cup chicken broth
½ teaspoon salt
2 tablespoons heavy cream
1 teaspoon unsalted butter

Simmer cauliflower, garlic, broth, and salt in a small saucepan, covered, until cauliflower is very tender, about 10 minutes.

Purée mixture with cream and butter in a food processor until smooth (use caution when blending hot liquids), or mash with a potato masher or a fork.

PHOTO ON PAGE 113

CAULIFLOWER CHEDDAR GRATIN WITH HORSERADISH CRUMBS

Serves 8
Active time: 35 min   Start to finish: 45 min

3 lb cauliflower (1 large head), cut into
  1½- to 2-inch florets
4 tablespoons unsalted butter
2 tablespoons all-purpose flour
1½ cups milk
6 oz sharp Cheddar, coarsely grated
  (2 cups)
½ cup finely chopped scallion greens
½ teaspoon salt
½ teaspoon black pepper
20 (2-inch square) saltine crackers
2 tablespoons drained bottled horseradish

Preheat oven to 450°F.

Cook cauliflower in a 5- to 6-quart pot of boiling salted water (see Tips, page 8) until just tender, 6 to 8 minutes. Drain cauliflower well in a colander and transfer to a buttered 2-quart baking dish.

While cauliflower is cooking, melt 2 tablespoons butter in a 3- to 4-quart heavy saucepan over moderately low heat and whisk in flour. Cook roux over low heat, whisking, 3 minutes. Add milk in a slow stream, whisking, and bring to a boil, whisking frequently.

Reduce heat and simmer sauce, whisking occasionally, 8 minutes. Remove from heat and add cheese, scallion greens, salt, and pepper, whisking until cheese is melted. Pour cheese sauce over cauliflower and stir gently to combine.

Coarsely crumble crackers into a bowl. Melt remaining 2 tablespoons butter in a small saucepan, then remove from heat and stir in horseradish. Pour over crumbs and toss to coat.

Sprinkle crumb topping evenly over cauliflower. Bake gratin in middle of oven until topping is golden brown, about 10 minutes.

CREAMY CORN WITH SUGAR SNAP PEAS AND SCALLIONS

Serves 16
Active time: 45 min   Start to finish: 1 hr

3 lb sugar snap peas, trimmed
12 ears corn, shucked
1 cup heavy cream
2 bunches scallions (white and pale
  green parts only), thinly sliced
1 tablespoon kosher salt
1 tablespoon black pepper

Cook sugar snaps in 6 batches in an 8-quart pot of boiling salted water (see Tips, page 8) until crisp-tender, about 1 minute (return to a boil between batches). Transfer with a slotted spoon to a large bowl of ice and cold water to stop cooking. Drain sugar snaps and pat dry with paper towels.

Cook corn in 2 batches in same pot of boiling water until just tender, about 3 minutes (return to a boil between batches). Transfer to bowl of ice and cold water to stop cooking. Drain corn and pat dry with paper towels. Cut off kernels and discard cobs.

Just before serving, boil cream and scallions in a wide 6- to 8-quart heavy pot over high heat until slightly thickened, about 2 minutes. Add sugar snaps, corn, kosher salt, and pepper and cook, tossing, until vegetables are coated and heated through, about 2 minutes.

Cooks' note:
• Sugar snaps and corn can be cooked 1 day ahead and chilled separately in sealed plastic bags lined with paper towels.

PHOTO ON PAGE 78

GRILLED CORN

Serves 1
Active time: 15 min   Start to finish: 35 min

1 or 2 ears corn
Softened butter for brushing

Prepare grill for cooking. If using a charcoal grill, open vents on bottom of grill.

Pull husks back from corn, keeping them attached at base, and discard silk. Push husks back around ears and soak in cold water 10 minutes.

When fire is hot (you can hold your hand 5 inches above rack for 1 to 2 seconds) drain corn and grill (in husks) on lightly oiled grill rack, uncovered, turning, 10 minutes. Pull back husks and grill corn, turning, until browned and tender, about 5 minutes more.

Brush corn with butter and season with salt.

Cooks' note:
• If serving with steak (page 147), start grilling corn 5 minutes after putting steak on grill.
PHOTO ON PAGE 112

CREAMED CORN WITH BASIL

Serves 6 to 8
Active time: 35 min   Start to finish: 35 min

8 large ears corn, husked
2 to 4 tablespoons crème fraîche or
  heavy cream
1 large shallot, finely chopped (¼ cup)
2 tablespoons unsalted butter
1 cup water
1 teaspoon salt
¼ teaspoon black pepper
2 to 3 tablespoons thinly sliced fresh basil

Working in a large bowl, cut kernels from cobs with a sharp knife and set aside. Scrape back of knife several times against cobs to extract remaining corn pulp, scraping into a large glass measure. (You should have at least ¾ cup of corn pulp. If not, add 2 tablespoons crème fraîche.) Transfer pulp to a blender and purée with 2 tablespoons crème fraîche until smooth.

Cook shallot in butter in a 12-inch heavy skillet over moderate heat, stirring occasionally, until softened, 3 to 4 minutes. Stir in kernels, then add corn purée, water, salt, and pepper and simmer, uncovered, stirring occasionally, until kernels are just tender, 3 to 4 minutes. Stir in basil (to taste).

OVEN-FRIED ONION RINGS

Serves 4
Active time: 20 min   Start to finish: 35 min

1 large egg white, lightly beaten
½ cup well-shaken low-fat buttermilk
¼ cup all-purpose flour
½ teaspoon salt
¼ teaspoon cayenne
1 large sweet onion (12 oz) such as Vidalia,
  cut crosswise into ⅓-inch-thick slices
1 tablespoon olive oil

Preheat oven to 450°F.

Whisk together egg white, buttermilk, flour, salt, and cayenne in a shallow bowl until smooth.

Separate onion slices into rings and pick out the 12 largest, reserving remainder for another use.

Heat 1 teaspoon oil in a 12-inch nonstick skillet over moderately high heat until hot but not smoking.

Working in batches of 4, dip rings into batter, letting excess drip off, then cook in skillet, turning once, until golden brown, 2 minutes total. (Use 1 teaspoon oil per batch.) Transfer rings as browned to a lightly oiled shallow baking pan (1 inch deep).

Bake rings in middle of oven, turning once, until crisp and deep golden, 12 to 15 minutes total.

Each (3-ring) serving about 74 calories and 2 grams fat

ROASTED STUFFED ONIONS

Makes 10 stuffed onions
Active time: 2 hr   Start to finish: 3½ hr

Many people consider stuffing the best part of a Thanksgiving meal, and they can be quite particular about it—some like it dense and moist from the turkey juices, others fluffy and browned from the oven. Now we've made sure everyone will be satisfied: This recipe makes enough stuffing for the turkey and the onions, with plenty left over for another baking dish of stuffing.

You can easily adapt the recipe to suit vegetarian guests—simply eliminate the bacon (use olive oil instead of bacon fat for sautéing the vegetables) and substitute vegetable stock for the turkey stock.

    10 medium red and yellow onions (4 lb)
     1 lb sliced bacon, cut crosswise into
         1-inch-wide pieces
     3 celery ribs, cut crosswise into
         ½-inch-thick slices
     1 teaspoon salt
     1 teaspoon black pepper
     3 garlic cloves, minced
    15 oz baby spinach, trimmed and coarsely
         chopped (14 cups)
     1 (9-inch) round loaf country-style bread
         (1¼ lb), cut into ½-inch cubes (10 cups),
         lightly toasted
     2 cups salted roasted cashews (10 oz),
         coarsely chopped
     1 stick (½ cup) unsalted butter, melted
    1¼ cups turkey giblet stock (page 169)

Make onion shells:
Cut a ½-inch-thick slice from tops of onions, discarding tops, and trim just enough from bottoms for onions to stand upright. Scoop out all but outer 2 or 3 layers from each using a small ice cream scoop or spoon (don't worry if you make a hole in the bottom), reserving scooped-out onion and onion shells separately.

Make stuffing:
Coarsely chop enough scooped-out onion to measure 3 cups.

Cook bacon in 2 batches in a 12-inch heavy skillet over moderate heat, stirring, until crisp, about 10 minutes, then transfer with a slotted spoon to paper towels to drain, reserving about ⅓ cup fat in skillet.

Add chopped onion, celery, salt, and black pepper to skillet and sauté over moderately high heat, stirring, until vegetables are softened, about 5 minutes. Add garlic and sauté, stirring, 1 minute. Transfer mixture to a large bowl and stir in spinach, bread, cashews, butter, 1 cup stock, and bacon, then cool completely.

Roast onions:
Preheat oven to 425°F.

Arrange onion shells, open sides up, in a 13- by 9- by 2-inch baking pan, then add ½ cup water and cover pan tightly with foil. Roast onions in middle of oven until tender but not falling apart, 25 to 30 minutes.

Stuff and bake onions:
Reduce oven temperature to 350°F.

Transfer shells to a work surface and pour off water in pan. Fill shells with stuffing, mounding it, and return to pan. Reserve 5 to 7 cups stuffing for turkey cavity, then put remaining stuffing in a buttered shallow 3½-quart baking dish and drizzle with remaining ¼ cup stock. Bake stuffed onions and stuffing in dish in middle of oven, uncovered, until heated through, about 25 minutes.

Cooks' notes:
· Stuffing can be prepared and onions can be stuffed 1 day ahead and chilled, covered. Bring stuffed onions to room temperature before baking.
· If you are making the entire *Thanksgiving with a Twist* menu (page 98) in a single oven, bake stuffed onions and stuffing in dish in upper third of oven (with beans and squash in lower third) while turkey is standing.

PHOTO ON PAGE 98

PEAS WITH SPINACH AND SHALLOTS

Serves 4
Active time: 15 min   Start to finish: 15 min

2 medium shallots, thinly sliced
2 garlic cloves, thinly sliced
1 tablespoon vegetable oil
1 tablespoon unsalted butter
10 oz frozen peas
¼ cup water
5 oz baby spinach
¾ teaspoon salt
¼ teaspoon black pepper

Cook shallots and garlic in oil and butter in a 12-inch nonstick skillet over moderate heat, stirring, until soft, about 6 minutes.

Stir in peas and water and cook, covered, stirring occasionally, until peas are tender, about 5 minutes.

Stir in spinach, salt, and pepper and cook, tossing, until spinach is just wilted, about 1 minute.

GRILLED BELL PEPPERS WITH CRIOLLA SAUCE

Serves 6
Active time: 45 min   Start to finish: 45 min

Criolla is traditionally served as a sauce for grilled meats, but we tossed it with bell peppers as an accompaniment or side dish.

4 orange bell peppers
2 medium tomatoes, finely chopped
1 medium white onion, finely chopped
1 fresh *serrano* chile, minced (including seeds)
1 large garlic clove, minced
1 tablespoon minced fresh flat-leaf parsley
2½ tablespoons olive oil
1½ tablespoons red-wine vinegar
1 teaspoon kosher salt

To roast peppers using a charcoal grill:
When fire is hot (you can hold your hand 5 inches above rack for 1 to 2 seconds), grill peppers on rack, turning with tongs, until skins are blackened, 10 to 12 minutes.

To roast peppers using a gas grill:
Preheat all burners on high, then adjust heat to moderately high. Grill peppers on rack, turning with tongs, until skins are blackened, 10 to 12 minutes.

Peel and sauce peppers:
Transfer peppers to a large bowl and cover tightly with plastic wrap, then let stand until cool enough to handle. Peel peppers, then halve lengthwise, discarding stems and seeds.

Stir together remaining ingredients, then add peppers and toss gently.

Cooks' notes:
• If you aren't able to grill, peppers can be roasted on racks of gas burners over high heat, turning with tongs. Or broil on broiler pan about 5 inches from heat, turning occasionally (about 15 minutes).
• Peppers in criolla sauce can be made 1 day ahead and chilled, covered. Bring to room temperature before serving.

POTATO GALETTE

Serves 1
Active time: 10 min   Start to finish: 30 min

A nonstick skillet and an adjustable-blade slicer make this elegant dish easy.

1 tablespoon unsalted butter
1 large russet (baking) potato (½ lb)
¼ teaspoon salt
¼ teaspoon black pepper

Special equipment: **a Japanese Benriner or other adjustable-blade slicer**

Melt butter in a 7½- to 8-inch nonstick skillet. Peel potato and cut crosswise into ⅛-inch-thick slices with slicer. Toss potato with melted butter, salt, and pepper in a bowl, then layer potato slices, overlapping slightly, in skillet.

Cover skillet with a lid, or tightly with foil, and cook over moderately low heat until underside is golden brown, about 10 minutes. Slide *galette* onto a dinner plate. Invert skillet over *galette*, then, holding plate tightly against skillet, flip *galette* into skillet. Cook, covered, until potato is tender when pierced with a paring knife, 10 to 12 minutes more.

HORSERADISH MASHED POTATOES

Serves 8
Active time: 15 min   Start to finish: 40 min

4 lb large yellow-fleshed potatoes such as
   Yukon Gold, peeled and quartered
1¾ cups half-and-half
¾ stick (6 tablespoons) unsalted butter,
   cut into tablespoon pieces
1½ teaspoons salt
½ teaspoon black pepper
¼ cup drained bottled horseradish

Special equipment: **a potato ricer or a food mill**
fitted with medium disk

Cover potatoes with salted cold water (see Tips, page 8) by 2 inches in a 5-quart heavy pot, then simmer, uncovered, until very tender, about 25 minutes.

While potatoes are simmering, bring half-and-half, butter, salt, and pepper just to a simmer, stirring until butter is melted. Keep hot, covered.

Drain potatoes in a colander, then immediately force through ricer into a large bowl. Stir in hot milk mixture, then horseradish.

Cooks' notes:
• If you don't have a ricer or food mill, you can use a handheld masher, but the consistency of the potatoes won't be as smooth.
• Mashed potatoes can be made 1 day ahead and chilled, covered. Bring to room temperature, then reheat in a microwave or double boiler, stirring occasionally.

SCALLION MASHED POTATOES

Serves 4
Active time: 30 min   Start to finish: 30 min

2 lb medium yellow-fleshed potatoes
   such as Yukon Gold
3 tablespoons unsalted butter
2 cups chopped scallion (2½ bunches)
⅔ cup whole milk
½ cup chopped fresh flat-leaf parsley
½ teaspoon salt
⅛ teaspoon black pepper

Peel and quarter potatoes, then cover with salted cold water (see Tips, page 8) by 1 inch in a large saucepan and simmer, uncovered, until tender, 15 to 20 minutes.

While potatoes are simmering, heat butter over moderately high heat in a large nonstick skillet and sauté chopped scallion, stirring, until just tender, about 6 minutes.

Drain potatoes in a colander and return to saucepan. Mash hot potatoes with milk using a potato masher until smooth, then stir in scallion, parsley, salt, and pepper.

CHIVE AND PARSLEY MASHED POTATOES

Serves 8 to 10
Active time: 30 min   Start to finish: 1¼ hr

For chive and parsley oil
1 cup chopped fresh chives
¾ cup chopped fresh flat-leaf parsley
½ cup plus 3 tablespoons olive oil
¼ teaspoon salt
For mashed potatoes
5 lb yellow-fleshed potatoes such as
   Yukon Gold
1½ cups milk
1 stick (½ cup) unsalted butter, cut
   into tablespoon pieces
1¼ teaspoons salt
¾ teaspoon black pepper

Make oil:
Purée chives and parsley with oil and salt in a blender until smooth, then pour through a fine-mesh sieve into a glass measure, pressing on and discarding solids.

Prepare potatoes:

Peel and quarter potatoes. Cover potatoes with salted cold water (see Tips, page 8) by 1 inch in a 5-quart heavy pot, then simmer, uncovered, until very tender, about 25 minutes.

While potatoes are simmering, bring milk, butter, salt, and pepper just to a simmer, stirring until butter is melted.

Drain potatoes in a colander and return to pot. Add hot milk mixture and mash with a potato masher until almost smooth, then stir in 4 tablespoons herb oil.

If desired, serve potatoes drizzled with some of remaining oil.

Cooks' notes:
· Oil can be made 4 days ahead and chilled, covered. Bring to room temperature before using.
· Potatoes can be made 1 day ahead and chilled, covered. Bring to room temperature before reheating in a microwave or double boiler, stirring occasionally.

PHOTO ON PAGE 100

CHEDDAR GARLIC STUFFED POTATOES

Serves 4
Active time: 15 min   Start to finish: 1¾ hr

1 medium head of garlic
4 medium russet (baking) potatoes (2 lb)
3 tablespoons unsalted butter, softened
⅓ cup sour cream
6 oz Cheddar, coarsely grated (1½ cups)

Preheat oven to 400°F.

Cut off and discard top third of garlic and wrap remainder in foil. Prick potatoes with a fork and bake with garlic on middle rack of oven 45 minutes. Remove garlic to cool and continue baking potatoes until tender, about 20 minutes more. (Leave oven on.)

Squeeze garlic cloves into a bowl and discard skins, then stir in butter, sour cream, and 1 cup Cheddar. Cutting lengthwise, remove top fourth of each potato and discard. Scoop flesh out of potatoes, leaving ¼-inch-thick shells, and add to cheese mixture. Mash with a fork to combine. Season with salt and pepper and divide among shells.

Arrange potatoes in a small baking pan and sprinkle with remaining Cheddar, then bake until heated through, 15 to 20 minutes.

WARM SMASHED POTATOES WITH MUSTARD SEED AND CAPER VINAIGRETTE

Serves 4
Active time: 20 min   Start to finish: 45 min

2½ lb medium yellow-fleshed potatoes such as Yukon Gold
1 tablespoon whole-grain or coarse-grain mustard
1 tablespoon white-wine vinegar
2 teaspoons finely chopped drained bottled capers
½ teaspoon salt
½ teaspoon black pepper
3 tablespoons finely chopped shallot
½ cup extra-virgin olive oil
⅓ cup chopped fresh flat-leaf parsley

Peel and quarter potatoes, then cover with salted cold water (see Tips, page 8) by 2 inches in a 5-quart pot and simmer, covered, until just tender, 20 to 25 minutes.

While potatoes are cooking, whisk together mustard, vinegar, capers, salt, pepper, and shallot. Add oil in a slow stream, whisking until emulsified.

Drain potatoes in a colander and cool slightly. Break up warm potatoes into smaller chunks with a spoon and stir in vinaigrette and parsley. Serve warm.

PARSLEY POTATOES

Serves 4
Active time: 20 min   Start to finish: 1 hr

1½ lb small (1½- to 2-inch) boiling potatoes
3 tablespoons unsalted butter, cut into pieces
2 tablespoons chopped fresh flat-leaf parsley
½ teaspoon kosher salt

Peel potatoes and cover with salted cold water (see Tips, page 8) by 2 inches in a 5-quart heavy saucepan. Simmer, uncovered, until just tender, 15 to 20 minutes. Drain in a colander and toss in a bowl with butter, parsley, and kosher salt.

PHOTO ON PAGE 86

STRAW POTATOES

Serves 6
Active time: 25 min   Start to finish: 25 min

**1 lb russet (baking) potatoes
6 cups vegetable oil for deep-frying**

Special equipment: **a Japanese Benriner or other adjustable-blade slicer fitted with julienne blade; a deep-fat thermometer**

Peel potatoes and cut lengthwise into ⅛-inch-thick julienne with slicer, then submerge in a large bowl of ice water. Rinse potatoes in several changes of cold water in bowl until water is clear. Drain in a colander, then spread out on several layers of paper towels and pat dry. Transfer potatoes to a large rack to air-dry 15 minutes.

While potatoes are drying, heat oil in a 5- to 6-quart heavy pot over moderately high heat until it registers 375°F on thermometer. Fry potatoes in 8 batches, stirring, until crisp and golden, 45 seconds to 1 minute per batch, transferring with a slotted spoon to dry paper towels to drain and seasoning with salt. Return oil to 375°F between batches.

Cooks' note:
• **Potatoes can be fried 1 day ahead, then cooled completely and kept in an airtight container at room temperature.**

PHOTO ON PAGE 64

MASHED POTATOES AND TURNIPS WITH HORSERADISH

Serves 6
Active time: 30 min   Start to finish: 1 hr

**2½ lb yellow-fleshed potatoes such as Yukon Gold
3 lb turnips or rutabagas, peeled and cut into 2-inch pieces
6 tablespoons unsalted butter, softened
2 tablespoons horseradish cream or drained bottled horseradish, or to taste
2 to 4 teaspoons sugar
½ cup chopped fresh flat-leaf parsley**

Cover potatoes with salted cold water (see Tips, page 8) by 2 inches in a large pot and simmer, uncovered, until very tender, 20 to 30 minutes (depending on size of potatoes). Drain potatoes in a colander and, when just cool enough to handle, peel. Transfer potatoes to a bowl.

While potatoes are cooking, cover turnips with salted cold water by 2 inches in a large pot and simmer, uncovered, until very tender, 10 to 20 minutes (depending on freshness of turnips).

Drain turnips in colander and immediately add to warm potatoes, then mash with butter and horseradish. Stir in sugar (to taste), parsley, and salt and black pepper to taste.

PHOTO ON PAGE 51

WILTED BABY SPINACH

Serves 6
Active time: 10 min   Start to finish: 10 min

**½ stick (¼ cup) unsalted butter
1½ lb baby spinach**

Heat butter in a wide 6-quart heavy pot over moderate heat until foam subsides, then cook spinach, stirring, until just wilted and bright green, 2 to 3 minutes. Season with salt and pepper.

PHOTO ON PAGE 64

SPAGHETTI SQUASH WITH MOROCCAN SPICES

Serves 4 (side dish)
Active time: 20 min   Start to finish: 20 min

Microwaving is one of the best ways to cook spaghetti squash; while a conventional oven might take over an hour, a microwave cooks the squash in a quarter of the time.

1 (3½- to 4-lb) spaghetti squash
2 garlic cloves, minced
½ stick unsalted butter, cut into pieces
1 teaspoon ground cumin
½ teaspoon ground coriander
⅛ teaspoon cayenne
¾ teaspoon salt
2 tablespoons chopped fresh cilantro

Pierce squash all over with a sharp small knife. Microwave in an 800-watt microwave at high power (100 percent) 6 to 7 minutes, then turn over and microwave at high until squash gives to gentle pressure, 8 to 10 minutes more. Cool 5 minutes.

While squash is cooling, cook garlic in butter in a small heavy saucepan over moderately high heat, stirring, until golden, about 1 minute. Stir in spices and salt and remove from heat.

Carefully halve squash lengthwise (it will emit steam) and discard seeds. Working over a bowl, scrape squash flesh with a fork, loosening and separating strands. Toss with spiced butter and cilantro.

ROASTED SPICED SWEET POTATOES

Serves 4 to 6
Active time: 10 min   Start to finish: 45 min

1 teaspoon coriander seeds
½ teaspoon fennel seeds
½ teaspoon dried oregano
½ teaspoon dried hot red pepper flakes
1 teaspoon kosher salt
2 lb medium sweet potatoes
3 tablespoons vegetable oil

Preheat oven to 425°F.

Coarsely grind coriander, fennel, oregano, and red pepper flakes in an electric coffee/spice grinder or with a mortar and pestle, then stir together with kosher salt.

Cut potatoes lengthwise into 1-inch wedges.

Toss wedges with oil and spices in a large roasting pan and roast in middle of oven 20 minutes. Turn wedges over with a spatula and roast until tender and slightly golden, 15 to 20 minutes more.

GRILLED SWEET POTATOES WITH LIME CILANTRO VINAIGRETTE

Serves 16
Active time: 20 min   Start to finish: 1 hr

4 lb sweet potatoes (8; preferably long)
¼ cup fresh lime juice
1½ teaspoons kosher salt
¼ teaspoon black pepper
½ cup olive oil
¼ cup chopped fresh cilantro

Cover potatoes with cold salted water (see Tips, page 8) in a large pot, then bring to a boil. Simmer until slightly resistant in center when pierced with a small knife, 25 to 30 minutes, then transfer to a large bowl of cold water to stop cooking. Drain well. When cool enough to handle, peel potatoes with small knife and quarter lengthwise.

Prepare gas or charcoal grill for cooking. If using charcoal, open vents on bottom of grill.

Whisk together lime juice, kosher salt, and pepper, then add oil in a slow stream, whisking, then whisk in cilantro.

When fire is hot (you can hold your hand 5 inches above rack for 1 to 2 seconds), grill potatoes in 2 or 3 batches on lightly oiled grill rack, uncovered, turning, until grill marks appear and potatoes are just tender, 3 to 6 minutes total.

Serve potatoes warm or at room temperature, drizzled with vinaigrette.

Cooks' notes:
· Potatoes can be boiled and peeled 1 day ahead and chilled, covered.
· Vinaigrette can be made 2 hours ahead and kept at room temperature.
· If you aren't able to grill, potatoes can be cooked in a well-seasoned ridged grill pan over moderately high heat, turning, until grill marks appear, 3 to 6 minutes total.

PHOTO ON PAGE 78

SWEET-POTATO AND PARMESAN CAKE

Serves 6
Active time: 1 hr   Start to finish: 1¾ hr

  **2 lb sweet potatoes (6 to 7 inches long),
     peeled**
 ⅓ **cup finely grated Parmigiano-Reggiano
     (1 oz)**
  2 tablespoons extra-virgin olive oil
 ¾ **teaspoon salt**
 ½ **teaspoon black pepper**

Preheat oven to 425°F.

Shave potatoes lengthwise into long, wide ribbons with a vegetable peeler and toss strips with remaining ingredients. Lightly oil a 9-inch metal pie pan. Arrange strips in overlapping layers radiating from center, letting slices overhang slightly if necessary.

Bake in lower third of oven until edges are browned, then cover edges with foil and bake until potatoes are tender and top of cake is crisp and brown, 45 to 50 minutes total.

Each serving about 176 calories and 6 grams fat
PHOTO ON PAGE 109

ZUCCHINI CURRY

Serves 6 (main course) or 8 (side dish)
Active time: 20 min   Start to finish: 35 min

 ½ **teaspoon yellow or brown mustard seeds**
 ½ **teaspoon cumin seeds**
  1 garlic clove, chopped
  **1 to 2 teaspoons chopped fresh jalapeño chile
     (including seeds)**
  2 teaspoons finely grated peeled fresh ginger
  2 teaspoons salt
  1 tablespoon curry powder
 ¼ **teaspoon ground coriander**
  3 tablespoons vegetable oil
  1 large onion, thinly sliced
  **6 medium green or Cocozelle zucchini (3 lb),
     cut crosswise into ½-inch-thick slices**
  **1 (13½- to 14-oz) can unsweetened coconut
     milk, well stirred**
 ¼ **cup chopped fresh cilantro**
 ½ **cup roasted cashews, chopped**

Accompaniment: **cooked basmati rice**

Toast mustard and cumin seeds (see Tips, page 8) and cool.

Pound garlic, jalapeño (to taste), and ginger to a paste with 1 teaspoon salt using a mortar and pestle (or mince and mash with a large heavy knife), then stir in curry powder, coriander, and mustard and cumin seeds.

Heat oil in a 6-quart heavy pot over moderately high heat until hot but not smoking, then sauté onion, stirring, until golden, about 8 minutes. Add curry paste and cook over moderately low heat, stirring, 2 minutes.

Add zucchini and cook, stirring, until it begins to appear moist, 3 to 5 minutes. Add coconut milk and remaining teaspoon salt and bring to a boil, then reduce heat and simmer, covered, stirring occasionally, until zucchini is just tender, 10 to 12 minutes.

Serve sprinkled with cilantro and cashews.

ZUCCHINI PANCAKES WITH BASIL CHIVE CREAM

Makes 15 pancakes (hors d'oeuvre or side dish)
Active time: 25 min   Start to finish: 45 min

For basil chive cream
 ¾ **cup sour cream**
  2 tablespoons water
 ¼ **cup chopped fresh basil**
  2 tablespoons chopped fresh chives
 ½ **teaspoon salt, or to taste**
For pancakes
  **4 cups coarsely grated zucchini
     (1 lb)**
 1¼ **teaspoons salt**
 ¼ **cup all-purpose flour**
 1½ **teaspoons sugar**
 ¼ **teaspoon black pepper**
  2 large egg whites
  **4 tablespoons vegetable or
     canola oil**

Make basil chive cream:
Blend sour cream, water, basil, chives, and salt in a blender until smooth and pale green. Chill until ready to serve.

Make pancakes:
Put zucchini in a colander and toss with salt. Let stand at room temperature 20 minutes, then wrap zucchini in a kitchen towel and twist towel to wring out as much liquid as possible. Transfer zucchini to a large bowl and stir in flour, sugar, and pepper.

Beat egg whites with a pinch of salt using an electric mixer until they just hold stiff peaks, then gently fold into zucchini mixture.

Heat 2 tablespoons oil in a 10-inch nonstick skillet over moderately high heat until hot but not smoking. Working in batches of 5, spoon 2 tablespoons batter per pancake into skillet, flattening slightly with back of spoon. Cook pancakes, turning once, until golden brown, about 3 minutes total, transferring to paper towels to drain and adding more oil to skillet as necessary.

Serve immediately, with basil chive cream.

HARVEST HASH

Serves 4 (side dish)

Active time: 40 min   Start to finish: 40 min

 1 russet (baking) potato (½ lb)
 3 medium parsnips (½ lb total),
    peeled and cut into ½-inch cubes
    (1¼ cups)
½ lb butternut squash, peeled and
    cut into ½-inch cubes (1¼ cups)
½ stick (¼ cup) unsalted butter,
    cut into pieces
 3 shallots (6 oz), halved lengthwise and
    thinly sliced crosswise (1⅓ cups)
 3 garlic cloves, chopped
½ teaspoon salt
¼ teaspoon black pepper
1½ to 2 teaspoons chopped fresh sage

Peel potato and cut into ½-inch cubes. Bring a 5- to 6-quart pot of salted water (see Tips, page 8) to a boil and cook potato until crisp-tender, about 5 minutes, then transfer with a slotted spoon to a colander. Cook parsnips and squash together in same boiling water until crisp-tender, about 3 minutes, then drain.

Heat butter in a 12-inch heavy skillet over moderately high heat, swirling skillet occasionally, until foam subsides and butter begins to brown, about 2 minutes. Add shallots and garlic and sauté, stirring occasionally, until shallots are golden brown, about 5 minutes. Add parcooked vegetables, salt, and pepper and sauté, stirring occasionally, until browned and tender, about 7 minutes. Stir in sage (to taste).

ROASTED CHERRY TOMATOES WITH MINT

Serves 4

Active time: 5 min   Start to finish: 15 min

 1 pt cherry or grape tomatoes (12 oz)
 1 tablespoon extra-virgin olive oil
¼ teaspoon salt
⅛ teaspoon black pepper
 2 teaspoons finely chopped fresh mint

Preheat oven to 425°F.

Toss tomatoes with oil, salt, and pepper in a small baking pan and roast in middle of oven until skins just begin to split, 5 to 10 minutes.

Sprinkle tomatoes with mint.

SALADS

main course salads

DUCK AND WILD RICE SALAD

Serves 6 to 8 (main course)
Active time: 1 hr   Start to finish: 2½ hr

For dressing
> **Finely grated zest of 1 orange**
> **⅔ cup fresh orange juice**
> **⅓ cup extra-virgin olive oil**
> **⅓ cup finely chopped shallot**
> **1 teaspoon mild honey**
> **1 teaspoon salt**
> **½ teaspoon black pepper**

For salad
> **2 cups wild rice (10 oz)**
> **3 tablespoons unsalted butter**
> **1 large onion, finely chopped**
> **4 cups water**
> **3 cups chicken broth**
> **10 oz sugar snap peas, trimmed and halved diagonally**
> **2 (14-oz) boneless magret duck breast halves with skin**
> **6 scallions, thinly sliced diagonally**
> **1 cup soft dried apricots (preferably California; 5 oz), cut into ¼-inch strips**
> **1½ cups pecans (4½ oz), chopped and toasted (see Tips, page 8)**
> **1 teaspoon salt**

Special equipment: **an instant-read thermometer**

Make dressing:
Whisk together all dressing ingredients in a large bowl and let stand at room temperature while making rice salad.

Cook rice:
Rinse rice well in a large medium-mesh sieve under cold water, then drain. Heat butter in a 4- to 5-quart heavy pot over moderate heat until foam subsides, then cook onion, stirring occasionally, until golden, about 5 minutes. Add rice and cook, stirring, until fragrant, about 3 minutes. Stir in water and broth and bring to a boil, then reduce heat and simmer, covered, until rice is tender, 1 to 1¼ hours. (Grains will split open but not all liquid will be absorbed.) Drain well in a colander and cool to warm before adding to dressing. (Spread rice out in a shallow baking pan to cool faster.)

Cook sugar snaps and duck while rice cooks:
Preheat oven to 375°F.

Cook sugar snaps in a 4-quart pot of boiling salted water (see Tips, page 8) until crisp-tender, about 2 minutes. Drain in sieve and rinse under cold water to stop cooking, then drain well.

Pat duck dry and season with salt and pepper. Score skin in a crosshatch pattern and put duck, skin sides up, in a lightly oiled shallow baking pan (1 inch deep). Roast in middle of oven until thermometer inserted horizontally into center registers 120°F (for medium-rare), about 25 minutes. Leave oven on.

Transfer duck to a cutting board and when just cool enough to handle, remove skin. Thinly slice skin (scored side down), keeping duck breast warm, loosely covered with foil. Bake skin in baking pan in middle of oven until very crisp, about 15 to 20 minutes, then transfer with a slotted spoon to paper towels to drain.

Cut duck breast halves in half horizontally (butterfly-style), then cut across the grain into thin slices. Add duck with any juices to dressing along with rice, sugar snaps, scallions, apricots, pecans, and salt and toss gently to combine.

Just before serving, scatter crisp duck skin on top.

PHOTO ON PAGE 111

POTATO, ITALIAN SAUSAGE, AND ARUGULA SALAD

Serves 4
Active time: 15 min   Start to finish: 35 min

⅓ cup thinly sliced red onion
1 lb small (1½- to 2-inch) boiling potatoes
1 lb sweet or hot Italian sausage links
4 tablespoons extra-virgin olive oil
2 tablespoons red-wine vinegar
1¼ teaspoons salt
½ cup drained bottled roasted red peppers, cut into ¼-inch strips
½ lb arugula, coarse stems discarded (4 cups)

Soak onion in cold water to cover 15 minutes. Drain and pat dry.

Meanwhile, cover potatoes with salted cold water (see Tips, page 8) by 2 inches in a 3-quart heavy saucepan and simmer, uncovered, until just tender, 15 to 25 minutes. Drain in a colander and cool slightly.

While potatoes are simmering, prick sausages once or twice with a fork, then cook in 1 tablespoon oil in a large heavy skillet over moderate heat, turning occasionally, until browned and cooked through, about 10 minutes. Transfer to paper towels to drain. When sausages are cool enough to handle, cut diagonally into ½-inch pieces.

Whisk together vinegar and salt in a large bowl until salt is dissolved. When potatoes are just cool enough to handle (but still warm), peel and cut into 1-inch cubes, adding to vinegar as cut, and toss gently.

Add onion, sausages, roasted peppers, arugula, remaining 3 tablespoons oil, and salt and pepper to taste to potatoes and toss well.

SHRIMP, AVOCADO, AND ENDIVE SALAD

Serves 2 to 4 (light main course)
Active time: 20 min   Start to finish: 20 min

3 tablespoons fresh lemon juice
2½ teaspoons salt
¾ lb large shrimp in shell (21 to 25 per lb), peeled and deveined
1 tablespoon chopped fresh tarragon
2 teaspoons Dijon mustard
¼ teaspoon black pepper

3 tablespoons olive oil
2 firm-ripe California avocados (preferably Hass)
1 lb Belgian endive (4 heads), cut crosswise into 1-inch pieces

Bring 2 quarts water, 1 tablespoon lemon juice, and 2 teaspoons salt to a boil in a 3-quart saucepan, then add shrimp and poach at a bare simmer, uncovered, until just cooked through, about 3 minutes. Transfer with a slotted spoon to a bowl of ice and cold water to stop cooking. Let shrimp chill in water 2 minutes, then drain and pat dry.

Whisk together tarragon, mustard, pepper, and remaining 2 tablespoons lemon juice, and remaining ½ teaspoon salt in a serving bowl. Add oil in a slow stream, whisking until emulsified.

Quarter avocados lengthwise, then pit, peel, and cut into bite-size pieces. Add shrimp, avocados, and endive to dressing and toss.

SHRIMP, JICAMA, AND APRICOT SALAD

Serves 4 (main course)
Active time: 30 min   Start to finish: 30 min

1 lb large shrimp in shell (21 to 25 per lb), peeled and deveined
¼ cup seasoned rice vinegar
½ teaspoon minced garlic
½ teaspoon minced peeled fresh ginger
2 tablespoons vegetable oil
1 lb jicama, peeled and cut into ⅛-inch-thick matchsticks
1 seedless cucumber (usually plastic-wrapped), cut into ⅛-inch-thick matchsticks
¾ lb firm-ripe apricots (4 large), cut into ¼-inch-thick wedges
¼ cup chopped fresh cilantro

Halve shrimp lengthwise by cutting down middle of backs and cook in a saucepan of boiling salted water (see Tips, page 8), stirring occasionally, until just cooked through, 1 to 2 minutes. Drain in a colander and spread on a large plate to cool.

Whisk together vinegar, garlic, ginger, and oil, then add shrimp and remaining ingredients and toss to combine well. Season salad with salt and pepper.

CURRIED CHICKEN SALAD

Serves 6
Active time: 25 min   Start to finish: 35 min

1¾ cups chicken broth
1½ lb skinless boneless chicken breast
½ cup mayonnaise
⅓ cup plain yogurt
5 teaspoons curry powder
1 tablespoon fresh lime juice
1 teaspoon honey
½ teaspoon ground ginger
½ teaspoon salt
¼ teaspoon black pepper
1 medium red onion, chopped (1 cup)
1 firm-ripe mango (¾ lb), peeled, pitted, and chopped
1 cup red seedless grapes (5 oz), halved
½ cup salted roasted cashews, coarsely chopped

Bring 4 cups water to a simmer with chicken broth in a 2- to 3-quart saucepan. Add chicken and simmer, uncovered, 6 minutes. Remove pan from heat and cover, then let stand until chicken is cooked through, about 15 minutes. Transfer chicken to a plate and cool 10 minutes. Chop into ½-inch pieces.

While chicken is cooling, whisk together mayonnaise, yogurt, curry, lime juice, honey, ginger, salt, and pepper in a large bowl. Add chicken, onion, mango, grapes, and cashews and stir gently to combine.

garlic

LAYERED COBB SALAD

Serves 4 to 6 (main course)
Active time: 1¼ hr   Start to finish: 1¼ hr

For dressing
3 tablespoons red-wine vinegar
1 tablespoon fresh lemon juice
2 teaspoons Dijon mustard
1 small garlic clove, minced
½ teaspoon salt
½ teaspoon sugar
¼ teaspoon black pepper
½ cup extra-virgin olive oil
For salad
3 skinless boneless chicken breast halves (1¼ lb total)
2 California avocados
1 head romaine, cut crosswise into ½-inch-wide slices (8 cups)
6 bacon slices, cooked until crisp, drained, and finely chopped
3 medium tomatoes (¾ lb), seeded and cut into ½-inch pieces
2 to 3 oz Roquefort, crumbled (½ to ¾ cup)
2 bunches watercress, coarse stems discarded
2 hard-boiled large eggs, halved and forced through a coarse-mesh sieve
¼ cup finely chopped fresh chives

Make dressing:
Whisk together all dressing ingredients except oil in a bowl, then add oil in a slow stream, whisking until emulsified.

Make salad:
Bring 5 cups water to a simmer in a 2-quart saucepan, then simmer chicken, uncovered, 6 minutes. Remove pan from heat and cover, then let stand until chicken is cooked through, about 15 minutes. Transfer chicken to a cutting board and cool completely. Cut into ½-inch cubes.

Halve, pit, and peel avocados. Cut into ½-inch cubes.

Spread romaine over bottom of a 6- to 8-quart glass bowl and top with an even layer of chicken. Sprinkle bacon over chicken, then continue layering with tomatoes, cheese (to taste), avocados, watercress, eggs, and chives.

Just before serving, pour dressing over salad and toss.

PHOTO ON PAGE 110

"PAELLA" COUSCOUS SALAD

Serves 6
Active time: 1 hr   Start to finish: 1½ hr

For salad
  2 tablespoons extra-virgin olive oil
  ½ lb Spanish chorizo (spicy cured pork
      sausage; preferably hot), cut into
      ¼-inch dice
  ½ cup finely chopped shallot
  1 large garlic clove, minced
  1½ cups chicken broth
  ½ cup dry white wine
  ¾ lb medium shrimp in shell (31 to 35 per lb),
      peeled and deveined
  ¾ lb sea scallops, tough muscle removed from
      side of each if necessary, halved crosswise
      (quartered if large)
  1 tablespoon fresh lemon juice
  1 (10-oz) box couscous (1½ cups)
  ¼ teaspoon crumbled saffron threads
  1 cup frozen peas, thawed
  1 large red bell pepper, finely diced
  1 cup coarsely chopped drained pimiento-
      stuffed green olives (5 oz)
  ⅓ cup finely chopped fresh flat-leaf parsley
For dressing
  ⅓ cup fresh lemon juice
  ⅓ cup extra-virgin olive oil
  2 large garlic cloves, chopped
  ¾ teaspoon salt
  ½ teaspoon black pepper
  ⅛ teaspoon cayenne

Accompaniment: **lemon wedges**

Make salad:
Heat oil in a large heavy skillet over moderately
high heat until hot but not smoking, then sauté chorizo
and shallot, stirring, until chorizo is golden brown on
edges, 3 to 4 minutes. Add garlic and sauté, stirring,
1 minute. Transfer mixture to a large bowl, scraping
out skillet with a rubber spatula.

Bring broth and wine to a boil in a 2½-quart
saucepan and cook shrimp, covered, until just cooked
through, about 45 seconds. Transfer shrimp with a slotted spoon to a small bowl. Bring liquid in saucepan
back to a boil and cook scallops, covered, until just
cooked through, about 2 minutes. Transfer scallops
with slotted spoon to bowl with shrimp and pour any

liquid accumulated in bowl back into pan. Add lemon
juice to seafood, then add salt and pepper to taste and
toss to combine.

Put couscous in a metal bowl. Reserve 1¾ cups
cooking liquid in saucepan and discard remainder.
Add saffron, then bring liquid to a boil and pour over
couscous. Let stand, covered tightly with plastic wrap,
5 minutes. Fluff with a fork and add to chorizo. Stir in
peas, bell pepper, olives, and seafood and toss.

Make dressing:
Blend lemon juice, oil, garlic, salt, black pepper,
and cayenne in a blender until smooth and pour over
seafood salad, tossing to combine well. Let stand
30 minutes at room temperature to allow couscous
to absorb dressing.

Stir in parsley and season salad with salt and pepper.

Cooks' note:
• Salad can be made (without parsley) 2 hours ahead
  and chilled, covered. Bring to room temperature and
  stir in parsley just before serving.
PHOTO ON PAGE 111

salads with greens

DANDELION SALAD WITH WARM BACON DRESSING

Serves 6
Active time: 15 min   Start to finish: 15 min

  1 lb tender dandelion greens, tough
      stems removed
  5 bacon slices
  1½ tablespoons finely chopped shallot
  1½ tablespoons cider vinegar
  ¼ teaspoon salt
  ⅛ teaspoon black pepper

Cut greens into 1½-inch lengths and transfer to a
large bowl.

Cook bacon in a large heavy skillet until golden
and crisp, then transfer to a cutting board, reserving fat
in skillet. Finely chop bacon.

Whisk together shallot, vinegar, salt, and pepper in
a small bowl, then whisk in 3 tablespoons hot bacon
fat. Toss greens with enough warm dressing to coat and
sprinkle with bacon. Serve immediately.
PHOTO ON PAGE 59

BITTER GREENS AND GRAPES WITH BLUE CHEESE DRESSING

Serves 6
Active time: 20 min   Start to finish: 20 min

For dressing
⅓ cup 1% fat cottage cheese
3 tablespoons nonfat plain yogurt
2 tablespoons well-shaken buttermilk
2 teaspoons water
½ teaspoon fresh lemon juice
½ teaspoon Worcestershire sauce
1½ oz blue cheese (scant ¼ packed cup)
⅛ teaspoon salt
⅛ teaspoon black pepper

For salad
6 oz frisée, torn into bite-size pieces (5 cups)
8 oz escarole, core and tough leaves discarded, torn into bite-size pieces (4½ cups)
1 head radicchio (¼ lb), cut into ½-inch pieces
1 cup red seedless grapes, halved

Make dressing
Purée all dressing ingredients in a blender until very smooth, about 1 minute.

Make salad:
Toss together frisée, escarole, and radicchio and divide greens among 6 plates. Top with grapes and drizzle with dressing.

Each serving about 69 calories and 2 grams fat

ROMAINE, RADISH, AND CUCUMBER SALAD WITH TAHINI DRESSING

Serves 4
Active time: 25 min   Start to finish: 25 min

For tahini dressing
¼ cup well-stirred tahini (Middle Eastern sesame paste)
¼ cup water
2½ tablespoons fresh lemon juice
2 tablespoons soy sauce
1 tablespoon mild honey
1 small garlic clove, minced
½ teaspoon salt
⅛ teaspoon cayenne

For salad
½ lb romaine, torn into bite-size pieces (6 cups)
1 bunch radishes (½ lb), trimmed, halved, and thinly sliced
½ seedless cucumber (usually plastic-wrapped), halved lengthwise and thinly sliced crosswise
4 scallions, thinly sliced

Make dressing:
Blend all dressing ingredients in a blender until smooth. (If desired, blend in more water, 1 teaspoon at a time, to thin dressing.)

Make salad:
Toss together all salad ingredients in a large bowl with just enough dressing to coat.

Cooks' note:
• Dressing keeps, covered and chilled, 3 days. Stir before using, thinning with additional water if necessary.

BABY GREENS WITH WARM GOAT CHEESE

Serves 1
Active time: 10 min   Start to finish: 25 min

1 large egg white
1 teaspoon water
2 (⅓-inch-thick) rounds soft mild goat cheese, cut from a cold log
2 tablespoons plain dry bread crumbs (preferably Japanese *panko*)
1 teaspoon cider vinegar
⅛ teaspoon salt
⅛ teaspoon Dijon mustard
Pinch of sugar
1 tablespoon plus 1 teaspoon extra-virgin olive oil
2 cups mesclun (1 oz)

Whisk together egg white and water. Dip cheese rounds in egg, letting excess drip off, then dredge in bread crumbs, pressing lightly to adhere. Chill 15 minutes.

Whisk together vinegar, salt, mustard, sugar, and a pinch of pepper in a small salad bowl. Add 1 tablespoon oil in a slow stream, whisking until emulsified.

Heat remaining teaspoon oil in a small nonstick skillet over moderately high heat until hot but not smoking, then sauté cheese, turning once, until golden, about 1 minute total. Remove skillet from heat.

Add greens to dressing and toss gently to coat. Serve salad topped with warm cheese.

Cooks' note:
• The easiest way to cut goat cheese is with a piece of dental floss.

PHOTO ON PAGE 113

FRISÉE AND ENDIVE SALAD WITH WARM BRUSSELS SPROUTS AND TOASTED PECANS

Serves 6
Active time: 45 min   Start to finish: 45 min

If you're making the whole vegetarian Thanksgiving menu, The Peaceable Feast, *(page 103) in one oven, roast the Brussels sprouts in the lower third of the oven while heating the crêpes in the upper third.*

For vinaigrette
  3 tablespoons white-wine vinegar
  2 tablespoons water
  1 tablespoon Dijon mustard
  ¼ cup minced shallot
  ½ teaspoon salt
  ¼ teaspoon black pepper
  6 tablespoons olive oil
For salad
  ½ stick (¼ cup) unsalted butter, cut into pieces
  1 lb Brussels sprouts (preferably small), trimmed and halved lengthwise (quartered if large)
  ½ cup pecan halves, halved lengthwise
  1 teaspoon salt
  6 oz frisée, trimmed and torn into bite-size pieces (4 cups)
  3 Belgian endives (1 lb), cut crosswise into ½-inch slices

Make vinaigrette:
Whisk together vinegar, water, mustard, shallot, salt, and pepper in a small bowl, then add oil in a slow stream, whisking.

Make salad:
Preheat oven to 400°F.

Melt butter in a large shallow baking pan (1 inch deep) in lower third of oven, about 3 minutes. Toss

sprouts in pan with butter, pecans, and salt. Arrange sprouts, cut sides down, in 1 layer and roast in lower third of oven until undersides of sprouts are golden and nuts are fragrant, 12 to 15 minutes.

Whisk vinaigrette, then transfer warm sprouts and nuts to a large bowl and toss with frisée, endive, and enough vinaigrette to coat. Serve immediately.

Cooks' notes:
• Vinaigrette can be made 2 hours ahead and kept at room temperature.
• Brussels sprouts and nuts can be roasted 2 hours ahead and kept at room temperature. Reheat in a 400°F oven until hot, about 5 minutes.

PHOTO ON PAGE 103

ESCAROLE SALAD WITH HAZELNUTS AND CURRANTS

Serves 4
Active time: 15 min   Start to finish: 30 min

  1 teaspoon minced garlic
  2 tablespoons extra-virgin olive oil
  3 tablespoons dried currants
  1 tablespoon cider vinegar
  ¼ teaspoon salt
  ⅛ teaspoon black pepper
  2 heads escarole (2 lb), dark outer leaves removed and pale green and yellow inner leaves torn into bite-size pieces (16 cups)
  ¼ cup loosely packed fresh flat-leaf parsley leaves
  ⅓ cup hazelnuts, toasted (see Tips, page 8) and chopped

Cook garlic in oil in an 8-inch nonstick skillet over moderate heat, stirring, until fragrant, about 30 seconds. Add currants and cook, stirring, 20 seconds, then whisk in vinegar, salt, and pepper.

Toss escarole, parsley, and nuts with warm dressing in a large bowl and serve immediately.

MESCLUN AND RICOTTA SALATA ON GRILLED GARLIC TOASTS

Serves 8
Active time: 40 min   Start to finish: 40 min

 2 large lemons
 4 teaspoons honey
 ⅛ teaspoon salt, or to taste
 ⅛ teaspoon black pepper, or to taste
 ¾ cup olive oil
 4 (½-inch-thick) slices country-style bread,
   halved diagonally
 1 large garlic clove, halved crosswise
 8 oz mesclun (8 cups)
 ¾ lb grape tomatoes, halved
 6 oz *ricotta salata*, thinly sliced

Remove zest from lemons in large strips with a vegetable peeler and cut any white pith from strips with a sharp knife. Cut enough zest into julienne strips to measure ¼ cup. Blanch zest in boiling water 1 minute, then drain in a sieve medium-mesh and plunge into a bowl of cold water to stop cooking. Drain and pat dry.

Squeeze enough juice from lemons to measure 6 tablespoons. Whisk together lemon juice, honey, salt, and pepper, then add ½ cup oil in a slow stream, whisking until emulsified.

Prepare charcoal or gas grill for cooking. If using charcoal, open vents on bottom of grill.

Brush both sides of bread slices with remaining ¼ cup oil and season with salt and pepper.

When fire is hot (you can hold your hand 5 inches above rack for 1 to 2 seconds), grill bread on lightly oiled grill rack, turning once, until golden, about 3 minutes total. Immediately rub 1 side of each slice with garlic.

Toss mesclun with tomatoes, half of zest, and enough dressing to coat, then season with salt and pepper.

Put toasts on salad plates and spoon some of remaining dressing over each. Layer cheese and salad alternately on each toast and sprinkle with remaining zest.

Cooks' note:
• Zest can be blanched (and dried) 1 day ahead and chilled, wrapped tightly in plastic wrap.
PHOTO ON PAGE 72

RADICCHIO, PEAR, AND FENNEL SALAD WITH ANISE ORANGE DRESSING

Serves 6
Active time: 20 min   Start to finish: 20 min

For dressing
 ⅓ cup fresh orange juice
 1 teaspoon sugar
 1 teaspoon anise seeds, coarsely ground with
   a mortar and pestle or in an electric
   coffee/spice grinder
 ½ teaspoon salt
 ¼ teaspoon black pepper
 ½ cup extra-virgin olive oil
For salad
 1 (1¼-lb) fennel bulb (sometimes called
   anise; preferably with fronds),
   quartered lengthwise
 2 pears
1¾ lb radicchio (2 medium heads),
   thinly sliced

Make dressing:
Whisk together all dressing ingredients in a large bowl until combined well.

Make salad:
Tear enough fennel fronds, if using, into small sprigs to measure ½ cup. Trim fennel stalks flush with bulb and discard stalks. Cut out and discard core of bulb, then cut bulb lengthwise into thin strips. Peel and core pears, then cut into 3-inch-long matchsticks. Add fennel strips and fronds to dressing along with pears and radicchio and toss well.

chicory salad with Oranges & red onions

BABY SPINACH AND MINT SALAD WITH BLACK-EYED PEAS

Serves 4
Active time: 25 min   Start to finish: 30 min

 1 cup frozen black-eyed peas
 1 cup water
 ¾ teaspoon salt
 ¼ teaspoon fennel seeds
 ⅛ teaspoon cayenne
 ⅛ teaspoon black pepper
 2 tablespoons fresh orange juice
 1 tablespoon fresh lemon juice
 1 tablespoon low-sodium fat-free
    chicken broth
 ½ teaspoon honey
 1½ teaspoons olive oil
 5 oz baby spinach
 1 cup loosely packed fresh mint
    (see Tips, page 8)

Special equipment: **an electric coffee/spice grinder**

Simmer peas, water, and ½ teaspoon salt in a 1-quart saucepan, uncovered, over moderate heat until peas are just tender, about 15 minutes. Drain in a colander and rinse under cold water, then spread peas out on a paper towel and pat dry.

Grind fennel seeds with cayenne and black pepper to a powder in grinder, then transfer to a small bowl. Add peas to spice mixture and toss to coat.

Whisk together juices, broth, honey, oil, and remaining ¼ teaspoon salt in a large bowl and add spinach and mint, tossing to coat.

Serve salad sprinkled with spiced peas.

Each serving about 89 calories and 2 grams fat

CHICORY SALAD WITH ORANGES AND RED ONIONS

Serves 8
Active time: 20 min   Start to finish: 25 min

 ⅓ cup red-wine vinegar
 1 tablespoon sugar
 1½ teaspoons salt
 1 medium red onion, sliced crosswise
    ⅛ inch thick and separated into rings
 2 medium navel oranges

 2 teaspoons whole-grain mustard
 1 tablespoon low-fat chicken stock or
    low-sodium fat-free chicken broth
 ¼ teaspoon black pepper
 1 tablespoon olive oil
 ½ lb chicory (curly endive), stems and
    center ribs discarded and leaves torn
    into bite-size pieces (10 cups)

Bring vinegar, sugar, and 1 teaspoon salt to a boil in a small saucepan, stirring frequently until sugar is dissolved, then remove from heat.

Cook onion in a saucepan of boiling salted water (see Tips, page 8) until crisp-tender, about 4 minutes, then drain in a colander. Rinse under cold water and drain again. Stir onion into vinegar mixture and marinate 10 minutes.

While onion is marinating, cut peel and white pith from oranges with a sharp knife, then cut oranges crosswise into ¼-inch-thick slices.

Drain onion in a medium-mesh sieve set over a salad bowl, reserving marinade and onion separately. Whisk mustard, stock, remaining ½ teaspoon salt, pepper, and oil into marinade. Add chicory, onion, and oranges and toss with dressing. Serve immediately.

Each serving about 46 calories and 2 grams fat
PHOTO ON PAGE 42

vegetable salads and slaws

BEET AND SARDINE SALAD

Serves 6
Active time: 15 min   Start to finish: 15 min

 ½ cup sour cream
 1 tablespoon bottled horseradish
    (not drained)
 2 tablespoons chopped fresh dill
 1 (16-oz) jar pickled sliced beets, drained
 1 tablespoon vegetable oil
 1 (3¾- to 4⅜-oz) can sardines in
    oil, drained

Stir together sour cream, horseradish, dill, and salt to taste. Cut beets into ½-inch cubes and toss with oil and salt to taste. Serve sardines on top of beets with sour cream mixture.

BEET AND SUGAR SNAP PEA SALAD

Serves 4 (first course or side dish)
Active time: 20 min   Start to finish: 20 min

½ small red onion, halved lengthwise,
   then thinly sliced lengthwise
3 tablespoons rice vinegar (not seasoned)
1 teaspoon ground coriander,
   lightly toasted (see Tips, page 8)
2 teaspoons sugar
1 teaspoon salt
2 tablespoons extra-virgin olive oil
1 (14- to 15-oz) can whole small beets,
   drained and quartered
¼ lb sugar snap peas, trimmed

Soak onion in cold water in a small bowl 10 minutes, then drain in a medium-mesh sieve.

Whisk together vinegar, coriander, sugar, and salt in a salad bowl, then add oil in a slow stream, whisking. Toss onion and beets with dressing.

Steam sugar snaps on a steamer rack over boiling water, covered, 2 minutes, then transfer to a bowl of ice water to stop cooking. Drain well in sieve and toss with beet mixture.

HEIRLOOM TOMATO SALAD

Serves 6
Active time: 15 min   Start to finish: 15 min

If you can't find heirloom tomatoes near you, this salad would also be delicious with any ripe tomato from garden or market.

1½ tablespoons red-wine vinegar
¾ teaspoon salt
½ teaspoon Dijon mustard
¼ teaspoon black pepper
¼ cup olive or vegetable oil
3 lb mixed heirloom tomatoes, halved if
   small or cut into ½-inch wedges if
   medium or large

Whisk together vinegar, salt, mustard, and pepper in a large bowl, then add oil in a slow stream, whisking constantly until dressing is emulsified. Add tomatoes and gently toss to coat. Season with salt and pepper.

PHOTO ON PAGE 90

BEET AND GOAT CHEESE SALAD

Serves 8
Active time: 30 min   Start to finish: 2½ hr

3 large red beets (1⅔ lb without greens)
2 large golden beets (1 lb without greens)
¼ cup minced shallot
2 tablespoons fresh lemon juice
¾ teaspoon salt
¼ teaspoon black pepper
¼ cup pistachio oil
4 oz soft mild goat cheese
3 tablespoons salted shelled pistachios
   (not dyed red), coarsely chopped
1 oz *mâche* (also called lamb's lettuce),
   trimmed (4 cups)

Special equipment: **a 2½-inch round cookie cutter (without handle; at least 2 inches high)**

Preheat oven to 425°F.

Separately wrap red and golden beets tightly in double layers of foil and roast in middle of oven until tender, 1 to 1½ hours. Unwrap beets.

While beets are cooling slightly, whisk together shallot, lemon juice, salt, and pepper in a small bowl, then add oil in a stream, whisking.

When beets are cool enough to handle, slip off and discard skins. Separately cut red and golden beets into ¼-inch dice and put in separate bowls. Add 2½ tablespoons dressing to each bowl and toss to coat.

Place cookie cutter in center of 1 of 8 salad plates. Put one eighth of red beets in cutter and pack down with your fingertips. Crumble 2 teaspoons goat cheese on top, then one eighth of golden beets, packing them down. Gently lift cutter up and away from stack. Make 7 more servings in same manner. Drizzle each plate with 1 teaspoon dressing and scatter with some pistachios.

Toss *mâche* with just enough remaining dressing to coat and gently mound on top of molded beets. Serve salad immediately.

Cooks' notes:
• Beets can be roasted and diced 1 day ahead and chilled, covered. Bring to room temperature before using.
• Molded beet salad (without mâche) can be assembled 45 minutes ahead and kept, covered, at cool room temperature.

PHOTO ON PAGE 104

ASPARAGUS WITH
TARRAGON SHERRY VINAIGRETTE

Serves 4
Active time: 20 min   Start to finish: 30 min

1½ lb medium asparagus, trimmed
1 tablespoon Sherry vinegar
2 teaspoons minced shallot
¼ teaspoon Dijon mustard
¼ teaspoon salt
⅛ teaspoon black pepper
3 tablespoons extra-virgin olive oil
1½ teaspoons finely chopped fresh tarragon
1 large egg, hard-boiled

Steam asparagus on a steamer rack set over boiling water, covered, until just tender, 3 to 5 minutes (depending on thickness), then transfer to a bowl of ice water to stop cooking. Drain well and pat dry with paper towels.

Whisk together vinegar, shallot, mustard, salt, and pepper in a small bowl, then add oil in a slow stream, whisking until emulsified. Whisk in tarragon.

Halve hard-boiled egg and force each half through a coarse-mesh sieve into a bowl. Toss asparagus with 1 tablespoon vinaigrette and divide among 4 plates. Spoon remaining dressing over asparagus and top with egg.

ZUCCHINI, TOMATO,
AND CORN SALAD

Serves 4
Active time: 30 min   Start to finish: 1 hr

1½ lb medium zucchini
1¼ teaspoons salt
1 cup fresh corn kernels (cut from 2 ears)
2 tablespoons fresh lemon juice
½ teaspoon sugar
¼ teaspoon black pepper
¼ cup extra-virgin olive oil
8 oz grape or cherry tomatoes, halved lengthwise (2 cups)
¼ cup thinly sliced fresh basil

Special equipment: **a Japanese Benriner or other adjustable-blade slicer fitted with julienne cutter or a julienne peeler**

Working with 1 zucchini at a time, cut lengthwise into very thin (julienne) strips with slicer, turning zucchini and avoiding core. Discard core.

Toss zucchini strips with 1 teaspoon salt and let drain in a colander set over a bowl, covered and chilled, 1 hour.

Gently squeeze handfuls of zucchini to remove excess water and pat dry with paper towels.

Cook corn in a small saucepan of boiling water until tender, about 3 minutes. Drain, then rinse under cold water and pat dry.

Whisk together lemon juice, sugar, pepper, and remaining ¼ teaspoon salt in a large bowl, then add oil in a slow stream, whisking. Add zucchini, corn, tomatoes, and basil and toss well.

Cooks' note:
· **Salad (without dressing and basil) can be made 4 hours ahead and kept, covered, at room temperature.**
PHOTO ON PAGE 85

FENNEL, TOMATO, AND FETA SALAD

Serves 6
Active time: 15 min   Start to finish: 15 min

2 medium fennel bulbs (sometimes called anise), stalks discarded
4 plum tomatoes (½ lb total), seeded and thinly sliced lengthwise
2 teaspoons drained bottled capers
⅓ cup crumbled feta (1½ oz)
½ teaspoon finely grated fresh lemon zest (see Tips, page 8)
1 to 1½ tablespoons fresh lemon juice
1 tablespoon extra-virgin olive oil
½ teaspoon salt
¼ teaspoon black pepper

Special equipment: **a Japanese Benriner or other adjustable-blade slicer**

Quarter fennel bulbs lengthwise, then cut lengthwise into paper-thin slices with slicer.
Toss fennel with remaining ingredients in a large bowl.

Cooks' note:
• **Salad can be made 1 hour ahead.**

Each serving about 74 calories and 4 grams fat

TOMATO, CUCUMBER, AND PITA SALAD

Serves 16
Active time: 1½ hr   Start to finish: 9½ hr (includes marinating)

We seasoned this salad—based on the Middle Eastern bread salad called fattoush—*with* za'atar, *a mixture of salt, sumac, sesame, and thyme.*

For marinated olives
1 cup Kalamata or other brine-cured black olives (5 oz), halved lengthwise and pitted
¾ cup extra-virgin olive oil
2 teaspoons minced garlic
1 tablespoon chopped fresh oregano or 1 teaspoon dried, crumbled
2 (2- by ½-inch) strips fresh lemon zest, thinly sliced crosswise
½ teaspoon coarsely ground black pepper
¼ teaspoon coarse salt

For pita toasts
4 (6-inch) pita loaves with pockets, split horizontally
¼ cup olive oil
2 tablespoons *za'atar* (recipe follows)
For salad
3 tablespoons fresh lemon juice
4 hearts of romaine (1½ lb), cut into 2-inch pieces
1 seedless cucumber (usually plastic-wrapped), peeled, halved lengthwise, cored, and thinly sliced crosswise
1 pt grape or cherry tomatoes, halved
¾ lb feta, coarsely crumbled (2½ cups)
3 tablespoons *za'atar* (recipe follows)

Marinate olives:
Stir together all olive ingredients in an airtight container and marinate olives, chilled, at least 8 hours. Bring to room temperature before using.
Make pita toasts:
Preheat oven to 350°F.
Brush rough sides of pita halves with oil and sprinkle with *za'atar.* Cut each round into 8 wedges, then halve each wedge diagonally. Arrange triangles, oiled sides up, on 2 baking sheets and bake in batches in middle of oven until crisp and pale golden, about 10 minutes. Cool on a rack.
Assemble salad:
Add lemon juice to marinated olives, then close container and shake vigorously. Divide olive mixture between 2 large salad bowls. Divide romaine, cucumber, tomatoes, feta, and pita toasts between bowls, then sprinkle with *za'atar* and toss.

Cooks' notes:
• **Olives can marinate up to 2 weeks.**
• **Pita toasts can be made 2 days ahead and kept in an airtight container at room temperature.**

ZA'ATAR

Makes about 5 tablespoons
Active time: 15 min   Start to finish: 15 min

This Middle Eastern spice mixture is so delicious we suggest doubling the recipe and using the extra for a snack: Dunk some bread (such as pita) in flavorful olive oil and then in the za'atar. Or sprinkle za'atar over plain yogurt and drizzle with olive oil, and you've got a terrific dip.

2 tablespoons minced fresh thyme
2 tablespoons sesame seeds, toasted
  (see Tips, page 8)
2 teaspoons ground sumac
½ teaspoon coarse salt

Stir together all ingredients in a small bowl.

Cooks' note:
• *Za'atar* keeps, chilled in a sealed plastic bag, 1 week.

POTATO SALAD
WITH MUSTARD VINAIGRETTE

Serves 8
Active time: 30 min   Start to finish: 1 hr

4 lb fingerling or small boiling potatoes
2 teaspoons sugar
4 tablespoons white-wine vinegar
⅓ cup finely chopped shallot
2 tablespoons coarse-grain Dijon mustard
  (not whole-grain)
2 tablespoons vegetable oil

Cover potatoes with salted cold water (see Tips, page 8) by 2 inches in a 5- to 6-quart pot and simmer, uncovered, until just tender, 20 to 25 minutes. Drain in a colander and cool slightly.

While potatoes are simmering, whisk together sugar and 3 tablespoons vinegar in a large bowl until sugar is dissolved.

When potatoes are just cool enough to handle, peel and cut diagonally into ½-inch-thick slices, adding to vinegar mixture as sliced and tossing gently to combine.

Whisk together shallot, mustard, and remaining tablespoon vinegar in a small bowl, then add oil in a slow stream, whisking until emulsified. Add dressing

to potatoes, then season with salt and pepper and stir gently with a rubber spatula.

Cooks' note:
• Potato salad can be made 1 day ahead and chilled, covered. Bring to room temperature, then stir and season before serving.
PHOTO ON PAGE 75

GREEN BEAN SALAD
WITH PUMPKIN SEED DRESSING

Serves 4 (side dish)
Active time: 25 min   Start to finish: 30 min

½ cup green (hulled) pumpkin seeds (not
  roasted; 2¼ oz) or pine nuts (2½ oz)
1 small garlic clove, minced
¼ cup extra-virgin olive oil
¼ cup water
1½ tablespoons fresh lemon juice
½ teaspoon ground cumin
½ teaspoon salt
2 tablespoons finely chopped fresh cilantro
¾ lb green beans (preferably *haricots verts*)
2 small tomatoes (½ lb total), halved, seeded,
  and cut lengthwise into ¼-inch-wide strips

Toast pumpkin seeds in a dry small heavy skillet over moderately low heat, stirring frequently, until puffed but not browned, about 6 minutes. (If using pine nuts, toast until pale golden, about 7 minutes.) Transfer to a plate to cool. Reserve 1 tablespoon seeds, then purée remaining seeds in a blender with garlic, oil, water, lemon juice, cumin, salt, and 1 tablespoon cilantro until smooth.

Cook beans in a large pot of boiling salted water (see Tips, page 8) until just tender, 4 to 6 minutes. Drain in a colander, then plunge into a bowl of ice and cold water to stop cooking. Drain beans and pat dry.

Arrange beans on a plate and drizzle with two thirds of dressing. Top with tomatoes and remaining dressing, then sprinkle with remaining tablespoon cilantro and reserved pumpkin seeds.

SPICY SAVOY SLAW

Makes about 6 cups
Active time: 20 min   Start to finish: 50 min

 5 tablespoons seasoned rice vinegar
 1 tablespoon sugar
 ½ teaspoon salt
 1 to 2 teaspoons minced fresh *serrano* chile
   (including seeds)
 1 teaspoon finely grated peeled fresh ginger
 1½ teaspoons Asian sesame oil
 1½ lb Savoy cabbage, thinly sliced (6 cups)
 ¼ lb snow peas, trimmed and very thinly
   sliced lengthwise (1 cup)
 ¼ red bell pepper, cut into thin matchsticks

  Whisk together vinegar, sugar, and salt in a large
bowl until sugar and salt are dissolved, then whisk
in chile, ginger, and sesame oil. Add remaining ingredients and toss well. Let stand, uncovered, at room
temperature, tossing occasionally, until wilted, about
30 minutes.

RED AND GREEN CABBAGE SLAW
WITH CARAWAY

Makes about 6 cups
Active time: 15 min   Start to finish: 1¼ hr

 ¼ cup cider vinegar
 1 tablespoon sugar
 1 teaspoon salt
 1½ tablespoons olive oil
 ¾ teaspoon caraway seeds, coarsely crushed
 ¼ teaspoon black pepper
 1 lb red cabbage, cored and thinly sliced
   (4 cups)
 1 lb green cabbage, cored and thinly sliced
   (4 cups)
 1 tart apple

  Whisk together vinegar, sugar, and salt in a large
bowl until sugar and salt are dissolved, then whisk in
oil, caraway, and pepper. Add cabbages and toss well.
Let stand, uncovered, at room temperature, tossing
occasionally, until wilted, about 1 hour.
  Core apple, then cut into thin matchsticks and toss
with slaw.

FIG AND CARROT SLAW

Makes about 3 cups
Active time: 20 min   Start to finish: 50 min

 3 tablespoons fresh lemon juice
 2 tablespoons sugar
 ½ teaspoon salt
 ¼ teaspoon ground cumin
 ⅛ teaspoon cayenne
 1 lb carrots, cut into julienne strips
   (4 cups)
 ½ cup thinly sliced soft dried Mission
   figs (6)

  Whisk together lemon juice, sugar, salt, cumin,
and cayenne in a large bowl until sugar and salt are
dissolved. Add carrots and figs and toss well. Let stand,
uncovered, at room temperature, tossing occasionally,
until carrots are wilted, about 30 minutes.

JICAMA SLAW

Serves 8
Active time: 30 min   Start to finish: 30 min

 1 medium red onion, finely chopped
   (¾ cup)
 1¼ teaspoons salt
 2½ tablespoons fresh lime juice
 ⅓ cup extra-virgin olive oil
 1 teaspoon sugar
 ¼ teaspoon black pepper
 2½ lb jicama, peeled and cut into julienne
   strips (9 to 10 cups)
 ⅓ cup finely chopped fresh cilantro

  Soak onion in 1 cup cold water with ½ teaspoon
salt 15 minutes (to make onion flavor milder). Drain in
a medium-mesh sieve, then rinse under cold water and
pat dry.
  Whisk together lime juice, oil, sugar, pepper, and
remaining ¾ teaspoon salt in a large bowl until combined well. Add onion, jicama, cilantro, and salt to taste
and toss well.

  Cooks' note:
• **Jicama can be cut into julienne strips 6 hours ahead
  and chilled, covered.**
  PHOTO ON PAGE 67

pasta and grain salads

SOBA SALAD

Serves 6
Active time: 45 min   Start to finish: 55 min

6 oz *soba* (Japanese buckwheat noodles)
1 teaspoon Asian sesame oil
1 medium red bell pepper, cut lengthwise
   into thin strips
½ seedless cucumber (usually plastic-wrapped;
   8 oz), cored and cut into ⅛-inch-thick
   matchsticks
½ lb jicama, peeled and cut into
   ⅛-inch-thick matchsticks
2 oz *mizuna* or chopped trimmed baby
   mustard greens (2 cups)
4 scallions, cut into 3-inch-long julienne strips
1 tablespoon seasoned rice vinegar
¼ teaspoon salt

Bring 4 quarts salted water (see Tips, page 8) to a
rolling boil in a 5- to 6-quart pot over moderately high
heat. Stir in noodles and ½ cup cold water. When water
returns to a boil, add another ½ cup cold water and
bring to a boil again, then repeat procedure once more.
Test noodles for doneness (*soba* should be just tender
but still firm and chewy throughout). Drain noodles in a
colander and rinse well under cold water, then drain
again, thoroughly. Toss noodles with sesame oil in a
large bowl.

Toss together remaining ingredients in another
bowl, then add to noodles and toss again to combine.

Each serving about 122 calories and 1 gram fat

GINGERED NOODLE SALAD
WITH MANGO AND CUCUMBER

Serves 6
Active time: 15 min   Start to finish: 30 min

*Bean thread noodles (also known as cellophane
noodles) come in varying widths. For this recipe
we like the wider (¼-inch) noodles.*

For vinaigrette
   6 tablespoons seasoned rice vinegar
   1½ tablespoons vegetable oil
   1½ teaspoons chopped peeled fresh ginger
   1 teaspoon minced fresh jalapeño chile
      (including seeds) or to taste
   1 garlic clove, chopped
For noodles
   8 oz bean thread (cellophane) noodles
   1 seedless cucumber (usually plastic-
      wrapped), halved lengthwise and thinly
      sliced diagonally
   1 bunch scallions, thinly sliced diagonally
      (1 cup)
   1 firm-ripe mango, peeled, pitted, and thinly
      sliced
   2 thin carrots, very thinly sliced diagonally
   1 cup loosely packed fresh cilantro sprigs

Make vinaigrette:
Blend all vinaigrette ingredients in a blender
until smooth.
   Prepare noodles:
Soak noodles in cold water in a bowl until pliable,
about 15 minutes, then drain in a colander. Cut noodles
in half with scissors.

Cook noodles in a 4-quart pot of boiling salted
water (see Tips, page 8), stirring occasionally, until just
tender, about 2 minutes. Drain noodles in colander and
rinse under cold water to stop cooking. Drain noodles
again well, then spread out on paper towels and blot
excess liquid.

Toss noodles with dressing in a bowl. Add cucumber, scallions, mango, and carrots and gently toss until
just combined. Serve topped with cilantro sprigs.

Each serving about 240 calories and 4 grams fat
PHOTO ON PAGE 108

SUSHI-ROLL RICE SALAD

Serves 4
Active time: 40 min   Start to finish: 1½ hr

1½ cups short-grain sushi rice
1¾ cups plus 1½ tablespoons water
¼ cup seasoned rice vinegar
1 tablespoon sugar
1 teaspoon salt
1 medium carrot
1¼ teaspoons wasabi paste (Japanese
   horseradish paste)
1½ tablespoons vegetable oil
½ large seedless cucumber (usually plastic-
   wrapped), peeled, halved lengthwise,
   cored, and chopped (1 cup)
3 scallions, thinly sliced diagonally
3 tablespoons drained sliced Japanese pickled
   ginger, coarsely chopped
1 tablespoon sesame seeds, toasted
   (see Tips, page 8)
1 firm-ripe California avocado
8 fresh *shiso* leaves (optional)
1 (6-inch) square toasted nori (dried laver),
   cut into very thin strips with scissors

Rinse rice in several changes of cold water in a bowl until water is almost clear, then drain in a colander 30 minutes.

Bring rice and 1¾ cups water to a boil in a 3- to 4-quart heavy saucepan, then simmer, covered, 2 minutes. Remove from heat and let rice stand, covered, 10 minutes (do not lift lid).

While rice is standing, bring vinegar, sugar, and salt just to a boil in a very small saucepan, stirring constantly until sugar is dissolved, then cool 2 minutes.

Spread rice in a large baking pan, then sprinkle with vinegar mixture and toss with a wooden spoon.

Shave thin lengthwise slices from carrot with a vegetable peeler, then cut slices diagonally into ¼-inch-wide strips.

Whisk together wasabi, remaining 1½ tablespoons water, and oil in a bowl, then add rice, carrot, cucumber, scallions, pickled ginger, and sesame seeds and toss gently.

Halve, pit, and peel avocado and cut crosswise into ¼-inch-thick slices. Arrange 2 *shiso* leaves (if using) on each of 4 plates. Top with avocado and rice mixture and sprinkle with nori strips.

PHOTO ON PAGE 81

LEBANESE TABBOULEH

Serves 4 to 6 (side dish)
Active time: 40 min   Start to finish: 40 min

Fine bulgur might seem like a specialty ingredient, but it is actually in most supermarkets under the name Near East Taboule Wheat Salad Mix—just toss away the seasoning packet.

½ cup fine bulgur
3 tablespoons olive oil
1 cup boiling-hot water
2 cups finely chopped fresh flat-leaf parsley
   (from 3 bunches)
½ cup finely chopped fresh mint
2 medium tomatoes, cut into ¼-inch pieces
½ seedless cucumber (usually plastic-
   wrapped), peeled, cored, and cut into
   ¼-inch pieces
3 tablespoons fresh lemon juice
¾ teaspoon salt
¼ teaspoon black pepper

Stir together bulgur and 1 tablespoon oil in a heat-proof bowl. Pour boiling water over, then cover bowl tightly with plastic wrap and let stand 15 minutes. Drain in a medium-mesh sieve, pressing on bulgur to remove any excess liquid.

Transfer bulgur to a bowl and toss with remaining 2 tablespoons oil and remaining ingredients until combined well.

creamy basil
dressing

salad dressings

CREAMY BASIL DRESSING

Makes about ½ cup
Active time: 10 min   Start to finish: 10 min

 1 cup loosely packed fresh basil
1½ tablespoons chopped shallot
 2 tablespoons balsamic vinegar
 ¾ teaspoon salt
 ¼ teaspoon black pepper
 2 tablespoons mayonnaise
 6 tablespoons extra-virgin olive oil

Blend all ingredients in a blender until smooth.

Cooks' note:
• **Dressing keeps, covered and chilled, 1 day.**

LIME MOLASSES VINAIGRETTE

Serves 4
Active time: 15 min   Start to finish: 15 min

 2 tablespoons fresh lime juice
 4 teaspoons mild molasses
 ¼ teaspoon Tabasco
 ½ teaspoon salt
 3 tablespoons olive oil
 1 scallion, finely chopped
 ¼ teaspoon ground cumin
   Pinch of ground allspice

Whisk together lime juice, molasses, Tabasco, and salt in a bowl.

Heat oil with scallion, cumin, and allspice in a small skillet over moderate heat until sizzling, then add to lime mixture in a slow stream, whisking until emulsified.

SAUCES AND CONDIMENTS

sauces

PLUM BARBECUE SAUCE

Makes about 1½ cups
Active time: 10 min   Start to finish: 1 hr

1 small onion, finely chopped
1 tablespoon vegetable oil
1 lb black plums (4), pitted and
   coarsely chopped
1¼ cups water
¼ cup plum jam
2 teaspoons balsamic vinegar
2 teaspoons Dijon mustard
¼ teaspoon black pepper
¼ teaspoon salt

Cook onion in oil in a 3- to 4-quart heavy saucepan over moderate heat, stirring occasionally, until golden, about 5 minutes. Stir in remaining ingredients and simmer, uncovered, stirring more frequently toward end of cooking, until plums fall apart and sauce is thickened, about 1 hour. Cool to room temperature.

Serve with pork or chicken.

COFFEE BOURBON BARBECUE SAUCE

Makes about 1 cup
Active time: 5 min   Start to finish: 15 min

1 cup strong brewed coffee
½ cup bourbon
½ cup packed light brown sugar
½ cup soy sauce
2 tablespoons cider vinegar
1 teaspoon Worcestershire sauce

Simmer all ingredients in a 2½- to 3-quart heavy saucepan, uncovered, stirring occasionally, until reduced to about 1 cup, 15 to 20 minutes (sauce will be thin). Cool to room temperature.

Serve with steak or chicken.

ASIAN BARBECUE SAUCE

Makes about 1 cup
Active time: 15 min   Start to finish: 15 min

6 tablespoons hoisin sauce
2 tablespoons rice vinegar (not seasoned)
1 tablespoon Asian fish sauce
1 tablespoon soy sauce
1 tablespoon honey
⅓ cup minced shallot
2 garlic cloves, minced
1 tablespoon minced peeled fresh ginger
⅛ teaspoon Chinese five-spice powder
⅓ cup sugar

Stir together all ingredients except sugar in a bowl.

Cook sugar in a dry heavy saucepan over moderate heat, undisturbed, until it begins to melt. Continue to cook, stirring occasionally with a fork, until sugar is melted into a deep golden caramel. Tilt pan and carefully pour in hoisin mixture (caramel will harden and steam vigorously). Cook over moderately low heat, stirring, until caramel is dissolved and sauce is thickened, 6 to 8 minutes. Cool to room temperature.

Serve with shrimp, swordfish, pork, or chicken.

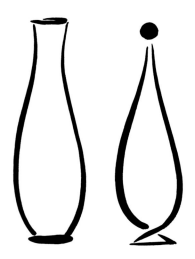

ROASTED PEPPER AND MAPLE BARBECUE SAUCE

Makes about ¾ cup
Active time: 5 min   Start to finish: 15 min

1 cup coarsely chopped drained bottled
    roasted red peppers (6 oz)
⅓ cup pure maple syrup
1 tablespoon cider vinegar
1 teaspoon chopped canned *chipotle* chiles
    in *adobo* plus 1 teaspoon *adobo* sauce
    (from can), or ½ teaspoon cayenne
½ teaspoon salt

Purée all ingredients in a blender until smooth, then simmer in a small heavy saucepan, stirring occasionally, until reduced to about ¾ cup, 8 to 10 minutes. Cool to room temperature.

Serve with shrimp or chicken.

condiments

BASIL LIME SYRUP

Makes about 1 cup
Active time: 10 min   Start to finish: 30 min

¾ cup sugar
    Zest of 1 lime, removed in strips
    with a vegetable peeler
½ cup fresh lime juice
¼ cup water
1 cup loosely packed fresh basil

Bring sugar, zest, juice, and water to a boil, stirring until sugar is dissolved. Remove from heat and let syrup stand, uncovered, 15 minutes.

Discard zest and transfer syrup to a blender. Add basil and blend 20 seconds. Pour through a fine-mesh sieve lined with a rinsed and squeezed paper towel into a bowl or glass measuring cup, then cool.

Cooks' notes:
• Use syrup in fruit salads or to flavor drinks.
• For a basil lime spritzer: Pour 2 tablespoons syrup
  into an ice-filled tall glass and top off with sparkling
  water. Stir, then garnish with a basil sprig.
• Syrup keeps, covered and chilled, 2 days.

KUMQUAT AND CRANBERRY COMPOTE

Serves 8 to 10 (condiment)
Active time: 20 min   Start to finish: 1½ hr

If you can't find kumquats, don't panic—the recipe works fine without them.

2 (12-oz) bags cranberries, thawed if frozen
9 oz kumquats, trimmed and quartered
    lengthwise (1½ cups)
1 cup water
1¼ cups sugar
2 tablespoons finely chopped peeled
    fresh ginger
2 whole star anise
¼ teaspoon salt

Stir together all ingredients in a 4-quart heavy saucepan and simmer, uncovered, stirring occasionally, until berries have burst, 10 to 12 minutes. Remove star anise and cool completely.

Cooks' note:
• Compote can be made 1 week ahead and chilled,
  covered.
PHOTO ON PAGE 100

SPICY CRANBERRY RELISH

Makes about 2½ cups
Active time: 10 min   Start to finish: 2¼ hr

1 lime
1 (12-oz) bag fresh cranberries (3 cups)
1 medium red onion, chopped
½ cup sugar
1 to 2 teaspoons minced fresh *serrano* chile
    (including seeds)

Finely grate 1 teaspoon zest from lime, then squeeze enough juice to measure 2 tablespoons.

Pulse cranberries with zest, juice, onion, sugar, and chile (to taste) in a food processor until finely chopped.

Chill relish, covered, stirring occasionally, at least 2 hours (to allow flavors to develop).

Cooks' note:
• Relish can chill up to 1 week.

ROASTED-BEET AND APPLE RELISH

Makes about 4 cups
Active time: 25 min   Start to finish: 4 hr

3 medium beets (1 lb total with greens),
    trimmed, leaving 1 inch of stems attached
⅓ cup cider vinegar
2 tablespoons sugar
½ teaspoon salt
¼ teaspoon black pepper
2 Granny Smith apples (1 lb total)
2 tablespoons drained bottled horseradish

Preheat oven to 425°F.

Tightly wrap beets in a double layer of foil and roast on a baking sheet in middle of oven until very tender, 1¼ to 1½ hours. Cool in foil package until warm (the steam makes beets easier to peel), about 20 minutes.

While beets are roasting, stir together vinegar, sugar, salt, and pepper in a large bowl until sugar and salt are dissolved. Cut apples into ¼-inch dice, then add to dressing with horseradish and toss well.

When beets are cool enough to handle, slip off skins and remove stems. Cut beets into ¼-inch dice and stir into apple mixture.

Chill relish, covered, stirring occasionally, at least 2 hours (to allow flavors to develop).

Cooks' note:
• Relish can be chilled up to 3 days.

PAPAYA SALSA

Makes about 4½ cups
Active time: 20 min   Start to finish: 20 min

2 lb papaya (2; preferably pink-fleshed
    strawberry variety), peeled, seeded,
    and cut into ¼-inch dice
1½ cups diced (¼ inch) fresh pineapple
    (from ½ small pineapple)
2 scallions, finely chopped
1 small garlic clove, minced
2 tablespoons fresh lime juice
½ teaspoon salt
¼ teaspoon black pepper

Stir together all ingredients.

BELL PEPPER AND DRIED APRICOT CHUTNEY

Makes about 2½ cups
Active time: 15 min   Start to finish: 3¼ hr

1 medium onion, chopped
1 red or orange bell pepper, cut into
    ½-inch pieces
1 cup dried apricots (6 oz), quartered
½ cup water
¾ cup cider vinegar
¼ cup plus 1 tablespoon sugar
1½ teaspoons curry powder (preferably
    Madras)
¼ teaspoon salt

Bring all ingredients to a boil in a nonreactive 2-quart saucepan, stirring occasionally. Reduce heat and simmer, covered, until chutney is thickened but still saucy, about 50 minutes. Cool chutney, uncovered, then chill, covered, stirring occasionally, at least 2 hours (to allow flavors to develop).

Cooks' note:
• Chutney can chill up to 1 week.

TOMATILLO SALSA

Makes about 3 cups
Active time: 20 min   Start to finish: 1¼ hr

This salsa goes well with the Cheddar shortcakes with corned beef hash (page 172).

1 lb fresh tomatillos, husked, rinsed,
    and chopped
1 fresh *serrano* chile, seeded (for less
    spiciness) and finely chopped
½ cup finely chopped white onion
1 garlic clove, minced
½ cup finely chopped fresh cilantro
1½ tablespoons fresh lime juice
1 teaspoon salt

Stir together all ingredients and let stand, covered, about 1 hour.

Cooks' note:
• Salsa can be made 1 day ahead and chilled, covered.

PINEAPPLE HABANERO SALSA

Makes about 2 cups
Active time: 25 min   Start to finish: 1 hr

For this salsa, we prefer the tang of a regular pineapple—not too ripe and not "extra sweet."

½ pineapple, peeled (reserving rind), cored, and coarsely chopped (2 cups)
2 tablespoons fresh pineapple juice, squeezed from reserved rind with your hands
2 tablespoons fresh lime juice
1 tablespoon molasses (not robust)
3 scallions, finely chopped
¼ to ½ teaspoon minced seeded *habanero* or Scotch bonnet chile
1 teaspoon chopped fresh thyme
¾ teaspoon salt
¼ teaspoon ground allspice

Toss all ingredients together in a bowl and let stand, stirring occasionally, 30 minutes, to allow flavors to blend.

Cooks' note:
• Salsa can be made 1 day ahead and chilled, covered. Bring to room temperature before serving.

SPICY PICKLED PLUMS

Serves 8 (condiment)
Active time: 20 min   Start to finish: 1 day (includes chilling)

These plums nicely complement pork or lamb chops. You can slip off the skins before eating if you like.

2 lb firm-ripe red or black plums
2 cups water
2½ cups sugar
1¾ cups red-wine vinegar
3 dried *chiles de árbol*
3 whole star anise
3 (1-inch) dried long peppers, or 1 (3-inch) piece peeled fresh ginger cut crosswise into ½-inch-thick slices

Slit skin of each plum lengthwise from top to bottom with a sharp paring knife evenly around plum in 4 to 6 places, then put in a heatproof jar.

Bring water to a boil with remaining ingredients in a 3-quart nonreactive saucepan, stirring until sugar is dissolved, then simmer, uncovered, stirring occasionally, 15 minutes.

Immediately pour pickling liquid over plums. Cool, uncovered, then chill, covered, at least 1 day.

Cooks' note:
• Pickled plums keep, chilled, 1 month.

BUTTERNUT SQUASH AND GINGER RELISH

Makes about 4 cups
Active time: 20 min   Start to finish: 2½ hr

½ cup unseasoned rice vinegar
¼ cup sugar
½ teaspoon salt
1 teaspoon finely grated peeled fresh ginger
¼ teaspoon cayenne
2 lb butternut squash, peeled, seeded, and coarsely shredded (5 cups)
1 bunch scallions, finely chopped (⅔ cup)

Stir together vinegar, sugar, and salt in a large bowl until sugar and salt are dissolved, then add remaining ingredients and toss well. Chill relish, covered, tossing occasionally, at least 2 hours (to allow flavors to develop).

Cooks' note:
• Relish can chill up to 2 days.

FRESH TOMATO AND ONION CHUTNEY

Serves 4 (makes about 1¼ cups)
Active time: 20 min   Start to finish: 1½ hr

1 small onion, finely chopped
1 teaspoon fine sea salt
½ lb tomatoes, chopped (1 cup)
4 teaspoons minced fresh jalapeño chile
   (including seeds)
1½ tablespoons fresh lemon juice
1 tablespoon fresh orange juice
1 teaspoon finely grated peeled fresh ginger
½ teaspoon mustard seeds
¼ teaspoon turmeric
1½ tablespoons olive oil
¼ teaspoon black pepper

Soak onion with ½ teaspoon sea salt in 1 cup cold water 15 minutes, then drain well in a medium-mesh sieve. Transfer to a bowl and stir in tomatoes, jalapeño, lemon juice, and orange juice.

Cook ginger, mustard seeds, and turmeric in oil in a small skillet over moderately low heat, stirring, until seeds begin to pop, about 2 minutes. Stir into tomatoes with pepper and remaining ½ teaspoon sea salt, then let stand at least 1 hour for flavors to develop.

Just before serving, drain chutney in sieve set over a bowl, discarding liquid.

Cooks' note:
• Chutney can be made 1 day ahead and chilled, covered. Bring to room temperature before serving.
PHOTO ON PAGE 96

dessert sauces

CARAMEL AND SCOTCH SAUCE

Makes about 1¼ cups
Active time: 30 min   Start to finish: 35 min

1 cup sugar
½ cup boiling-hot water
¼ cup Scotch

Cook sugar in a dry 2-quart heavy saucepan over moderately low heat, stirring slowly with a fork until sugar is melted and pale golden. Cook caramel, without stirring, until deep golden, then remove pan from heat.

Carefully add boiling water and Scotch (mixture will bubble up and vigorously steam), then cook over low heat, stirring with a wooden spoon, until caramel is melted and sauce is smooth. Serve warm.

Cooks' note:
• Sauce can be made 2 days ahead and chilled, covered. Reheat before serving.

HOT FUDGE SAUCE

Makes about 1½ cups
Active time: 5 min   Start to finish: 5 min

1 stick (½ cup) unsalted butter
1 cup semisweet chocolate chips (6 oz)
½ cup light corn syrup
¼ teaspoon distilled white vinegar

Bring all ingredients to a boil with a pinch of salt in a 2-quart heavy saucepan over moderately high heat, whisking until smooth.

DESSERTS

cakes

KEY LIME CHEESECAKE WITH MANGO RIBBONS

Serves 8 to 10

Active time: 1 hr   Start to finish: 8 hr (includes cooling)

If you can't find fresh Key limes in your area, you can substitute bottled Key lime juice. We've tried several different kinds in our test kitchen, and the only one we like so far is Manhattan brand.

For crust
  1¼ **cups fine graham cracker crumbs (5 oz)**
  3 **tablespoons sugar**
  ½ **stick (¼ cup) unsalted butter, melted**
For filling
  2 **(8-oz) packages cream cheese at room temperature**
  1 **cup plus 2 tablespoons sugar**
  ¾ **cup fresh Key lime juice (strained from about 1½ lb Key limes) or bottled**
  ½ **cup sour cream**
  ½ **teaspoon vanilla**
  2½ **tablespoons all-purpose flour**
  ¼ **teaspoon salt**
  3 **large eggs**
For topping
  2 **large firm-ripe mangoes**
  1 **tablespoon fresh Key lime juice (strained) or bottled**
  ½ **cup chilled heavy cream**
  1 **tablespoon sugar**

Special equipment: **a 9- to 9½-inch springform pan; a Japanese Benriner or other adjustable-blade slicer**

Make crust:
  Preheat oven to 350°F and butter bottom and side of springform pan.
  Stir together crumbs, sugar, and butter in a bowl with a fork until combined well, then press evenly onto bottom and one third up side of pan. Bake crust in middle of oven 8 minutes and cool in pan on a rack.
  Make filling:
  Reduce oven temperature to 325°F.
  Beat cream cheese with an electric mixer at medium speed until fluffy, then beat in sugar. Add lime juice, sour cream, and vanilla and beat until smooth. Mix in flour and salt at low speed, scraping down side as needed, until just incorporated, then add eggs all at once and mix just until incorporated.
  Pour filling into crust and set springform pan in a shallow baking pan. Bake cake in middle of oven until set in center, 1 hour to 1 hour and 10 minutes. Cool completely in springform pan on rack. (Cake will continue to set as it cools.)
  Run a thin knife around edge of cake and remove side of pan. If desired, transfer cake with a large metal spatula to a serving plate.
  Make topping:
  Peel mangoes and, leaving fruit whole, slice very thinly lengthwise (slightly less than ⅛ inch thick) with slicer (use caution—peeled mango is slippery). Halve wide slices lengthwise. Gently toss mango slices with lime juice.
  Beat cream with sugar in a bowl with electric mixer until it just holds stiff peaks, then spread over top of cheesecake. Bending and curling mango slices, arrange them decoratively over cream.

  Cooks' note:
· **Cheesecake (without topping) can be made 1 day ahead and chilled, covered. If desired, bring to room temperature. Add topping just before serving.**
  PHOTO ON PAGE 67

BANANA BOSTON CREAM PIE

Serves 8
Active time: 1 hr   Start to finish: 2¼ hr

For cake layers
1¼ cups cake flour (not self-rising)
1 teaspoon baking soda
½ teaspoon baking powder
½ teaspoon salt
2 tablespoons unsalted butter, softened
½ cup sugar
2 large eggs, separated
1 teaspoon vanilla
¾ cup well-shaken low-fat buttermilk

For filling
2 large egg yolks
3 tablespoons sugar
2 tablespoons cornstarch
⅛ teaspoon salt
1 cup fat-free (skim) milk
1 teaspoon unsalted butter
½ teaspoon vanilla
1 firm-ripe banana

For chocolate glaze
½ cup evaporated skim milk
¼ cup sugar
1 tablespoon light corn syrup
1 oz semisweet chocolate, coarsely chopped
3 tablespoons unsweetened cocoa powder
    (not Dutch-process)
2½ tablespoons boiling-hot water
½ teaspoon vanilla

Special equipment: **a standing electric mixer**

Make cake layers:
Preheat oven to 350°F. Lightly butter 2 (8-inch) round cake pans and dust with flour, knocking out excess flour.

Sift together flour, baking soda, baking powder, and salt.

Beat together butter and sugar in standing mixer at high speed until lightened, about 5 minutes. Add yolks 1 at a time, beating well after each addition, then beat in vanilla. Reduce speed to low, then add half of flour mixture and mix until just blended. Add buttermilk, mixing until just combined, then add remaining flour mixture, mixing until smooth. Transfer batter to a large shallow bowl. Clean mixing bowl and beaters.

Beat whites with a pinch of salt in mixer until they just hold stiff peaks, then fold into batter gently but thoroughly.

Divide batter between pans, smoothing tops. Bake in middle of oven until cake is springy to the touch and a tester comes out clean, 15 to 20 minutes. (Layers will be about ¾ to 1 inch high.) Cool in pans on racks 5 minutes. Run a sharp thin knife around edges, then invert onto racks and cool completely.

Make custard for filling:
Whisk together yolks, sugar, cornstarch, salt, and 2 tablespoons milk in a bowl. Bring remaining milk to a boil in a 2-quart heavy saucepan and add to yolk mixture in a slow stream, whisking constantly. Pour custard into saucepan and bring to a boil over moderately low heat, whisking constantly, then boil, whisking constantly, 2 minutes. Remove from heat and whisk in butter and vanilla. Transfer custard to a bowl and chill, its surface covered with wax paper, until cold, about 2 hours.

Make glaze:
Stir together evaporated milk, sugar, and corn syrup in a small heavy saucepan and simmer, stirring constantly, until caramel-colored and slightly thickened, about 6 minutes (be careful not to burn). Remove from heat and add chopped chocolate, whisking until glaze is smooth.

Stir together cocoa, hot water, and vanilla in a small bowl, then stir into glaze. Chill, covered, until cool, about 15 minutes.

Assemble cake:
Place 1 cake layer, upside down, on a platter. Whisk custard until smooth and spread ⅔ cup over top of cake. Cut banana into ¼-inch-thick slices and arrange evenly over custard, then spread remaining custard over banana. Top with remaining cake layer, upside down. Pour chocolate glaze over top (some glaze may drip onto platter).

Cooks' notes:
• Cake, custard, and glaze can be made 1 day ahead and kept separately. Wrap cake layers well in plastic wrap and keep at room temperature.
• Cake can be assembled 2 hours ahead and chilled.

Each serving about 293 calories and 7 grams fat
PHOTO ON PAGE 44

STREUSEL SOUR CREAM COFFEECAKES

Serves 6
Active time: 30 min   Start to finish: 1½ hr

¾ cup granulated sugar
2½ cups all-purpose flour
½ teaspoon salt
1 cup packed light brown sugar
2 sticks (1 cup) cold unsalted butter, cut into ½-inch cubes
1 teaspoon cinnamon
1½ cups pecans (6 oz), toasted (see Tips, page 8) and chopped
1 cup sour cream
1 whole large egg
1 large egg yolk
1 teaspoon vanilla
1 teaspoon baking soda
1½ teaspoons finely grated fresh orange zest

Special equipment: **2 muffin tins, each with 12 (½-cup) muffin cups**

Preheat oven to 350°F.

Stir together granulated sugar, flour, salt, and ¾ cup brown sugar in a large bowl. Blend in 1½ sticks (¾ cup) butter with your fingertips or a pastry blender until mixture resembles coarse meal with some pea-size butter lumps. Transfer ¾ cup flour mixture to a bowl and blend in cinnamon, remaining ½ stick (¼ cup) butter, and remaining ¼ cup brown sugar with your fingertips or pastry blender until crumbly. Stir in pecans, then chill streusel topping 15 minutes.

Whisk together sour cream, whole egg, yolk, vanilla, baking soda, and zest, then stir into remaining flour mixture until just combined (batter will be stiff).

Divide batter among 18 well-buttered muffin cups (they'll be about two-thirds full; butter tops of tins as well). Sprinkle each with streusel topping, pressing it lightly into batter. Bake coffeecakes in middle of oven until golden brown and a toothpick inserted in center comes out clean, 20 to 25 minutes. Cool in pans on racks 30 minutes. Loosen cakes with a sharp small knife, then carefully remove cakes from pans.

Cooks' note:
• **Cakes can be made 1 day ahead, then cooled completely and kept in an airtight container at room temperature.**
PHOTO ON PAGE 49

CHOCOLATE CHIP ZUCCHINI CAKE

Serves 8 to 10
Active time: 20 min   Start to finish: 1¼ hr

2½ cups all-purpose flour plus additional for dusting
1 teaspoon baking soda
½ teaspoon baking powder
½ teaspoon salt
2 sticks (1 cup) unsalted butter, softened
1 cup packed light brown sugar
1 teaspoon vanilla
3 large eggs at room temperature
2 cups coarsely grated zucchini (8 oz)
1 cup semisweet chocolate chips
½ cup walnuts, toasted (see Tips, page 8) and chopped

Special equipment: **a 3-quart bundt or fleur-de-lis pan**

Preheat oven to 350°F. Butter bundt pan well and dust with some flour, knocking out excess.

Sift together 2½ cups flour, baking soda, baking powder, and salt into a bowl. Beat together butter and brown sugar in a large bowl with an electric mixer at high speed until pale and fluffy, about 3 minutes, then beat in vanilla. Reduce speed to medium and add eggs 1 at a time, beating well after each addition and scraping down side of bowl occasionally, then beat until very smooth and fluffy, about 2 minutes more.

Reduce speed to low and add all but ½ cup flour mixture, mixing until just combined.

Toss zucchini, chocolate chips, and walnuts with remaining ½ cup flour mixture and add to batter, then mix with a rubber spatula (batter will be thick).

Spoon batter into bundt pan, smoothing top. Bake in middle of oven, rotating pan halfway through baking, until side begins to pull away from pan and a tester comes out clean, 45 to 50 minutes total.

Cool cake in pan on a rack 30 minutes, then run a thin knife around outer and inner edges. Invert rack over pan, then invert cake onto rack. Cool completely.

Cooks' note:
• **Cake keeps 3 days in an airtight container at room temperature.**

CHOCOLATE CHESTNUT TORTE WITH CHOCOLATE COGNAC MOUSSE

Serves 8
Active time: 1¾ hr   Start to finish: 5 hr

For the torte in our photograph (page 105), we used 3 (8-inch) round cake pans and then trimmed each layer into a 7-inch round for a dramatically tall effect. Our recipe here skips the trimming and simply uses the 8-inch layers as they are.

We liked this particular recipe with Lindt or Ghirardelli bittersweet chocolate, which is around 50 percent cocoa solids. We tested the ganache with chocolate containing a higher percentage, and found the flavor too intense and the consistency less velvety.

For ganache filling and frosting
>   2 cups heavy cream
>   ½ stick (¼ cup) unsalted butter
>   16 oz fine-quality bittersweet chocolate (not unsweetened), finely chopped
>   6 marrons glacés (candied chestnuts), finely chopped

For cake layers
>   9 oz bottled whole shelled roasted chestnuts (1½ cups)
>   2 cups cake flour (not self-rising)
>   1½ teaspoons baking soda
>   ½ teaspoon salt
>   2 sticks (1 cup) unsalted butter, softened
>   1½ cups packed light brown sugar
>   4 large eggs
>   1 teaspoon vanilla
>   ¾ cup sour cream

For chocolate Cognac mousse
>   ¾ stick (6 tablespoons) unsalted butter, cut into pieces
>   8 oz fine-quality bittersweet chocolate (not unsweetened), finely chopped
>   5 tablespoons Cognac
>   ¾ cup chilled heavy cream
>   2 large egg whites
>   ¼ cup granulated sugar

Garnish: **caramelized chestnuts (recipe follows)**
Special equipment: **3 (8-inch) round cake pans; an 8-inch round of cardboard, covered with foil if not wax-coated**

Make ganache:
Bring cream and butter to a simmer in a 3- to 4-quart heavy saucepan, then reduce heat to low. Whisk in chocolate until smooth and remove from heat. Transfer ganache to a bowl and chill, covered, stirring every 30 minutes, until thickened but spreadable, about 2 hours. (If ganache becomes too stiff, let stand at room temperature until slightly softened.)

Make cake layers while ganache chills:
Preheat oven to 350°F. Butter cake pans and line bottom of each with a round of parchment or wax paper. Butter paper and dust pans with flour, knocking out excess flour.

Pulse chestnuts with flour, baking soda, and salt in a food processor until finely ground.

Beat butter and brown sugar in a large bowl with an electric mixer at medium-high speed until pale and fluffy, about 3 minutes in a standing mixer or about 6 minutes with a handheld. Add eggs 1 at a time, beating well after each addition, then beat in vanilla (mixture will look a little separated). Reduce speed to low and add flour mixture and sour cream alternately in 3 batches, beginning and ending with flour and mixing until just combined.

Divide batter evenly among pans and bake in middle of oven until pale golden and springy to the touch, about 30 minutes. Cool cakes in pans on racks, then invert onto racks and remove parchment.

Make mousse and assemble torte:
Melt butter and chocolate in a double boiler or a metal bowl set over a saucepan of barely simmering water, stirring until smooth, and stir in Cognac. Transfer to a bowl and chill, covered, stirring occasionally, until thickened to the consistency of softened butter, about 1 hour. (If mixture becomes too stiff, let stand at room temperature until softened.)

Beat cream in a bowl with cleaned beaters until it just holds soft peaks, then chill, covered, while beginning to assemble torte.

Put 1 cake layer on cardboard round on a rack set in a shallow baking pan (1 inch deep). Spread ½ cup ganache evenly over top of layer and sprinkle with all of chopped marrons glacés. Top marrons glacés with another ¼ cup ganache and cover with another cake layer.

Beat egg whites with a pinch of salt using cleaned beaters at medium-high speed until they just hold soft peaks. Add sugar and beat at high speed until whites just hold stiff peaks. Stir whipped cream into chocolate Cognac mixture, then stir in one third of whites to lighten. Fold in remaining whites gently but thoroughly.

Spoon mousse immediately onto cake layer (it sets quickly), spreading evenly, then top with third cake layer. Chill torte, covered, until mousse layer is firm, about 1 hour. Keep remaining ganache at a spreadable consistency at room temperature, chilling, covered, if it becomes too soft.

Glaze cake:

Reserve 1¼ cups ganache in a metal bowl, then spread remainder over top and side of torte to seal in crumbs. Chill until firm, about 1 hour.

Set bowl of reserved ganache over a saucepan of barely simmering water, stirring until ganache reaches a pourable consistency. Remove bowl from heat and cool 5 minutes. Pour ganache evenly over top of torte, making sure it coats all of side. Shake rack gently to smooth glaze (let excess drip into baking pan). Transfer cake on cardboard to a cake stand or plate using 2 large heavy metal spatulas and chill until set. Garnish just before serving.

Cooks' notes:
- Cake layers can be made 3 days ahead, cooled completely, then chilled, individually wrapped well in plastic wrap.
- Ganache can be made 3 days ahead and chilled, covered. Let stand at room temperature 2 to 3 hours to soften to a spreadable consistency.
- Torte can be assembled 2 days ahead and chilled, covered with a cake dome.
- The egg whites in this recipe are not cooked. If salmonella is a problem in your area, you can use reconstituted powdered egg whites such as Just Whites.

PHOTO ON PAGE 105

CARAMELIZED CHESTNUTS

Makes 10
Active time: 25 min   Start to finish: 1½ hr

10 bottled whole shelled roasted chestnuts (3 oz)
1 cup sugar

Preheat oven to 350°F.

Bake chestnuts on a baking sheet in middle of oven until slightly dried and a shade darker, about 30 minutes. Cool chestnuts completely on a rack.

Cook sugar in a dry 10- to 12-inch nonstick skillet over moderate heat, swirling and shaking skillet (to help sugar melt evenly), until caramel is deep golden.

Remove from heat, then prop skillet up against a ramekin or metal cookie cutter, tilting it just enough for caramel to pool. Add 1 chestnut to caramel and evenly coat by turning with 2 forks, then transfer with forks to a sheet of foil to cool. Coat remaining chestnuts in same manner. (If caramel starts to harden, melt over moderately low heat, stirring.) Once completely cooled, peel chestnuts from foil.

Cooks' note:
- Caramelized chestnuts can be made 8 hours ahead (they will "weep" if stored longer) and kept in an airtight container at cool room temperature.

CHOCOLATE RASPBERRY ICEBOX CAKE

Serves 1
Active time: 15 min   Start to finish: 4¼ hr (includes chilling)

⅓ cup chilled heavy cream
½ teaspoon sugar
⅛ teaspoon vanilla
5 chocolate wafers such as Nabisco Famous
⅓ cup fresh raspberries

Garnish: **grated bittersweet chocolate (not unsweetened)**

Beat chilled cream with sugar and vanilla in a small deep bowl with an electric mixer until it just holds stiff peaks.

Spread 1 heaping teaspoon cream onto each of 4 wafers. Arrange enough raspberries side by side (as close together as possible) on 1 cream-topped wafer to form an even layer. Stack 2 cream-topped wafers on a plate (cream sides up) and top with berry wafer, then carefully spread another teaspoon cream over berries. Top with last cream wafer and cover cream with remaining plain wafer. Frost top and sides of cake with remaining cream. Cover with an inverted bowl and chill at least 4 hours.

Serve cake with remaining berries.

Cooks' note:
- Cake can chill up to 1 day.

PHOTO ON PAGE 112

MOCHA CAKE WITH
MALTED SEMIFREDDO

Serves 4
Active time: 1½ hr   Start to finish: 10 hr (includes freezing)

For cake
>   4 teaspoons instant-espresso powder or
>   instant-coffee granules
>   3 tablespoons hot water
>   8 oz fine-quality bittersweet chocolate
>   (not unsweetened), chopped
>   6 large eggs, separated
>   ⅔ cup granulated sugar
>   ¼ teaspoon salt
>   2 tablespoons unsweetened Dutch-process
>   cocoa powder

For semifreddo
>   3 large eggs at room temperature for
>   30 minutes
>   ⅓ cup packed light brown sugar
>   ⅔ cup chilled heavy cream
>   ½ teaspoon vanilla
>   ⅓ cup malted milk powder

Garnish: **unsweetened Dutch-process cocoa
    powder and chocolate curls**
Special equipment: **an 8½- by 4½-inch metal loaf
    pan; an instant-read thermometer**

Make cake:

Preheat oven to 350°F. Oil a 15- by 10- by 1-inch baking pan and line bottom lengthwise with a large piece of wax paper, allowing a 2-inch overhang on each end.

Stir together espresso powder and hot water in a heavy saucepan until coffee is dissolved. Add chocolate and melt over low heat, stirring, until smooth. Remove from heat and cool to room temperature.

Beat together yolks, ⅓ cup sugar, and ⅛ teaspoon salt in a large bowl with a handheld electric mixer at moderately high speed until mixture is thick and pale, 5 to 7 minutes. Beat in melted chocolate.

Beat whites with remaining ⅛ teaspoon salt in another large bowl with cleaned beaters until they just hold soft peaks. Gradually add remaining ⅓ cup sugar and beat until whites just hold stiff peaks. Stir one third of whites into chocolate mixture to lighten, then fold in remaining whites gently but thoroughly.

Spread cake batter evenly in baking pan and bake in middle of oven until puffed and top is dry to the touch and springs back when gently pressed, 12 to 14 minutes. Cover cake with 2 layers of dampened paper towels and let stand in pan on a rack 3 minutes, then remove towels and cool completely. Loosen edges with a sharp knife.

Sift cocoa powder evenly over top of cake and overlap 2 layers of wax paper lengthwise over cake. Invert a baking sheet over cake, then invert cake onto it, gently peeling off wax paper now on top.

Lightly oil loaf pan and line with 2 (24-inch-long) crisscrossed sheets of plastic wrap, letting excess hang over all sides. Using outside of loaf pan as a stencil, cut a rectangle from cake to line bottom of pan. Cut another rectangle for top of cake. Cut 2 pieces of cake to line long sides of pan, then 2 more for short sides. Fit all cake pieces (except top piece) into pan, cocoa sides against pan, pressing gently to help adhere. Wrap top piece of cake in plastic wrap and cover cake in pan with plastic-wrap overhang, then freeze cake while making *semifreddo*.

Make semifreddo:

Beat together eggs and brown sugar in a metal bowl set over a saucepan of simmering water with electric mixer at medium speed until mixture registers 160°F on thermometer, 6 to 8 minutes. Remove bowl from heat and chill mixture until cool, 10 minutes.

Mix together cream, vanilla, and malted milk powder in a separate bowl at low speed with electric mixer until powder is dissolved, then increase speed to moderately high and beat until it just holds soft peaks. Stir one third of cream into egg mixture to lighten, then fold in remaining cream gently but thoroughly.

Assemble cake:

Spoon *semifreddo* into cake-lined pan, spreading evenly and smoothing top, and cover with top piece of cake. Freeze, covered with plastic-wrap overhang, until firm, at least 8 hours.

Before serving, let cake stand at room temperature 5 minutes. Unwrap plastic and invert cake onto a long platter, using plastic wrap to help pull cake from pan. Sift cocoa evenly over top to garnish, then top with chocolate curls and cut into ½-inch-thick slices. Serve immediately.

Cooks' note:
- **Assembled cake can be frozen in pan up to 2 days.**
PHOTO ON PAGE 87

UPSIDE-DOWN PEAR GINGERBREAD CAKE

Serves 6
Active time: 30 min   Start to finish: 1½ hr

For topping
2½ firm pears (preferably Bosc)
½ stick (¼ cup) unsalted butter
¾ cup packed light brown sugar
For cake
2½ cups all-purpose flour
1½ teaspoons baking soda
1 teaspoon ground cinnamon
1 teaspoon ground ginger
½ teaspoon ground cloves
¼ teaspoon salt
1 cup molasses (preferably mild)
1 cup boiling-hot water
1 stick (½ cup) unsalted butter, softened
½ cup packed light brown sugar
1 large egg, lightly beaten

Special equipment: **a well-seasoned 10-inch cast-iron skillet or a 12-inch deep nonstick skillet (handle wrapped with a double layer of foil if not ovenproof)**
Accompaniment: **vanilla ice cream**

Make topping:
Peel and core pears and cut each into 8 wedges.
Melt butter in skillet over moderate heat until foam subsides. Reduce heat to low, then sprinkle brown sugar over bottom of skillet and cook, undisturbed, 3 minutes (not all sugar will be melted). Arrange pears decoratively over sugar and cook, undisturbed, 2 minutes. Remove from heat.
Make cake:
Preheat oven to 350°F.
Whisk together flour, baking soda, cinnamon, ginger, cloves, and salt in a bowl. Whisk together molasses and boiling water in a small bowl. Beat together butter, brown sugar, and egg in a large bowl with an electric mixer at medium speed until creamy, about 2 minutes, then reduce speed to low and alternately mix in flour mixture and molasses in 3 batches until smooth.
Pour batter over topping in skillet, spreading evenly and being careful not to disturb pears. Bake in middle of oven until a tester comes out clean, 40 to 50 minutes. Cool cake in skillet on a rack 5 minutes. Run a thin knife around edge of skillet, then invert a large plate with a lip over skillet and, using pot holders to hold skillet and plate tightly together, invert cake onto plate. Replace any pears that stick to skillet. Serve warm or at room temperature.

PHOTO ON PAGE 50

NECTARINE CAKE SQUARES

Serves 6 to 8
Active time: 20 min   Start to finish: 1 hr

This is best eaten the day it's made.

1½ cups all-purpose flour
1½ teaspoons baking powder
½ teaspoon baking soda
¼ teaspoon salt
1 stick (½ cup) unsalted butter, softened
1 cup plus 3 tablespoons granulated sugar
1 teaspoon vanilla
¼ teaspoon almond extract
2 large eggs
½ cup sour cream
2 medium firm-ripe nectarines (14 to 16 oz), quartered lengthwise and pitted
1 tablespoon fresh lemon juice
2 teaspoons confectioners sugar for dusting

Preheat oven to 350°F. Butter and flour a 13- by 9- by 2-inch metal baking pan, knocking out excess flour.
Sift together flour, baking powder, baking soda, and salt into a small bowl. Beat together butter and 1 cup granulated sugar in a large bowl with an electric mixer at medium-high speed until pale and fluffy, about 2 minutes, then beat in vanilla and almond extract. Add eggs 1 at a time, mixing at low speed after each addition until just combined. Add flour mixture and sour cream alternately in 3 batches, mixing after each addition until just combined. Spread batter in pan, smoothing top.
Cut nectarines lengthwise into ⅛-inch slices and toss with lemon juice and remaining 3 tablespoons granulated sugar in a bowl. Arrange slices, overlapping slightly, in 4 crosswise rows over batter. Cover surface of cake with a piece of buttered wax paper (paper helps fruit glaze itself) and bake in middle of oven 15 minutes. Remove paper and bake until a tester comes out clean, 20 to 25 minutes more.
While cake is still warm, dust generously with confectioners sugar, then cool completely on a rack.

PHOTO ON PAGE 91

cookies and bars

COCONUT CRISPS

Makes 16 dessert crisps
Active time: 10 min   Start to finish: 15 min

1 tablespoon unsalted butter, melted
1 tablespoon vegetable oil
2 (17- by 12-inch) phyllo sheets, thawed
  if frozen, covered with 2 overlapping
  pieces of plastic wrap and then a damp
  kitchen towel
2 teaspoons sugar
⅓ cup sweetened flaked coconut

Preheat oven to 400°F.

Stir together butter and oil. Arrange 1 phyllo sheet on a work surface with a long side nearest you, keeping remaining sheet covered. Brush with some butter mixture and sprinkle all over with 1 teaspoon sugar. Top with remaining sheet of phyllo, then brush with remaining butter mixture and sprinkle with remaining teaspoon sugar.

Cut phyllo in half crosswise and stack. Cut stack into quarters and cut each quarter diagonally twice (in an X) to form 4 triangles (for a total of 16 triangles). Arrange triangles, spaced evenly, on 2 ungreased baking sheets and sprinkle with coconut. Bake in middle and lower third of oven, switching position of sheets halfway through baking, until golden and crisp, 5 to 6 minutes total.

Each (2-crisp) serving about 68 calories and 4 grams fat

OATMEAL COCONUT RASPBERRY BARS

Makes 24 bars
Active time: 20 min   Start to finish: 1¾ hr

1½ cups sweetened flaked coconut
1¼ cups all-purpose flour
 ¾ cup packed light brown sugar
 ¼ cup granulated sugar
 ½ teaspoon salt
1½ sticks (¾ cup) cold unsalted butter,
  cut into pieces
1½ cups old-fashioned oats
 ¾ cup seedless raspberry jam

Preheat oven to 375°F.

Spread ¾ cup coconut evenly on a baking sheet and toast in middle of oven, stirring once, until golden, about 8 minutes, then cool.

Blend together flour, sugars, and salt in a food processor, then add butter and blend until a dough begins to form. Transfer to a bowl and knead in oats and toasted coconut until combined well.

Reserve ¾ cup dough, then press remainder evenly into bottom of a buttered 13- by 9-inch metal baking pan and spread jam over it. Crumble reserved dough evenly over jam, then sprinkle with remaining ¾ cup (untoasted) coconut.

Bake in middle of oven until golden, 20 to 25 minutes, then cool completely in pan on a rack. Loosen from sides of pan with a sharp knife, then lift out in 1 piece and transfer to a cutting board.

Cut into 24 bars.

Cooks' note:
· Bars can be made 3 days ahead and kept in an airtight container at room temperature.
PHOTO ON PAGE 47

TINY CHOCOLATE CHIP COOKIES

Makes about 150 (1½-inch) cookies
Active time: 45 min   Start to finish: 45 min

1¼ sticks (10 tablespoons) unsalted butter,
  softened
⅔ cup packed light brown sugar
¾ teaspoon salt
½ teaspoon baking soda
1 large egg
½ teaspoon vanilla
1 cup all-purpose flour
1¼ cups semisweet chocolate chips (7½ oz)

Preheat oven to 400°F.

Beat together butter, sugar, salt, and baking soda in a large bowl with an electric mixer until fluffy, then beat in egg and vanilla. Add flour and mix at low speed until just combined. Fold in chocolate chips.

Drop barely rounded ½ teaspoons of dough about 1½ inches apart onto ungreased large baking sheets and bake in batches in middle of oven until golden brown, 6 to 7 minutes. Transfer cookies as baked to a rack to cool.

CHILE LIME TUILES

Makes about 24 cookies
Active time: 40 min   Start to finish: 2¼ hr

½ cup sugar
5 tablespoons unsalted butter, cut into pieces
3 tablespoons light corn syrup
⅓ cup all-purpose flour
¾ teaspoon *ancho* chile powder
2 teaspoons finely grated fresh lime zest
1 tablespoon fresh lime juice

Special equipment: **4 (12-inch-long) wooden spoons or 12- by ½-inch wooden dowels; parchment paper**

Bring sugar, butter, and corn syrup to a boil in a 1-quart heavy saucepan over moderate heat, stirring, then boil 1 minute. Remove from heat and stir in remaining ingredients until smooth. Cool dough to room temperature.

Preheat oven to 350°F. Place wooden spoons parallel to each other 2 inches apart on a metal rack.

Roll a level teaspoon of dough into a ball, then into a log. Arrange 3 logs about 3 inches apart on a parchment-lined baking sheet, then pinch and stretch each to form an 8- to 9-inch-long strip (about ⅛ inch wide).

Bake in middle of oven until flat and golden, 7 to 9 minutes. While first sheet is baking, form remaining strips on more sheets of parchment. Slide parchment paper with baked cookies from sheet to a rack and cool cookies 30 seconds. Working quickly, slide a long thin metal spatula under each cookie and drape across spoon handles to form a wavy shape. (If cookies harden on paper before being draped, slide them back onto hot baking sheet for a moment to soften.) Bake and drape remaining cookies in same manner.

Cooks' note:
• **Cookies keep in an airtight container at room temperature 1 week.**
PHOTO ON PAGE 97

VANILLA THINS

Makes about 30 cookies
Active time: 20 min   Start to finish: 1½ hr

½ **stick (¼ cup) unsalted butter, softened**
¼ **cup sugar**
⅛ **teaspoon salt**
1 **large egg**
½ **teaspoon vanilla**
¼ **cup plus 1 teaspoon all-purpose flour**

Preheat oven to 350°F.

Beat butter, sugar, and salt with an electric mixer at moderately high speed until pale and fluffy, about 2 minutes. Add egg and vanilla and mix at low speed until just combined. Add flour and mix until just combined.

Drop level teaspoons of batter about 3 inches apart on buttered baking sheets. Bake cookies in batches in middle of oven until just golden around edges, 6 to 8 minutes. Cool on baking sheet on a rack 1 minute, then transfer with a metal spatula to rack to cool completely.

Cooks' note:
• **Cookies can be made 3 days ahead and kept, layered between sheets of wax paper in an airtight container, at room temperature.**
PHOTO ON PAGE 83

confections

PANFORTE

Makes 1 (9-inch) cake
Active time: 40 min   Start to finish: 4 hr (includes cooling)

Panforte—a classic Italian Christmas treat—is a dense, rich confection loaded with nuts and dried fruit (hence its name, which means "strong bread"). This recipe yields a generous amount, but it keeps so well that you can enjoy the leftovers long after the holidays.

4 teaspoons unsweetened Dutch-process
    cocoa powder plus additional for dusting
⅔ cup all-purpose flour
1 teaspoon ground cinnamon
½ teaspoon ground ginger
⅛ teaspoon ground cloves
¼ teaspoon salt
1 cup whole almonds, toasted
    (see Tips, page 8)
1 cup whole hazelnuts, toasted
    (see Tips, page 8) and loose skins rubbed
    off with a kitchen towel
1 cup soft pitted prunes (dried plums; 8 oz),
    quartered
1 cup soft dried figs (preferably Mission;
    8 oz), each cut into 6 pieces
1 cup soft raisins (8 oz)
¾ cup sugar
⅔ cup honey

Special equipment: **a 9-inch springform pan; parchment paper; a candy thermometer**

Preheat oven to 300°F.

Line springform pan with parchment, using a round for bottom and a strip for side. Butter paper well and dust with cocoa powder, knocking out excess.

Whisk together flour, spices, salt, and 4 teaspoons cocoa in a large bowl, then stir in nuts and fruit.

Bring sugar and honey to a boil in a 2-quart heavy saucepan over moderate heat, stirring until sugar is dissolved, then boil without stirring until thermometer registers 238 to 240°F, about 2 minutes.

Immediately pour honey over fruit mixture and quickly stir until combined (mixture will be very thick and sticky). Quickly spoon mixture into springform pan, spreading evenly with back of spoon. Dampen your hands and press mixture firmly and evenly into pan to compact as much as possible. Bake in middle of oven until edges start to rise slightly and become matte, 50 to 55 minutes.

Cool panforte completely in pan on a rack, then remove side of pan and invert, peeling off paper. If making ahead, wrap panforte (see cooks' note, below). To serve, cut with a serrated knife into small pieces.

Cooks' note:
• **Panforte is best made at least 1 week ahead and chilled in a large sealed plastic bag. It can be made 1 month ahead and chilled, wrapped in parchment and then kept in a sealed plastic bag.**
PHOTO ON PAGE 107

CHOCOLATE EARL GREY TRUFFLES

Makes about 34 truffles
Active time: 45 min   Start to finish: 2¾ hr

⅔ cup heavy cream
2 tablespoons unsalted butter, cut into
    4 pieces and softened
2 teaspoons loose Earl Grey tea leaves
6 oz fine-quality bittersweet chocolate
    (not unsweetened), chopped
1 cup unsweetened Dutch-process
    cocoa powder

Bring cream and butter to a boil in a small heavy saucepan and stir in tea leaves. Remove from heat and let steep 5 minutes.

Meanwhile, finely grind chocolate in a food processor and transfer to a bowl. Pour cream through a fine-mesh sieve onto chocolate, pressing on and discarding tea leaves, then whisk until smooth. Chill ganache, covered, until firm, about 2 hours.

Spoon level teaspoons of ganache onto a baking sheet. Put cocoa in a bowl, then dust your palms lightly with it. Roll each piece of ganache into a ball (wash your hands and redust as they become sticky). Drop several balls at a time into bowl of cocoa and turn to coat. Transfer as coated to an airtight container, separating layers with wax paper.

Cooks' note:
• **Truffles can be made 1 week ahead and chilled, or 1 month ahead and frozen in an airtight container.**
PHOTO ON PAGE 107

MERINGUE PETITS FOURS WITH ANISE CREAM AND POMEGRANATE

Makes about 48 meringues
Active time: 30 min   Start to finish: 3½ hr

For meringues
> 2 large egg whites
> ⅛ teaspoon salt
> ½ cup superfine granulated sugar

For cream and topping
> 2 teaspoons regular granulated sugar
> ½ teaspoon anise seeds
> ½ cup chilled heavy cream
> ¼ cup pomegranate seeds

Special equipment: **a pastry bag fitted with ⅓-inch plain tip; parchment paper; an electric coffee/spice grinder**

Make meringues:
Preheat oven to 175°F.

Beat egg whites with salt using an electric mixer at high speed until they just hold stiff peaks. Add superfine granulated sugar a little at a time, beating at high speed, and continue to beat until whites hold stiff, glossy peaks.

Spoon meringue into pastry bag. Pipe 1¼-inch-wide disks (about ⅓ inch high) about ½ inch apart on a parchment-lined baking sheet.

Bake meringues in middle of oven until dry but still white, about 1½ hours, then cool in turned-off oven (with door closed) 1 hour. Transfer meringues on baking sheet to a rack to cool completely.

Whip cream and assemble petits fours:
Finely grind regular granulated sugar with anise in coffee/spice grinder. Beat cream in a bowl with cleaned beaters until it just holds soft peaks, then add anise sugar, beating until it just holds stiff peaks.

Peel meringues from parchment, then dollop 1 teaspoon cream onto each meringue and top with 3 pomegranate seeds.

Cooks' note:
• Baked meringues (without cream) and anise sugar can be made 1 week ahead and kept separately in airtight containers at room temperature.
• Meringues can be topped 30 minutes ahead and kept at cool room temperature.

NEW ORLEANS PRALINE PIECES

Makes 18 (2-inch) confections
Active time: 40 min   Start to finish: 1½ hr

Have your equipment meticulously clean—even a trace of oil can adversely affect texture. Watch carefully for visual cues to doneness, using our cooking times only as guidelines. Do the soft-ball test (see below), as well as taking the temperature of the syrup.

> ¾ cup granulated sugar
> ¾ cup packed light brown sugar
> ½ cup heavy cream
> 2 tablespoons unsalted butter, cut into bits
> ¼ teaspoon salt
> 1¼ cups pecan pieces (5 oz), toasted
>   (see Tips, page 8)

Special equipment: **a candy thermometer with a clamp**

Butter a 9-inch square metal baking pan.

Sift granulated sugar through a medium-mesh sieve into a bowl to remove any lumps or large crystals, then push brown sugar through sieve into bowl. Pour sugars into a 2½- to 3-quart heavy saucepan, being careful not to get sugar on side of pan.

Add cream, butter, and salt and cook over very low heat, stirring frequently with a wooden spoon and washing down any sugar crystals on side of pan with a pastry brush dipped in cold water, until sugar is dissolved, 10 to 15 minutes (do not let simmer).

Clamp on candy thermometer, then boil syrup over moderately high heat, undisturbed, until it registers 236°F and a teaspoon of syrup dropped into a small bowl of cold water holds a very soft ball when pressed between your fingers, 3 to 6 minutes.

Remove pan from heat, leaving thermometer in place, and cool, undisturbed, until syrup registers 220°F, 1 to 3 minutes. Stir syrup with cleaned and dried wooden spoon until thickened and creamy, 1 to 2 minutes, then immediately stir in pecans. Working very fast (syrup hardens quickly), pour into baking pan, scraping sides of saucepan with wooden spoon.

Let mixture harden at room temperature, about 45 minutes. Cut and break into pieces.

Cooks' note:
• Praline pieces keep, layers separated by wax paper, in an airtight container in a cool place 3 days.

pies and tarts

GRAPEFRUIT TART

Serves 6
Active time: 1½ hr   Start to finish: 3 hr   (includes making pastry)

Sweet pastry dough (recipe follows)
For filling
  4 grapefruit (preferably 2 pink and 2 red)
  8 oz mascarpone cheese at room temperature
  3 tablespoons finely chopped candied ginger
  4 tablespoons confectioners sugar

Special equipment: **a 9- to 10-inch round tart pan (1 inch deep) with removable bottom; pie weights or raw rice**

Roll out dough with a floured rolling pin into a 13-inch round on a floured surface and fit into tart pan (if pastry breaks, press together with your fingers). Trim excess dough, leaving a ½-inch overhang, then fold overhang inward and press against side of pan to reinforce edge. Lightly prick bottom of shell all over with a fork. Chill 30 minutes.

Preheat oven to 375°F.

Line shell with foil and fill with pie weights. Bake in middle of oven 10 minutes, then carefully remove foil and weights and bake shell until golden, 13 to 15 minutes more. Transfer shell in pan to a rack to cool.

Make filling just before serving:

Cut peel, including all white pith, from fruit with a sharp paring knife, then cut segments free from membranes and pat dry with paper towels. Squeeze 3 tablespoons juice from membranes into a bowl. Whisk together mascarpone, candied ginger, 2 tablespoons juice, and 2 tablespoons confectioners sugar. Add remaining tablespoon juice if mixture is too thick.

Spread ginger mascarpone evenly in tart shell and top decoratively with fruit. Dust with remaining 2 tablespoons confectioners sugar and serve immediately.

Cooks' note:
• **Tart shell can be made 1 day ahead and kept, loosely covered with plastic wrap, at room temperature.**

SWEET PASTRY DOUGH

Makes enough dough for a 9- to 10-inch tart
Active time: 30 min   Start to finish: 1½ hr

  1¼ cups all-purpose flour
  1½ tablespoons sugar
  ¼ teaspoon salt
  7 tablespoons cold unsalted butter, cut into bits
  1 large egg yolk
  ½ teaspoon vanilla
  ½ teaspoon fresh lemon juice
  2½ tablespoons cold water

Whisk together flour, sugar, and salt in a large bowl. Blend together flour and butter with your fingertips or a pastry blender until most of mixture resembles coarse meal with small (roughly pea-size) butter lumps. Beat together yolk, vanilla, lemon juice, and water with a fork and stir into flour with fork until combined well.

Gently knead with floured hands in bowl until a dough forms. Turn out dough onto a floured surface and gently knead 4 or 5 times.

Form dough into a ball, then flatten into a disk and chill, wrapped in plastic wrap, at least 1 hour.

Cooks' note:
• **Dough can be chilled up to 2 days.**

APRICOT RASPBERRY PIE

Serves 8
Active time: 40 min   Start to finish: 2¼ hr

  ¼ cup cornstarch
  ¼ teaspoon salt
  1¼ cups sugar
  Pastry dough (recipe follows)
  1½ lb firm-ripe apricots (8 large), cut into ½-inch-thick wedges
  1½ cups raspberries (7 oz)
  1 large egg, lightly beaten

Place a baking sheet in middle of oven and preheat oven to 450°F.

Whisk together cornstarch, salt, and 1 cup plus 2 tablespoons sugar in a large bowl.

Roll out 1 piece of dough (keep remaining piece chilled) on a lightly floured surface with a lightly floured rolling pin into a 13-inch round and fit into a

9-inch glass pie plate (4-cup capacity). Trim edge, leaving a ½-inch overhang. Chill shell while rolling out dough for top crust. Roll out remaining piece of dough into an 11-inch round.

Stir apricots into sugar mixture until combined, then gently stir in raspberries and spoon filling into pie shell.

Cover pie with pastry round and trim with kitchen shears, leaving a ½-inch overhang. Crimp edge decoratively. Brush top of pie with egg and sprinkle all over with remaining 2 tablespoons sugar. Cut 3 steam vents in top crust with a sharp small knife.

Bake pie on hot baking sheet 15 minutes. Reduce oven temperature to 375°F and continue to bake until crust is golden brown and filling is bubbling, about 45 minutes more. Cool pie on a rack at least 2 hours before serving.

Cooks' note:
- Pie can be made 1 day ahead and kept at room temperature.

PASTRY DOUGH

Makes enough for 1 double-crust 9-inch pie
Active time: 10 min   Start to finish: 1¼ hr

2½ cups all-purpose flour
1½ sticks (¾ cup) cold unsalted butter,
    cut into ½-inch cubes
¼ cup cold vegetable shortening
½ teaspoon salt
4 to 6 tablespoons ice water

Blend together flour, butter, shortening, and salt in a bowl with your fingertips or a pastry blender (or pulse in a food processor) until mixture resembles coarse meal with some small (roughly pea-size) butter lumps.

Drizzle 4 tablespoons ice water evenly over and gently stir with a fork (or pulse in a food processor) until incorporated.

Gently squeeze a small handful: If it doesn't hold together, add more water, 1 tablespoon at a time, stirring (or pulsing) after each addition until incorporated and continuing to test. (Do not overwork dough, or pastry will be tough.)

Turn out dough onto a work surface and divide into 4 portions. With heel of your hand, smear each portion once or twice in a forward motion to help distribute fat. Gather dough and form into 2 balls, then flatten each into a 5-inch disk. Wrap disks separately in plastic wrap and chill until firm, at least 1 hour.

Cooks' note:
- Dough can be chilled up to 1 day.

MAPLE BUTTERMILK PIE

Serves 6
Active time: 30 min   Start to finish: 3½ hr

1 (9-inch) baked pie shell (page 236)
2 cups well-shaken buttermilk
⅔ cup Grade B maple syrup
6 large egg yolks
¼ cup all-purpose flour
3 tablespoons maple sugar
1 teaspoon vanilla
¼ teaspoon salt

Accompaniment: **lightly sweetened whipped cream**

Preheat oven to 325°F. Put pie shell (in pie plate) in a shallow baking pan.

Whisk together remaining ingredients in a bowl until just combined, then pour three fourths of custard into shell. Carefully put pan in middle of oven and pour in remaining custard with a cup.

Bake until just set in center, about 55 minutes, then transfer pie to a rack to cool slightly. Serve warm or at room temperature.

Cooks' note:
- Pie can be made 4 to 6 hours ahead and kept at room temperature.
PHOTO ON PAGE 61

BAKED PIE SHELL

Makes 1 (9-inch) pie shell
Active time: 25 min   Start to finish: 2¾ hr

1¼ cups all-purpose flour
¾ stick (6 tablespoons) cold unsalted
    butter, cut into ½-inch cubes
2 tablespoons cold vegetable shortening
¼ teaspoon salt
3 to 4 tablespoons ice water

Special equipment: **a pastry or bench scraper; a
    9-inch glass or ceramic pie plate; pie
    weights or raw rice**

Blend together flour, butter, shortening, and salt in
a bowl with your fingertips or a pastry blender (or pulse
in a food processor) just until most of mixture resembles coarse meal with small (roughly pea-size) butter
lumps. Drizzle evenly with 3 tablespoons ice water and
gently stir with a fork (or pulse in food processor) until
incorporated.

Squeeze a small handful: If it doesn't hold together,
add more ice water, ½ tablespoon at a time, stirring (or
pulsing) until just incorporated, then test again. (Do not
overwork dough, or pastry will be tough.)

Turn out mixture onto a lightly floured surface and
divide into 4 portions. With heel of your hand, smear
each portion once or twice in a forward motion. Gather
dough together with pastry scraper and form into a ball,
then flatten into a 5-inch disk. Chill, wrapped in plastic
wrap, until firm, at least 1 hour.

Roll out dough with a floured rolling pin into a
12-inch round on a lightly floured surface and fit into
pie plate. Trim excess dough, leaving a ½-inch overhang, then fold overhang under pastry and press against
rim to reinforce edge. Decoratively crimp edge and
lightly prick bottom and side with a fork. Chill until
firm, about 30 minutes.

Preheat oven to 375°F.

Line chilled shell with foil and fill with pie
weights. Bake in middle of oven until pastry is pale
golden along rim and set underneath weights, about
20 minutes. Carefully remove foil and weights and
bake shell until pale golden all over, about 10 minutes
more. Cool completely in plate on a rack.

PECAN CRANBERRY TART

Serves 6 to 8
Active time: 45 min   Start to finish: 4 hr

1¼ cups pecans (5 oz), chopped
¾ cup sugar
¾ cup light corn syrup
2 tablespoons unsalted butter
3 large eggs
¼ teaspoon salt
1 teaspoon vanilla
1 cup fresh or frozen cranberries
    (not thawed; 3½ oz), chopped
1 baked (10-inch) tart shell (recipe follows)

Preheat oven to 350°F.

Lightly toast pecans in a shallow baking pan in
middle of oven until fragrant but not darker, about
5 minutes, then cool. Leave oven on.

Cook ½ cup sugar in a dry 2-quart heavy saucepan
over moderate heat, undisturbed, until it begins to melt.
Continue to cook, stirring occasionally with a fork (to
help sugar melt evenly), until sugar is melted into a
deep golden caramel. Tilt pan and carefully add corn
syrup (caramel will harden and steam vigorously).
Cook over moderately low heat, stirring, until caramel
is dissolved. Remove pan from heat and add butter,
stirring constantly until melted, then cool caramel
until it stops bubbling.

Whisk together eggs, salt, vanilla, and remaining
¼ cup sugar, then add caramel in a slow stream,
whisking constantly.

Spread pecans and cranberries evenly in tart shell
and pour caramel over them, tapping pecans and cranberries down to coat thoroughly. Bake tart in middle of
oven until filling is set, 30 to 35 minutes. Cool completely in pan on a rack before removing rim of pan.

TART SHELL

Makes enough dough for 1 (10-inch) tart shell
Active time: 25 min   Start to finish: 2¾ hr (includes chilling)

1¼ **cups all-purpose flour**
¾ **stick (6 tablespoons) cold unsalted butter,**
   cut into ½-inch cubes
2 **tablespoons cold vegetable shortening**
¼ **teaspoon salt**
2 **to 4 tablespoons ice water**

Special equipment: **a pastry or bench scraper;**
   a 10- by 1-inch round tart pan with
   a removable fluted rim; pie weights or
   raw rice

Blend together flour, butter, shortening, and salt in
a bowl with your fingertips or a pastry blender (or
pulse in a food processor) until mixture resembles
coarse meal with some small (roughly pea-size) butter
lumps. Drizzle evenly with 2 tablespoons ice water and
gently stir with a fork (or pulse in processor) until
incorporated.

Squeeze a small handful: If it doesn't hold together,
add more ice water, ½ tablespoon at a time, stirring (or
pulsing) until just incorporated, then test again. (Do not
overwork mixture, or pastry will be tough.)

Turn out mixture onto a lightly floured surface and
divide into 4 portions. With heel of your hand, smear
each portion once or twice in a forward motion. Gather
dough together with scraper and press into a ball, then
flatten into a 5-inch disk. Chill, wrapped in plastic
wrap, until firm, at least 1 hour.

Roll out dough with a floured rolling pin into a
14-inch round on a lightly floured surface, then fit into
tart pan. Trim excess dough, leaving a ½-inch overhang, then fold overhang inward and press against side
of pan to reinforce edge. Lightly prick bottom and sides
of shell with fork. Chill 30 minutes.

Preheat oven to 425°F.

Line shell with foil and fill with pie weights. Bake
in middle of oven until pastry is set and golden, about
12 minutes. Carefully remove foil and weights and
bake shell until golden all over, 5 to 10 minutes more.
Cool shell in pan on a rack.

Cooks' note:
• **Dough can be chilled up to 1 day.**

SOUR CHERRY STRUDELS

Serves 6
Active time: 30 min   Start to finish: 1½ hr

5 **cups fresh or frozen (not thawed) pitted**
   sour cherries (1½ lb)
¾ **cup plus 1½ teaspoons granulated sugar**
2½ **tablespoons cornstarch**
15 **(17- by 12-inch) phyllo sheets, thawed**
   if frozen
1 **stick (½ cup) unsalted butter, melted**

Garnish: **confectioners sugar**
Accompaniment: **vanilla ice cream or lightly**
   sweetened whipped cream

Bring cherries (with any juices), ¾ cup sugar, and
cornstarch to a boil in a 2½- to 3-quart heavy saucepan,
stirring occasionally, then simmer 2 minutes. Transfer
filling to a bowl and cool completely.

While cherry filling cools, arrange 3 phyllo sheets
in 1 layer on a work surface and let dry 15 minutes.
Keeping 12 remaining sheets stacked, halve crosswise,
then stack halves. Cover stack with a piece of plastic
wrap and a dampened kitchen towel. Finely crumble
3 dried phyllo sheets into a bowl.

Preheat oven to 400°F.

Arrange 1 piece of phyllo on work surface with a
short side nearest you (keep remaining sheets covered)
and brush with some butter. Top with 3 more phyllo
pieces, brushing each with butter.

Sprinkle 2 tablespoons crumbled phyllo over lower
third of buttered phyllo, leaving a 2-inch border along
bottom and sides, then top with a rounded ⅓ cup filling.
Fold bottom edge of phyllo up over filling and fold in
sides to enclose filling completely, then roll up phyllo
to form a strudel, about 4½ by 2½ inches. Transfer,
seam side down, to a buttered baking sheet. Brush top
with some butter, then sprinkle lightly with ¼ teaspoon
sugar. Cut 2 (1-inch) vents diagonally across top of
strudel, about 1½ inches apart, with a paring knife.
Make 5 more strudels in same manner.

Bake strudels in middle of oven until golden brown
and crisp, 20 to 25 minutes. Transfer to a rack and cool
30 minutes.

Cooks' notes:
• **Strudels can be baked 2 hours ahead and kept on rack**
  at room temperature.
• **Filling can be made 1 day ahead and chilled, covered.**

BERRY TART WITH GINGER CREAM

Serves 16 to 24
Active time: 1 hr   Start to finish: 2½ hr

Don't worry—you won't need a giant oven for this king-size tart. It's made in 4 quadrants, baked one at a time. And because the recipe uses packaged puff pastry, it's fairly simple to prepare.

2 large egg yolks
4 tablespoons water
4 (17¼-oz) packages frozen puff pastry
   sheets, thawed but kept chilled
2 (8-oz) packages cream cheese
½ cup granulated sugar
½ cup chopped crystallized ginger (4 oz)
2 pt strawberries (1 lb), hulled, then
   halved or quartered if large
¾ cup red currant jelly
4 pt blueberries (2½ lb)

Garnish: **confectioners sugar**
Special equipment: **parchment paper and a large flat board (at least 20 inches square) for serving**

Prepare and bake pastry in 4 quadrants:
Stir together yolks and 2 tablespoons water for egg wash. Put a baking sheet in freezer.

Unfold 1 pastry sheet on a 12-inch square of parchment and brush all over with egg wash. Prick entire surface evenly with a fork.

Unfold second pastry sheet on a cutting board. Cut out a 1¼-inch-wide right-angle strip along 2 adjacent edges with a sharp knife, reserving remaining square for another use. Place right angle on 1 corner on top of 2 adjacent edges of pricked pastry to form first quadrant of tart. Transfer pastry on parchment to baking sheet already in freezer and chill until firm, about 10 minutes.

Transfer pastry on parchment from freezer to cutting board and trim a ¼-inch-wide strip from all 4 edges using tip of small knife and a ruler and cutting all the way through pastry. Make ¼-inch-long vertical cuts through double layers of edge about ½ inch apart (to help sides rise evenly). Return pastry on parchment to baking sheet in freezer and chill until firm but not solid, about 10 minutes more.

Preheat oven to 450°F and heat another baking sheet on lowest rack in oven until hot, about 2 minutes.

Remove baking sheet from oven and transfer pastry on parchment from freezer to hot sheet. Bake pastry on lowest rack of oven until puffed and deep golden brown (a little darker than usual so double edges are cooked through), 14 to 16 minutes. Transfer pastry on parchment to a rack to cool.

Repeat procedure with remaining 3 packages puff pastry to make remaining 3 quadrants of tart.

Make ginger cream:
Blend cream cheese and granulated sugar in a food processor until sugar is dissolved and mixture is smooth. Add ginger and pulse until finely chopped and mixture is combined well.

Prepare fruit and assemble tart:
If very puffed, gently flatten inner parts of pastry (single layer) slightly with your palm. Fit quadrants together on flat board to form a giant square tart shell, trimming inside edges of each quadrant slightly with a serrated knife to help quadrants fit together smoothly. "Glue" inner edges together with a little ginger cream, then spread remaining ginger cream evenly over tart, leaving double edges as a border.

Arrange strawberries in a decorative pattern over cream. Bring jelly to a boil with remaining 2 tablespoons water, whisking until smooth, then simmer glaze 1 minute. Toss three fourths of glaze with blueberries in a large bowl and spoon blueberries onto tart to cover cream between strawberries, mounding slightly. Brush strawberries with remaining glaze.

Cooks' notes:
· All 4 quadrants of pastry can be prepared (but not baked) 1 day ahead and stacked in freezer between sheets of parchment paper. Let each section stand at room temperature until no longer frozen solid but still firm, about 5 minutes, before baking.
· Ginger cream can be made 1 day ahead and chilled, covered.
· Tart can be assembled 3 hours before serving and kept at cool room temperature.
PHOTO ON PAGE 79

PORT-GLAZED GRAPE TARTS WITH PECAN CRUST

Makes 2 (11- by 8-inch) tarts
Active time: 45 min   Start to finish: 1¾ hr

Our food editors loved shavings of Stilton cheese on these tarts. We understand that nobody has much room for dessert after a big meal, much less one with cheese, but these tarts are actually quite light and refreshing: The Stilton lends depth and provides a savory counterpoint to the sweet grapes and crust.

For tart shells
  ½ cup pecans (2 oz), lightly toasted
    (see Tips, page 8)
  ½ cup packed light brown sugar
  2 cups all-purpose flour
  2 sticks (1 cup) cold unsalted butter,
    cut into tablespoon pieces
  1 teaspoon cinnamon
  1 teaspoon ground ginger
  ¾ teaspoon salt
For grape filling
  2 cups Ruby Port
  1½ cups Concord grape jelly
  ¾ teaspoon fresh lemon juice, or to taste
  5 lb small red seedless grapes, stems
    discarded (12½ cups)

Special equipment: **2 (11¼- by 8- by 1-inch)
  rectangular tart pans with removable
  bottoms, or 2 (10-inch) round fluted tart
  pans with removable bottoms**

Make tart shells:
Preheat oven to 350°F.
  Pulse pecans with brown sugar in a food processor until finely ground (do not allow to become a paste). Add flour, butter, cinnamon, ginger, and salt and pulse until mixture begins to form large lumps. Divide mixture between tart pans and press evenly over bottom and up sides with floured fingers. Chill until firm, about 30 minutes.
  Bake tart shells in lower third of oven until golden brown, about 25 minutes. Transfer shells in pans to racks to cool completely. Carefully remove sides of pans, keeping shells on pan base.
Make filling while shells cool:
  Simmer Port and jelly, stirring occasionally, until reduced to about 1½ cups, about 30 minutes, then stir in lemon juice. Immediately toss grapes with 1 cup glaze in a large bowl until well coated, then mound in tart shells.
  Just before serving, drizzle tarts with more glaze and serve remainder on the side.

  Cooks' notes:
  • Tart shells can be made 2 days ahead and kept in pans, loosely covered, at room temperature. Remove sides of tart pans before filling.
  • Port glaze can be made 2 days ahead and chilled, covered. Reheat before proceeding.
  • Tarts can be assembled 4 hours ahead.
  PHOTO ON PAGE 101

ROASTED RHUBARB TARTS WITH STRAWBERRY SAUCE

Serves 6
Active time: 25 min   Start to finish: 1 hr

1 sheet frozen puff pastry (from a 17¼-oz package), thawed
1 lb rhubarb stalks, trimmed and cut crosswise into 1-inch pieces
½ cup confectioners sugar
1 (10-oz) package frozen strawberries in heavy syrup, thawed
¾ cup crème fraîche or sour cream

Bake pastry:
Preheat oven to 425°F.

Unfold puff pastry sheet and gently roll out with a floured rolling pin on a very lightly floured surface into a 12-inch square. Trim edges with a sharp knife, then cut pastry into 6 rectangles (about 6 by 4 inches each). Arrange rectangles 1 to 2 inches apart on an ungreased baking sheet and prick them all over with a fork.

Bake in middle of oven until pastry is puffed and golden, 13 to 15 minutes. Cool pastry on baking sheet on a rack.

Roast rhubarb while pastry cools:
Reduce oven temperature to 375°F.

Arrange rhubarb in 1 layer in a lightly oiled shallow 15- by 10-inch baking pan (preferably nonstick) and sift 2 tablespoons confectioners sugar evenly over it. Roast rhubarb in middle of oven until tender, 15 to 25 minutes, then cool in pan on a rack.

Make strawberry sauce and cream filling while rhubarb roasts:
Purée strawberries with syrup in a food processor, then force purée through a fine-mesh sieve into a bowl.

Sift 5 tablespoons confectioners sugar over crème fraîche and whisk to combine.

Assemble tarts:
Sift remaining tablespoon confectioners sugar over pastry rectangles. Make a 3-inch lengthwise trough in the center of each rectangle by gently tapping with back of a teaspoon. Divide cream filling among troughs and top with rhubarb, then drizzle with strawberry sauce.

Cooks' note:
• Strawberry sauce and cream filling can be made 1 day ahead and chilled separately, covered.

LIME CUSTARD TART

Serves 8
Active time: 45 min   Start to finish: 6½ hr
(includes cooling and chilling)

For crust
1 cup plus 2 tablespoons all-purpose flour
¼ cup sugar
½ teaspoon salt
¾ stick (6 tablespoons) unsalted butter, softened
1 large egg, lightly beaten
For custard
6 large eggs
1 cup heavy cream
1 cup sugar
⅔ cup fresh lime juice

Garnish: **confectioners sugar**
Special equipment: **an 8-inch fluted tart pan (2 inches deep) with a removable bottom; pie weights or raw rice**

Make crust:
Pulse together all crust ingredients in a food processor or beat with an electric mixer until a dough forms. Press dough evenly onto bottom and up side of tart pan with floured fingers. Chill shell until firm, about 30 minutes.

Preheat oven to 350°F.

Line shell with foil and fill with 1 inch of pie weights, then bake in middle of oven until edge is pale golden, about 22 minutes. Carefully remove foil and bake shell until edge is golden and bottom is pale golden, about 20 minutes more. Cool completely in pan on a rack.

Make custard:
Reduce oven temperature to 300°F.

Mix together all custard ingredients in a bowl with a whisk (do not beat) until just combined. Set tart shell (in tart pan) in a shallow baking pan and pour three fourths of custard into shell. Carefully put tart in middle of oven and pour remaining custard into shell with a small cup.

Bake tart until just set in center, about 1 hour. Cool tart completely in tart pan on rack, then chill, covered, until cold, at least 2 hours. Just before serving, remove side of pan.

Cooks' notes:
• Tart shell can be baked 3 days ahead and kept, wrapped in plastic wrap, at cool room temperature.
• Tart can be chilled up to 2 days.

PHOTO ON PAGE 107

frozen desserts

COCONUT TUILE CONES
WITH PASSION-FRUIT ICE CREAM

Serves 8
Active time: 1 hr   Start to finish: 5 hr (includes making ice cream)

½ stick (¼ cup) unsalted butter
¼ cup packed light brown sugar
3 tablespoons light corn syrup
¼ cup all-purpose flour
½ cup sweetened flaked coconut

Accompaniment: **passion-fruit ice cream (recipe follows)**
Garnish: **sliced star fruit**
Special equipment: **a small metal offset spatula**

Bring butter, brown sugar, and corn syrup to a boil over moderate heat, stirring. Add flour and cook, stirring constantly, until dough is slightly thickened, about 1 minute. Stir in coconut and cool to room temperature, about 45 minutes.

Preheat oven to 375°F. Crumple foil to form a solid cone (about 6 inches long and 3 inches across widest part) for shaping cookies.

Drop 2 (1-tablespoon) portions of dough 6 inches apart on a buttered baking sheet and pat each into a 5-inch round with your fingertips. Bake in middle of oven until golden, 6 to 8 minutes (cookies will spread to about 6 inches).

Let cookies stand on baking sheet until just firm enough to hold their shape, about 2 minutes. Gently loosen cookies from baking sheet with offset spatula,

then turn over so smooth sides are facing up. Roll 1 cookie onto cone and cool on cone until cookie holds cone shape, about 15 seconds, then carefully slip off onto a rack to cool completely. Shape remaining cookie in same manner. (If cookies become too brittle to roll onto cone, return baking sheet to oven for a few seconds to soften.) Make and shape more cookies with remaining dough.

Put 3 small scoops ice cream into each cone and put cones on plates.

Cooks' notes:
• Cones can be made 3 days ahead and kept in an airtight container at room temperature.
• Cookies can be shaped into cups instead: Transfer cookies to inverted glasses with spatula and gently mold around glasses.

PHOTO ON PAGE 71

PASSION-FRUIT ICE CREAM

Makes about 2 quarts
Active time: 15 min   Start to finish: 3¼ hr

This recipe makes more ice cream than you'll need to fill the cones (see preceding recipe), but it's so delicious you'll have no trouble getting rid of the leftovers.

1½ cups sugar
3 large eggs
3 cups heavy cream
1¼ cups thawed frozen passion-fruit pulp

Special equipment: **an instant-read thermometer; an ice cream maker**

Whisk together sugar and eggs. Heat cream in a 2½- to 3-quart heavy saucepan over moderate heat until it just reaches a boil, then add hot cream to egg mixture in a slow stream, whisking. Pour custard into saucepan.

Cook custard over moderately low heat, stirring constantly, until it registers 170°F on thermometer (do not let boil). Pour custard through a fine-mesh sieve into a clean bowl and cool completely. Stir in passion-fruit pulp, then chill, covered, until cold.

Freeze custard in ice cream maker. Transfer to an airtight container and put in freezer to harden.

Cooks' note:
• Ice cream can be made 1 week ahead.

ice cream

INDIVIDUAL CHOCOLATE RASPBERRY BAKED ALASKAS

Serves 6
Active time: 1¼ hr   Start to finish: 5½ hr

4 oz fine-quality bittersweet chocolate (not
   unsweetened), chopped
1 stick (½ cup) unsalted butter, cut into
   tablespoon pieces
2¼ cups sugar
3 whole large eggs
⅛ teaspoon salt
½ cup unsweetened cocoa powder
   Raspberry ice cream (recipe follows),
      slightly softened
8 large egg whites

Special equipment: **6 (8-oz) shallow ceramic
   or glass gratin dishes**

Make cake:
   Preheat oven to 375°F. Butter an 8-inch square baking pan. Line bottom with wax paper and butter paper.
   Melt chocolate and butter in a metal bowl set over
a saucepan of barely simmering water, stirring, until
smooth. Remove bowl from pan and whisk ¾ cup sugar
into chocolate mixture. Whisk in whole eggs and salt,
then sift cocoa over and whisk until just combined.
   Pour batter into baking pan, spreading evenly, and
bake in middle of oven until a tester comes out with a
few crumbs adhering, 20 to 25 minutes. Cool cake in

pan on a rack 5 minutes, then invert onto rack and cool
completely.
   Cut cake into 6 equal pieces, then arrange 1 piece
in each gratin dish, trimming to fit. Top each piece of
cake with a large scoop of ice cream (about ½ cup),
then freeze, covered, just until ice cream is hard, about
25 minutes (do not let ice cream become rock hard
unless making ahead—see cooks' note, below).
   Make meringue just before serving:
   Preheat oven to 450°F.
   Beat egg whites and a pinch of salt with an electric
mixer until they just hold soft peaks. Add remaining
1½ cups sugar a little at a time, beating at high speed,
and continue beating until whites just hold stiff, glossy
peaks, about 5 minutes in a standing mixer or about
12 minutes with a handheld.
   Remove gratin dishes from freezer and mound
meringue over ice cream and cake, spreading to edge
of gratin dish. Bake on a baking sheet in middle of
oven until golden brown, about 6 minutes. Serve
immediately.

   Cooks' notes:
 • Ice cream and cake can be frozen in gratin dishes,
   covered, up to 1 day. Let soften at room temperature
   15 minutes before covering with meringue.
 • The egg whites in this recipe will not be fully cooked,
   which may be of concern if salmonella is a problem in
   your area.
   PHOTO ON PAGE 65

RASPBERRY ICE CREAM

Makes about 1½ quarts
Active time: 30 min   Start to finish: 4 hr

*This recipe will yield more than you need for the baked
Alaskas (recipe precedes), but who would mind a little
extra ice cream in the house?*

2 (10-oz) boxes frozen raspberries
   in heavy syrup, thawed
2 teaspoons fresh lemon juice
½ cup sugar
1½ teaspoons cornstarch
1¼ cups whole milk
2 large egg yolks
¼ teaspoon vanilla
1 cup chilled heavy cream

Special equipment: **an ice cream maker**

Purée thawed raspberries with syrup and fresh lemon juice in a food processor, then force through a medium-mesh sieve into a bowl, pressing hard on and discarding solids.

Whisk together sugar and cornstarch in a bowl, then whisk in milk, yolks, and a pinch of salt. Cook custard in a 2½- to 3-quart heavy saucepan over moderate heat, whisking, until it just reaches a boil, then reduce heat and simmer, whisking, 1 minute. (Custard will look curdled.) Pour custard through a fine-mesh sieve into a bowl, then stir in vanilla and cool, stirring occasionally.

Stir berry purée and cream into custard and chill, covered, until cold, at least 2 hours.

Freeze in ice cream maker, then transfer to an airtight container and put in freezer to harden.

Cooks' note:
- **Ice cream keeps 1 week.**

MERINGUE NAPOLEONS WITH LIME ICE CREAM AND BLACKBERRIES

Serves 6
Active time: 1¾ hr   Start to finish: 12 hr
(includes making ice cream)

This recipe yields more meringue squares than you'll need. The extras can replace any that break—and they also make a delicious snack. Before starting, you'll need to make a template. Instructions are in the recipe.

For meringues
   3 large egg whites
   ⅛ teaspoon salt
   ¾ cup sugar
For blackberry sauce
   2 cups blackberries (about 10 oz)
   2 to 3 tablespoons sugar
For filling
   Lime ice cream (page 244)
   1 cup blackberries (about 5 oz)

Garnish: **confectioners sugar and finely grated fresh lime zest**
Accompaniment: **lightly sweetened whipped cream**
Special equipment: **parchment paper; 1 (5-inch) square of ⅛-inch-thick cardboard; a small metal offset spatula**

Make meringues:
Preheat oven to 175°F and line 2 large baking sheets with parchment paper. Make a template from cardboard: Trace a 5-inch square on a section of cardboard. Trim the cardboard to size and trace a 3-inch square inside the box. Cut out the center square with an X-Acto knife or scissors. If using scissors, snip through one outside edge of the "frame" so you don't bend it. Tape it together once you are through cutting.

Beat whites with salt in a bowl with an electric mixer at medium-high speed until they just hold soft peaks. Gradually add half of sugar, beating at high speed, and continue to beat until whites hold stiff, glossy peaks. Fold in remaining half of sugar gently but thoroughly.

Spread about 1 teaspoon meringue onto corners of each piece of parchment and turn paper over, pressing on corners to adhere parchment to baking sheets.

Starting in 1 corner, place template flat against 1 baking sheet and spoon a heaping tablespoon meringue into center. Holding template down firmly, spread meringue evenly with offset spatula to fill opening, then gently lift template straight up from sheet to make a clean edge. Form 17 more meringues in same manner (9 per sheet), scraping excess meringue from template as necessary. Discard any leftover meringue.

Bake in upper and lower thirds of oven until dry to the touch, very pale, and crisp, about 1¼ hours. Cool meringues on sheets 5 minutes, then carefully peel them from parchment and transfer to racks to cool.
Make blackberry sauce:
Purée berries with sugar (to taste) in a blender or food processor, then force through a fine-mesh sieve into a bowl to remove seeds.
Assemble napoleons:
Sprinkle 6 meringue squares with confectioners sugar. Put 1 unsugared meringue square on each of 6 plates and top with small scoops of ice cream and berries, then cover with a sugared meringue square. Spoon a dollop of whipped cream onto each napoleon and grate a bit of lime zest over top. Divide sauce among plates.

Cooks' notes:
- **Meringues (without confectioners sugar) can be made 4 days ahead and kept in an airtight container at room temperature.**
- **Blackberry sauce can be made 1 day ahead and chilled, covered.**
PHOTO ON PAGE 57

LIME ICE CREAM

Makes about 1 quart
Active time: 45 min   Start to finish: 8¾ hr (includes freezing)

2 tablespoons finely grated fresh lime zest
    (see Tips, page 8)
1 cup sugar
1½ cups heavy cream
1½ cups whole milk
½ cup plus 2 tablespoons fresh lime juice
6 large egg yolks
⅛ teaspoon salt

Special equipment: **a candy or instant-read**
    thermometer; an ice cream maker

Blend zest and ½ cup sugar in a food processor
30 seconds, then stir together with cream and milk in
a heavy saucepan. Bring to a boil over moderate heat,
stirring occasionally, and remove from heat. Steep,
covered, 30 minutes.

Bring remaining ½ cup sugar and ¼ cup plus
2 tablespoons lime juice to a boil in a 2-quart heavy
saucepan, stirring until sugar is dissolved, then boil,
swirling pan occasionally, until syrup just begins to
turn very pale golden. Remove from heat and whisk
in steeped cream.

Whisk yolks with salt in a large bowl and add
cream mixture in a slow stream, whisking. Return to
saucepan and cook over moderately low heat, stirring
constantly with a wooden spoon, until custard coats
back of spoon and thermometer registers 170°F (do not
let boil).

Pour through a fine-mesh sieve into a clean bowl
and cool, stirring occasionally. Stir in remaining ¼ cup
lime juice and chill custard, covered, until cold, at least
3 hours.

Freeze custard in ice cream maker. Transfer ice
cream to an airtight container and put in freezer
to harden.

Cooks' notes:
• Custard can chill up to 1 day.
• Ice cream can be made 1 week ahead.

GREEN TEA ICE CREAM

Makes about 1 quart
Active time: 30 min   Start to finish: 5 hr

2 cups heavy cream
1 cup whole milk
¼ teaspoon salt
6 large eggs
⅔ cup sugar
2 tablespoons *matcha* (powdered Japanese
    green tea)

Special equipment: **an instant-read thermometer;**
    an ice cream maker

Bring cream, milk, and salt to a boil in a 3- to
4-quart heavy saucepan and remove from heat.

Whisk together eggs, sugar, and *matcha* in a bowl,
then add 1 cup hot cream mixture in a slow stream,
whisking vigorously. Whisk custard into remaining
cream mixture in saucepan and cook over moderately
low heat, stirring constantly with a wooden spoon, until
thick enough to coat back of spoon and registers 170°F
on thermometer (do not let boil).

Immediately pour custard through a fine-mesh sieve
into a metal bowl, then cool to room temperature, stirring
occasionally. Chill, covered, until cold, at least 1 hour.

Freeze in ice cream maker, then transfer to an airtight container and put in freezer to harden.

PHOTO ON PAGE 83

MOLASSES ICE CREAM

Makes about 1 quart
Active time: 10 min   Start to finish: 1¾ hr

3 oz cream cheese, softened
½ cup packed light brown sugar
⅓ cup molasses (not robust)
2 cups half-and-half

Special equipment: **an ice cream maker**

Blend cream cheese, brown sugar, and molasses in
a food processor or blender until smooth. With motor
running, add half-and-half, blending until combined.

Freeze in ice cream maker, then transfer ice cream
to an airtight container and put in freezer to harden.

BLUEBERRY ALMOND PRALINE SUNDAE

Serves 6
Active time: 30 min   Start to finish: 30 min

1 cup sugar
¼ teaspoon salt
¾ cup sliced almonds, toasted
   (see Tips, page 8)
⅓ cup apricot jam
2 tablespoons water
1 teaspoon fresh lemon juice
3 cups blueberries (14 oz)
⅛ teaspoon almond extract
1 qt vanilla ice cream

Line a large baking sheet with foil, then lightly oil foil.

Cook sugar with salt in a dry 10-inch heavy skillet over moderate heat, undisturbed, until it begins to melt. Continue to cook, stirring occasionally with a fork, until sugar is melted into a deep golden caramel. Immediately remove from heat and stir in almonds with a wooden spoon, then quickly pour onto baking sheet, spreading out praline mixture with back of spoon before it hardens.

Cool praline on baking sheet 5 minutes, then break into large pieces. Put praline pieces in a heavy-duty sealable plastic bag and break into smaller pieces with a rolling pin.

Bring jam, water, and lemon juice to a boil, stirring, over moderate heat. Add 1½ cups blueberries and simmer until berries burst, 8 to 10 minutes. Add remaining 1½ cups blueberries and simmer, stirring gently, just until heated through, about 2 minutes. Remove from heat and stir in almond extract.

Top scoops of ice cream with warm blueberry sauce and praline.

ROASTED APRICOT SORBET

Makes about 3 cups
Active time: 20 min   Start to finish: 3¾ hr

¾ cup sugar
½ cup water
⅓ cup dried apricots, chopped
1¼ lb firm-ripe apricots (7 large)
2 tablespoons fresh lemon juice
⅛ teaspoon almond extract

Special equipment: **an ice cream maker**

Preheat oven to 350°F.

Bring sugar, water, and dried apricots to a boil in a 3-quart heavy saucepan over moderate heat, stirring, until sugar is dissolved. Remove from heat and let stand until apricots are softened, about 1 hour.

While dried apricots are standing, roast whole fresh apricots in a small roasting pan in middle of oven until soft, about 1 hour. Cool in pan, then peel and pit when cool enough to handle.

Purée dried apricot mixture, roasted apricots, lemon juice, and almond extract in a blender until very smooth, 1½ to 2 minutes. Force purée through a fine-mesh sieve into a bowl, pressing hard on solids and then discarding them. Chill purée, covered, until cold, at least 2 hours.

Freeze in ice cream maker, then transfer to an airtight container and put in freezer to harden.

Cooks' notes:
• **Purée can be chilled up to 8 hours.**
• **Sorbet keeps 1 week.**

COFFEE GRANITA WITH SAMBUCA CREAM AND CHOCOLATE SHAVINGS

Serves 8
Active time: 15 min   Start to finish: 5 hr (includes freezing)

4 cups hot strong brewed coffee
1 cup superfine granulated sugar
1 cup chilled heavy cream
4 teaspoons confectioners sugar
4 to 5 teaspoons Sambuca
½ cup fine-quality bittersweet chocolate
    shavings (not unsweetened; cut with
    a vegetable peeler from a 3-oz bar)

Stir together coffee and granulated sugar until sugar is dissolved, then chill until cold, about 1 hour.

Pour into an 8- to 9-inch baking pan (1½- to 2-quart capacity) and freeze, stirring and crushing lumps with a fork every 30 minutes, until evenly frozen, about 4 hours.

Scrape granita with fork to lighten texture.

Beat cream with confectioners sugar and Sambuca (to taste) in a bowl with an electric mixer until it just holds soft peaks. Spoon Sambuca cream into 8 glasses and top each serving with a scant cup of granita (do not pack when measuring).

Sprinkle with chocolate shavings.

Cooks' note:
• Granita can be made 3 days ahead and kept frozen, covered. Scrape with a fork just before serving.
PHOTO ON PAGE 75

RHUBARB LAMBRUSCO GRANITA

Serves 6 (makes about 7 cups)
Active time: 30 min   Start to finish: 8½ hr

1 cup Lambrusco wine
½ cup water
¾ cup plus 2 tablespoons superfine
    granulated sugar
1 lb rhubarb stalks, trimmed and cut
    crosswise into ½-inch pieces (3 cups)
1 teaspoon fresh lemon juice

Bring wine to a boil with water and sugar, stirring, in a 4-quart heavy pot. Add rhubarb and cook at a bare simmer, covered, stirring occasionally, until very tender and beginning to fall apart, 5 to 7 minutes.

Purée in a food processor with lemon juice until smooth, then force through a medium-mesh sieve into an 8- to 9-inch baking pan, pressing hard on and discarding solids.

Freeze, stirring and crushing lumps with a fork every 1½ hours, until evenly frozen, about 8 hours total. Scrape granita with a fork to lighten texture, crushing any lumps.

Serve immediately or freeze, covered, up to 3 days (rescrape to lighten texture again if necessary).

GRAPEFRUIT STAR ANISE GRANITA

Serves 4 (makes about 4 cups)
Active time: 15 min   Start to finish: 7 hr

⅓ cup water
½ cup sugar
2 whole star anise
2½ cups fresh red or pink grapefruit juice

Bring water, sugar, and star anise to a boil, stirring until sugar is dissolved. Discard star anise and cool syrup. Stir syrup into juice.

Freeze in a shallow metal pan, stirring and crushing lumps with a fork every 40 minutes, until liquid is frozen and granular, about 6 hours. Just before serving, scrape with a fork, breaking up lumps.

Cooks' note:
• Granita can be made 1 week ahead and kept frozen, covered.

PEACH PRALINE BOMBES
WITH PEACH SYRUP

Serves 6
Active time: 2 hr   Start to finish: 14½ hr (includes freezing)

For peach ice cream
  2 lb very ripe peaches, left unpeeled
  ¾ cup sugar
  2 tablespoons fresh lemon juice
  1½ cups heavy cream
  6 large egg yolks
  ¼ teaspoon salt
  ½ teaspoon vanilla extract
  ¼ teaspoon almond extract
For almond praline filling
  ⅓ cup sugar
  3 tablespoons water
  **⅓ cup whole blanched almonds, lightly
     toasted (see Tips, page 8), cooled,
     and coarsely chopped**
  ⅔ cup chilled heavy cream
  ½ teaspoon vanilla extract
For peach syrup
  1½ lb very ripe peaches, left unpeeled
  ½ cup sugar
  1 teaspoon fresh lemon juice

Garnish: **peach slices**
Special equipment: **an instant-read thermometer;
     an ice cream maker; 6 (8- to 9-oz)
     paper cups**

Make peach custard for ice cream:
  Slice peaches ¼ inch thick, then toss with ¼ cup sugar and lemon juice in a bowl. Let stand 30 minutes.
  While peaches are standing, bring cream just to a boil in a heavy saucepan. Whisk together yolks, remaining ½ cup sugar, and salt in a bowl, then add cream in a slow stream, whisking. Pour into saucepan and cook over moderately low heat, stirring constantly with a wooden spoon, until it coats back of spoon and registers 170°F on thermometer (do not let boil). Pour through a fine-mesh sieve into a clean bowl and cool, stirring occasionally.
  Purée peaches in batches in a blender until very smooth and force through sieve into custard, pressing hard on and discarding solids. Whisk in extracts and chill, covered, until cold, 2 to 3 hours. (Do not chill longer than 3 hours or custard will discolor.)

Make praline while custard chills:
  Lightly butter a small baking sheet or a sheet of foil.
  Bring sugar and water to a boil in a small heavy saucepan, stirring until sugar is dissolved. Boil syrup without stirring, washing down any sugar crystals on side of pan with a pastry brush dipped in cold water, until syrup turns a golden caramel. Remove from heat and stir in almonds. Pour praline onto baking sheet and cool completely.
  Break praline into pieces and pulse in a food processor until finely ground with some small pieces remaining.
Freeze ice cream:
  Freeze peach custard in ice cream maker, then transfer to a bowl and keep in freezer while assembling praline bombes.
Assemble bombes:
  Beat chilled cream in a bowl with an electric mixer until it just holds stiff peaks, then fold in vanilla and crushed praline.
  Spoon about ½ cup ice cream into 1 paper cup and spread it evenly over bottom and about two-thirds of the way up side of cup, forming a well. Spoon a rounded ¼ cup praline filling into well and top with another ¼ cup ice cream, spreading evenly to cover filling. Cover cup tightly with foil and put in freezer. Make 5 more bombes in same manner. Freeze bombes at least 8 hours and up to 2 days.
Make peach syrup:
  Chop peaches, then bring to a boil with sugar in a 3- to 4-quart saucepan over moderate heat, covered, stirring occasionally until sugar is dissolved. Reduce heat and simmer, covered, until peaches are very soft and have given off liquid, about 15 minutes. Pour peaches and syrup through sieve into a bowl, pressing on and discarding solids. Stir in lemon juice and cool syrup. Chill, covered, until cold.
  To serve, carefully tear off each paper cup. Invert bombes onto plates and halve each with a sharp knife. Let stand about 5 minutes to soften slightly, then drizzle about 2 tablespoons peach syrup around each serving.

Cooks' notes:
• **Bombes can be frozen up to 2 days.**
• **Peach syrup can be chilled up to 3 days.**
• **You can substitute ⅔ cup crushed *amaretti* (Italian
   almond macaroons) for the almond praline in the
   filling (this will result in a stronger almond flavor).**
PHOTO ON PAGE 94

fruit finales

APPLE, PRUNE, AND BRANDY CRISP

Serves 4
Active time: 15 min   Start to finish: 45 min

½ cup brandy
1 cup pitted prunes (dried plums; 8 oz),
   halved
⅔ cup all-purpose flour
½ cup packed light brown sugar
¾ stick (6 tablespoons) cold unsalted butter,
   cut into ½-inch cubes
¼ teaspoon salt
⅛ teaspoon cinnamon
⅔ cup old-fashioned oats
6 McIntosh apples (2¼ lb)

Accompaniment: **vanilla ice cream**

Preheat oven to 425°F.

Bring brandy to a boil in a small saucepan and remove from heat. Stir in prunes and let stand while making topping.

Pulse together flour, 6 tablespoons brown sugar, butter, salt, and cinnamon in a food processor until mixture resembles coarse meal. Add oats and pulse once or twice to just combine.

Peel, quarter, and core apples and cut into ½-inch wedges. Transfer apples to a 1½-quart shallow baking dish and toss with prune mixture and remaining 2 table-spoons brown sugar.

Sprinkle topping evenly over apple filling and bake in middle of oven until topping is golden brown and filling is bubbling, about 30 minutes.

GRAPEFRUIT AMBROSIA

Serves 4
Active time: 30 min   Start to finish: 30 min

5 lb grapefruit (preferably half pink and
   half red; about 6 total)
1 cup sweetened flaked coconut
2 tablespoons Campari
2 tablespoons sugar
½ cup salted shelled natural pistachios,
   toasted (see Tips, page 8) and
   coarsely chopped

Cut peel, including all white pith, from fruit with a sharp paring knife and cut segments free from membranes. Halve grapefruit segments crosswise, then transfer to a bowl. Stir in coconut, Campari, sugar, and a pinch of salt and chill 15 minutes.

Just before serving, stir in nuts.

Cooks' note:
• Ambrosia (without nuts) can be made 4 hours ahead and chilled, covered.

CARAMELIZED ORANGES

Serves 6
Active time: 10 min   Start to finish: 35 min

9 medium navel oranges
½ cup sugar
½ cup water
1 tablespoon unsalted butter

Squeeze enough juice from 3 oranges to measure 1 cup.

Bring sugar and water to a boil in a 1½-quart heavy saucepan over moderate heat, stirring until sugar is dissolved. Boil syrup, without stirring, washing down any sugar crystals with a pastry brush dipped in cold water, until syrup around edges begins to turn golden brown, about 10 minutes. Tilt pan and carefully add orange juice (caramel will harden and vigorously steam). Simmer, stirring, until caramel is completely dissolved, about 2 minutes.

Cut peel, including all white pith, from remaining 6 oranges with a sharp paring knife and cut each orange crosswise into thirds.

Heat one third of butter (1 teaspoon) in a 12-inch nonstick skillet over moderately high heat until hot but not smoking, then sauté 6 orange slices, turning once, until golden, 4 to 6 minutes total and transfer to a plate. Sauté remaining orange slices in butter in same manner, wiping out skillet between batches if necessary. Return all orange slices to skillet along with caramel sauce and cook over moderate heat until heated through, about 1 minute.

Each serving about 181 calories and 2 grams fat

BROWN SUGAR APRICOTS WITH VANILLA YOGURT

Serves 4
Active time: 5 min Start to finish: 25 min

 1½ **lb fresh apricots, halved and pitted**
  2 **tablespoons packed light brown sugar**
  8 **oz vanilla nonfat yogurt**

Special equipment: **a 12- by 8- by 2-inch disposable aluminum roasting pan**

Prepare grill for cooking. If using a charcoal grill, open vents on bottom of grill and on lid.

Arrange apricots, cut sides up, in disposable roasting pan and sprinkle with brown sugar, patting and pressing with fingers to help evenly adhere.

When fire is low (you can hold your hand 5 inches above rack for 4 to 5 seconds), cook apricots in pan, covered with grill lid, without turning, until sugar is melted and apricots are softened, about 5 minutes.

Serve apricots with yogurt on the side.

Cooks' note:
• **Apricots can also be broiled on lightly oiled rack of a broiler pan 4 to 5 inches from heat 2 to 3 minutes.**

Each serving about 118 calories and less than 1 gram fat

FRUIT GRATIN WITH CALVADOS AND MASCARPONE

Serves 6
Active time: 15 min Start to finish: 1¼ hr

 1½ **lb small (2½-inch) Gala, Empire, or Golden Delicious apples**
 1½ **lb firm-ripe Seckel (9), Forelle (6), or Bartlett (3) pears**
  2 **tablespoons unsalted butter**
  ½ **cup Calvados or Cognac**
  5 **tablespoons packed light brown sugar**
 24 **dried apricots (preferably California; 5 oz)**
 18 **pitted prunes (dried plums; 7 oz)**
  6 **(2- by ¼-inch) strips fresh lemon zest**
  1 **cup mascarpone cheese (8 oz)**
  2 **tablespoons confectioners sugar**

Special equipment: **a melon-ball cutter**

Preheat oven to 400°F.

Halve apples lengthwise (quarter if large), leaving stem intact, and core halves with melon-ball cutter. Halve Seckel and Forelle pears or quarter Bartletts lengthwise, then core with melon-ball cutter and trim root ends.

Melt butter in a 14- by 9-inch oval gratin dish or other 2½- to 3-quart shallow baking dish in middle of oven, about 2 minutes. Stir in Calvados and 3 tablespoons brown sugar, then add fresh and dried fruit and zest and turn gently to coat. Cover dish tightly with foil and bake in middle of oven, gently turning fruit and basting occasionally with juices, until apples and pears are tender but not falling apart, about 1 hour. Remove dish from oven.

Preheat broiler.

Spoon ⅓ cup baking juices from baking dish into a bowl and stir in mascarpone and remaining 2 tablespoons brown sugar. Rearrange fruit, cut sides up, in baking dish to form an even layer, if necessary, and spoon mascarpone mixture over fruit. Put confectioners sugar in a fine-mesh sieve and sift over fruit. Broil gratin 3 inches from heat until confectioners sugar is caramelized, 1 to 2 minutes.

Cooks' note:
• **Fruit can be baked 2 hours ahead and cooled, uncovered, then kept, covered with foil, at room temperature. Reheat in oven before adding mascarpone and broiling.**

CANTALOUPE CONSERVE

Serves 6 to 8 (dessert)
Active time: 25 min   Start to finish: 45 min

Spooning this conserve over yogurt makes a light, sweet summer dessert.

½ cup sugar
¼ cup water
2 tablespoons fresh lemon juice
1 large ripe cantaloupe, seeds and rind
   discarded and flesh cut into 1-inch
   pieces (4 cups)
⅓ cup golden raisins

Accompaniment: **plain yogurt**

Bring sugar, water, and lemon juice to a boil, stirring occasionally until sugar is dissolved, then boil, uncovered, until slightly thickened, about 5 minutes. Stir in cantaloupe and raisins and simmer, uncovered, stirring frequently, until cantaloupe is translucent and syrup is thickened, 15 to 20 minutes.

Transfer conserve to a metal bowl, then set bowl in a larger bowl of ice and cold water to cool, stirring occasionally.

BROILED PLUMS WITH MAPLE SYRUP AND CINNAMON TOASTS

Serves 6
Active time: 15 min   Start to finish: 30 min

6 (½-inch-thick) slices from a challah or large
   brioche loaf
¾ stick (6 tablespoons) unsalted butter, melted
3 tablespoons sugar
1 teaspoon cinnamon
6 firm-ripe medium red or black plums
   (1½ lb), halved lengthwise and pitted
¾ cup pure maple syrup, warmed

Preheat oven to 450°F.
Brush 1 side of each bread slice with butter and arrange slices, buttered sides up, on a baking sheet. Stir together sugar and cinnamon and sprinkle evenly over bread. Toast bread in middle of oven until crisp and golden brown on top, about 7 minutes. Halve toasts diagonally.

Preheat broiler.
Dip cut side of each plum half in maple syrup, then put plums, cut sides up, on a buttered broiler pan. Broil plums 4 to 5 inches from heat until golden, 3 to 5 minutes. Heat remaining syrup over moderate heat until hot.

Serve plums on cinnamon toasts, drizzled with remaining syrup.

PINEAPPLE, KIWIFRUIT, AND ORANGE IN MINT SYRUP

Serves 6
Active time: 30 min   Start to finish: 1¾ hr
(includes chilling syrup)

½ cup sugar
½ cup water
1 cup loosely packed fresh mint leaves (any
   size) plus 2 tablespoons small leaves
3 navel oranges
1 ripe pineapple (preferably labeled "extra
   sweet"), peeled, cored, and cut into
   ¾-inch pieces
4 kiwifruit, peeled and each cut into 8 wedges

Bring sugar, water, and 1 cup mint to a boil in a small saucepan, stirring until sugar is dissolved. Remove from heat and let steep, covered, 10 minutes.

Pour syrup through a medium-mesh sieve into a large serving bowl, pressing on and discarding mint, then cool syrup.

Cut peel and white pith from oranges with a sharp knife. Holding oranges over bowl of syrup to catch any juices, cut sections free from membranes, letting them fall into syrup, and squeeze membranes to extract as much juice as possible. Stir in pineapple, kiwis, and small mint leaves.

Cooks' note:
• **Fruit in mint syrup may be made 1 day ahead and
  chilled, covered.**
PHOTO ON PAGE 52

CHOCOLATE CHERRY CHARLOTTES

Serves 6
Active time: 1 hr   Start to finish: 3½ hr

You might wonder why we freeze the chocolate filling for these charlottes before baking them. The coldness prevents the chocolate from overcooking in the oven.

⅔ cup dried sour cherries
¼ cup kirsch
2 tablespoons sugar
2 to 3 drops almond extract
½ cup heavy cream
3½ oz fine-quality bittersweet chocolate
(not unsweetened), chopped
7 tablespoons unsalted butter, softened
1½ fresh loaves challah or large brioche
(1½ lb total), sliced ½ inch thick

Accompaniment: **lightly sweetened whipped cream**
Special equipment: **a 2-inch round cookie cutter;
6 (5- to 6-oz) charlotte molds or ramekins**

Bring cherries, kirsch, and sugar to a boil in a small saucepan, stirring occasionally. Remove from heat and let stand, covered, 15 minutes. Stir in almond extract.

Heat cream, chocolate, and a pinch of salt in another small heavy saucepan over low heat, stirring, until chocolate is melted and smooth, about 3 minutes. Remove from heat and add 1 tablespoon butter, stirring until incorporated, then stir in cooked cherries with any liquid. Transfer filling to a metal bowl and freeze, stirring occasionally, until firm but not solid, 2½ hours.

Preheat oven to 350°F.

Cut out 12 rounds from bread slices with cookie cutter, then cut 42 (2- by 1½-inch) rectangles from trimmings and remaining slices.

Spread 1 side of each round and rectangle with some of remaining butter. Put 6 rounds, buttered sides down, in molds and line sides with rectangles (5 to 7 per mold), buttered sides against mold, arranging them vertically and slightly overlapping, pressing gently to adhere. Trim any overhang flush with rims.

Divide chocolate cherry filling among molds and top with 6 remaining bread rounds, buttered sides up, pressing gently to fit inside bread rim.

Bake charlottes in molds on a baking sheet in middle of oven until bread is golden, about 25 minutes. Cool 5 minutes, then invert plates over charlottes and invert charlottes onto plates. Serve warm.

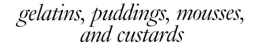

gelatins, puddings, mousses, and custards

MAPLE PUMPKIN POTS DE CRÈME

Makes 10 individual custards
Active time: 30 min   Start to finish: 3 hr

1 cup heavy cream
¾ cup whole milk
¾ cup pure maple syrup
½ cup canned solid-pack pumpkin
7 large egg yolks
½ teaspoon cinnamon
⅛ teaspoon freshly grated nutmeg
⅛ teaspoon salt

Special equipment: **10 (2- to 3-oz) custard cups
or ramekins**

Preheat oven to 325°F.

Whisk together cream, milk, syrup, and pumpkin in a heavy saucepan and bring just to a simmer over moderate heat.

Whisk together yolks, cinnamon, nutmeg, and salt in a bowl.

Add hot pumpkin mixture to yolks in a slow stream, whisking constantly. Pour custard through a fine-mesh sieve into a large measuring cup, then divide among custard cups (you may have some custard left over, depending on size of cups). Bake custards in a hot water bath (see Tips, page 8), pan covered tightly with foil, in middle of oven until a knife inserted in center of a custard comes out clean, 35 to 40 minutes. Transfer custards to a rack to cool completely.

Chill, covered, until cold, at least 2 hours.

Cooks' note:
• *Pots de crème* **can be chilled up to 2 days.**

MANGO FOOL

Serves 6
Active time: 15 min   Start to finish: 9¼ hr (includes chilling)

There are many varieties of mango grown on the African continent—comparatively, the selection of fresh mangoes here in the United States is limited. For this recipe, we recommend using canned slices of Alphonso mango, an Indian cultivar renowned for its bright orange flesh and very intense flavor.

1¼ teaspoons unflavored gelatin (less than
    1 envelope)
1 cup whole milk
1 large egg
½ cup sugar
1 (30-oz) can Alphonso mango slices
    in syrup, drained
1½ tablespoons fresh lime juice
1 cup chilled heavy cream

Special equipment: **an instant-read thermometer**

Sprinkle gelatin over 3 tablespoons milk in a small bowl and let soften while making custard.

Bring remaining milk just to a boil in a small heavy saucepan, then remove from heat. Whisk together egg and ¼ cup sugar until combined well, then add hot milk in a slow stream, whisking.

Pour custard into pan and cook over moderately low heat, stirring constantly with a wooden spoon, until thermometer registers 170°F and custard coats back of spoon (do not boil), about 2 minutes. Stir in gelatin mixture and cook over low heat, stirring, until dissolved, about 1 minute (do not boil). Pour custard through a medium-mesh sieve into a bowl and cool, stirring occasionally.

Purée mangoes with remaining ¼ cup sugar and lime juice in a blender until very smooth and force through sieve into custard. Stir until combined well, then chill until cold but not set, about 1 hour.

Beat cream with an electric mixer until it just holds stiff peaks, then fold into mango custard gently but thoroughly. Chill, covered, at least 8 hours.

Before serving, spoon fool into 6 dishes.

Cooks' note:
• **Fool can be chilled up to 1 day.**
PHOTO ON PAGE 40

STRAWBERRY PANNA COTTAS WITH STRAWBERRY COMPOTE

Serves 6
Active time: 25 min   Start to finish: 8¼ hr (includes chilling)

For panna cottas
3 cups sliced strawberries (1 lb)
1¾ cups well-shaken low-fat buttermilk
6 tablespoons sugar
2½ teaspoons unflavored gelatin
    (from two ¼-oz envelopes)
¼ cup whole milk
¼ cup heavy cream
For compote
2½ cups strawberries (preferably small;
    ¾ lb), trimmed
¼ cup fresh orange juice
2 teaspoons superfine granulated sugar

Special equipment: **6 (6-oz) stainless-steel or ceramic molds**

Make panna cottas:
Blend sliced strawberries, buttermilk, and sugar in a blender until very smooth, then pour through a fine-mesh sieve into a bowl, pressing hard on and discarding solids.

Sprinkle gelatin over milk in a small bowl and let stand 1 minute to soften.

Bring cream to a boil in a small saucepan. Remove pan from heat and add gelatin mixture, stirring until gelatin is dissolved.

Whisk cream mixture into strawberry purée and pour into molds. Chill panna cottas, covered, until firm, at least 8 hours.

To unmold, dip molds in a small bowl of hot water 2 or 3 seconds, then invert panna cottas onto dessert plates and remove molds. Let stand at room temperature 20 minutes to soften slightly.

Make compote while panna cottas stand:

Halve strawberries lengthwise if small or quarter if large. Whisk together orange juice and superfine sugar in a bowl until sugar is dissolved, then add strawberries, tossing to coat.

Serve panna cottas with compote.

Cooks' note:
• **Panna cottas can be chilled in molds up to 2 days.**

Each serving about 146 calories and 3 grams fat

PHOTO ON PAGE 108

KAFFIR LIME MOUSSE WITH HONEYDEW WATER

Serves 4

Active time: 40 min   Start to finish: 10 hr (includes chilling)

For mousse
⅔ **cup chilled heavy cream**
¼ **cup sugar**
3 **(2- by 1¼-inch) fresh or frozen *kaffir* lime leaves**
1½ **teaspoons finely grated fresh lime zest**
¾ **teaspoon unflavored gelatin (from a ¼-oz envelope)**
1 **tablespoon water**
½ **teaspoon fresh lime juice**
1 **cup plain whole-milk yogurt**
For honeydew water
3 **cups (1-inch) pieces honeydew flesh (2 lb)**
2 **tablespoons Midori (melon liqueur)**
1 **tablespoon fresh lime juice**
1 **teaspoon unflavored gelatin**
1 **tablespoon water**
2 **tablespoons sugar**

Garnish: **fresh green *shiso* leaves**

Accompaniment: **chile lime *tuiles* (page 231)**
Special equipment: **cheesecloth**

Make mousse:

Stir together ⅓ cup cream, sugar, lime leaves, zest, and a pinch of salt in a small heavy saucepan and bring to a bare simmer over moderately low heat, stirring until sugar is dissolved. Remove from heat and let steep, covered, 25 minutes.

Sprinkle gelatin over water and lime juice in a bowl and let soften 1 minute. Return cream mixture to a simmer, then pour through a fine-mesh sieve into gelatin, pressing on and discarding solids. Stir until gelatin is dissolved, about 1 minute. Gradually add yogurt, whisking, and chill, covered, 30 minutes. (Mixture will not be gelled.)

Beat remaining ⅓ cup cream in a chilled bowl with whisk until it just holds soft peaks. Fold into yogurt mixture and chill, covered, at least 8 hours. (Mousse will be softly set.)

Make honeydew water:

Blend honeydew, Midori, lime juice, and a pinch of salt in a blender at high speed until smooth, about 1 minute. Pour through sieve lined with dampened cheesecloth into a bowl. Let drain, undisturbed, 30 minutes, then discard foam remaining in cheesecloth.

Sprinkle gelatin over water in a small saucepan and let soften 1 minute. Add 2 tablespoons melon juice and sugar, then cook over low heat, stirring, until gelatin and sugar are dissolved, 1 to 2 minutes. Gradually whisk in 1⅛ cups melon juice (reserve remainder for another use if desired), then transfer to a bowl and chill, covered, at least 8 hours. (Honeydew water will be barely set.)

Assemble dessert:

Spoon honeydew water onto 4 dessert plates and top with *shiso* leaves. Spoon mousse onto leaves.

Cooks' note:
• **Mousse and honeydew water can be made 3 days ahead and chilled separately, covered.**

PHOTO ON PAGE 97

ORANGE YOGURT PARFAITS WITH SHREDDED WHEAT CRISPS

Serves 6
Active time: 25 min   Start to finish: 25 hr
(includes draining yogurt)

    3 cups low-fat plain yogurt
1½ large shredded wheat biscuits, coarsely
       crumbled
1½ tablespoons unsalted butter, melted
    2 teaspoons sugar
    ½ cup water
    ¼ cup honey
    6 (3- by ½-inch) strips orange zest
       (see Tips, page 8)
    ¼ cup strained fresh orange juice
    ⅓ cup chilled heavy cream

Drain yogurt in a paper-towel-lined large medium-mesh sieve set over a bowl, covered and chilled, 24 hours. Discard any liquid in bowl.

Preheat oven to 350°F.

Toss shredded wheat with butter and sugar in a bowl, then spread evenly on a baking sheet and bake in middle of oven until deep golden, about 12 minutes. Cool completely.

Simmer water, honey, zest, and orange juice in a small saucepan, uncovered, until reduced to about ½ cup, 8 to 10 minutes. Remove from heat and let steep, covered, 10 minutes. Cool syrup, then pour through sieve into a small bowl, reserving zest.

Finely chop half of zest and stir into yogurt in a bowl along with 4 tablespoons syrup. Thinly slice remaining zest for garnish.

Beat cream in a small deep bowl with a whisk or an electric mixer until it just holds stiff peaks, then fold into yogurt. Divide yogurt among 6 small dessert dishes, then drizzle remaining syrup over it and top with wheat crisps and sliced zest.

Cooks' notes:
• Wheat crisps and syrup can be made 1 day ahead. Keep wheat crisps in an airtight container at room temperature and chill syrup, covered.
• Yogurt mixture can be made 3 hours ahead (without syrup topping and wheat crisps) and chilled, covered.

Each serving about 179 calories and 10 grams fat

DRIED CHERRY AND RAISIN RICE PUDDING

Serves 6
Active time: 15 min   Start to finish: 3½ hr (includes chilling)

    1 cup water
    ¼ teaspoon salt
    ½ cup long-grain white rice
    3 cups 1% fat milk
    ⅓ cup sugar
    1 large whole egg
    2 large egg whites
    1 teaspoon vanilla
    ⅛ teaspoon ground cardamom
    ⅓ cup golden raisins
    ⅓ cup dried tart cherries

Special equipment: **an instant-read thermometer**

Bring water with salt to a boil in a 2-quart heavy saucepan and stir in rice. Cover pan and reduce heat to low, then cook rice until water is absorbed, about 15 minutes. Stir in milk and sugar and cook over very low heat, covered, until mixture resembles a thick soup, 50 minutes to 1 hour.

Whisk together whole egg, egg whites, vanilla, cardamom, and a pinch of salt. Whisk about 1 cup hot rice mixture into egg mixture, then stir mixture into remaining rice. Cook over low heat (do not let boil), whisking constantly, until thermometer registers 170°F, 1 to 2 minutes. Remove from heat and stir in raisins and cherries.

Transfer pudding to a 2-quart dish or 6 (8-ounce) ramekins and chill, its surface covered with wax paper, until cool but not cold, 1 to 2 hours.

Each serving about 192 calories and 2 grams fat

PHOTO ON PAGE 109

CHOCOLATE SOUFFLÉ

Serves 2 to 4
Active time: 20 min   Start to finish: 45 min

⅓ cup sugar plus additional for sprinkling
5 oz bittersweet chocolate (not unsweetened),
   chopped
3 large egg yolks at room temperature
   30 minutes
6 large egg whites

Accompaniment: **lightly sweetened whipped cream**
Special equipment: **a 5½- to 6-cup glass or
ceramic soufflé dish**

Preheat oven to 375°F. Generously butter soufflé
dish and sprinkle with sugar, knocking out excess.

Melt chocolate in a metal bowl set over a saucepan
of barely simmering water, stirring occasionally until
smooth. Remove bowl from heat and stir in yolks
(mixture will stiffen).

Beat whites with a pinch of salt in a large bowl
with an electric mixer at medium speed until they just
hold soft peaks. Add ⅓ cup sugar, a little at a time, continuing to beat at medium speed, then beat at high
speed until whites just hold stiff peaks. Stir about 1 cup
whites into chocolate mixture to lighten, then add mixture to remaining whites, folding gently but thoroughly.

Spoon into soufflé dish and run the end of your
thumb around inside edge of soufflé dish (this will
help soufflé rise evenly). Bake in middle of oven until
puffed and crusted on top but still jiggly in center,
24 to 26 minutes. Serve immediately.

Cooks' note:
• Soufflé can be assembled up to 30 minutes before
baking and kept, covered with an inverted large bowl
(do not let bowl touch soufflé), at room temperature.

CHOCOLATE RUM PUDDING

Serves 1
Active time: 10 min   Start to finish: 40 min

1 large egg yolk
1 tablespoon plus ½ teaspoon sugar
1½ teaspoons all-purpose flour
⅓ cup whole milk
6 tablespoons heavy cream
1½ oz fine-quality bittersweet chocolate
   (not unsweetened)
1 to 2 teaspoons dark rum
¼ teaspoon instant-espresso powder (optional)

Vigorously whisk together yolk, 1 tablespoon
sugar, flour, and a pinch of salt until well blended.
Heat milk and 3 tablespoons cream in a small heavy
saucepan until hot but not boiling. Add about one third
of hot milk to yolk mixture in a slow stream, whisking
constantly. Add remaining milk, whisking, then transfer
to saucepan. Bring to a simmer, whisking constantly,
then continue to simmer, still whisking constantly, until
thickened, about 1 minute.

Remove from heat and add chocolate, rum (to
taste), and espresso powder (if using). Let stand until
chocolate is melted, about 30 seconds, then whisk until
smooth. Transfer to a glass and chill, covered, at least
30 minutes (to cool quickly to room temperature).

Just before serving, vigorously whisk remaining
3 tablespoons cream with remaining ½ teaspoon sugar
in a small bowl until it holds soft peaks. Top pudding
with whipped cream.

Cooks' note:
• Pudding can be made 1 day ahead and chilled,
covered. Bring to room temperature before serving.
PHOTO ON PAGE 113

BEVERAGES

alcoholic

BLACKBERRY HERB COCKTAILS

Makes 6 drinks
Active time: 10 min   Start to finish: 1½ hr

2 cups fresh blackberries
¼ cup plus 2 tablespoons sugar
⅔ cup water
1½ tablespoons finely chopped fresh rosemary
1 (750-ml) bottle Prosecco (Italian sparkling white wine), chilled

Garnishes: **fresh rosemary sprigs and blackberries**

Simmer blackberries, sugar, water, and rosemary in a small heavy saucepan, uncovered, stirring occasionally, until thickened and reduced by about two thirds, about 20 minutes.

Pour into a very fine sieve set over a glass measure and let stand 5 minutes (there will be about ⅓ cup). Discard solids (do not press on them). Chill syrup, covered, until cold.

Divide Prosecco among 6 small Champagne flutes, then pour 1½ teaspoons syrup into each drink.

Cooks' notes:
• This recipe makes more syrup than you'll need for 6 drinks. Use additional for extra cocktails or stir it into sparkling water or lemonade for delicious nonalcoholic drinks.
• Syrup keeps, covered and chilled, 3 days.
PHOTO ON PAGE 92

CITRUS CHAMPAGNE COCKTAIL

Makes 1 drink
Active time: 2 min   Start to finish: 2 min

When selecting the Champagne for this cocktail, we wanted something moderately dry but with a hint of sweetness. Demi-sec (a French term meaning "half dry") Champagnes and sparkling wines provide the perfect balance.

2 teaspoons Mandarine Napoléon (tangerine) liqueur or Cointreau
6 oz demi-sec Champagne or sparkling wine, chilled

Garnish: **thin slices of kumquat**

Pour liqueur into a Champagne flute and swirl around to coat inside of glass. Top off with chilled Champagne.

PEAR CHAMPAGNE COCKTAIL

Makes 1 drink
Active time: 2 min   Start to finish: 2 min

We chose to garnish our cocktail with Seckel or Forelle pear slices because of their small size—they fit perfectly in the Champagne flutes. Be sure to lower the slices slowly into the flute or the Champagne will bubble over.

1 teaspoon *poire William* or other pear eau-de-vie
6 oz demi-sec Champagne or sparkling wine, chilled

Garnish: **thin slices of pear**

Pour eau-de-vie into a Champagne flute and swirl around to coat inside of glass. Top off with chilled Champagne.

PINK DAIQUIRIS

Makes 6 drinks
Active time: 10 min   Start to finish: 10 min

9 oz white rum (1 cup plus 2 tablespoons)
6 tablespoons fresh lime juice
1½ teaspoons grenadine
4½ tablespoons superfine granulated sugar

Garnish: **lime slices**

Stir together all ingredients in a pitcher until sugar is dissolved, then add about 2 cups ice cubes and stir until very cold. Pour daiquiris through a medium-mesh sieve into Martini glasses.

Cooks' note:
• For a more striking presentation, you can spread some sugar on a plate, then rub rims of glasses with a wedge of lime and dip into sugar.

PHOTO ON PAGE 69

FRAISES DES BOIS ROYALES

Serves 6
Active time: 5 min   Start to finish: 1 hr

If you can't find fraises des bois *liqueur in your local liquor store, you can substitute cassis or Chambord, though the cocktail will taste somewhat different.*

¼ cup *fraises des bois* liqueur
1 tablespoon grenadine
2 (750-ml) bottles demi-sec
Champagne, chilled

Stir together liqueur and grenadine and chill, covered, until cold, about 1 hour.

Just before serving, divide grenadine mixture among 6 Champagne flutes, then slowly top off with Champagne. Stir gently.

GIN GIMLET AND TONIC

Makes 1 drink
Active time: 5 min   Start to finish: 5 min

1½ oz gin (3 tablespoons)
2 teaspoons Rose's lime juice
Tonic water, chilled

Garnish: **lime slice**

Fill a glass with ice cubes, then add gin and lime juice. Top off with tonic water and stir to combine.

PHOTO ON PAGE 85

FIZZY SOUR CHERRY LEMONADE

Makes 8 drinks
Active time: 20 min   Start to finish: 20 min

We've spiked this lemonade with vodka to make a refreshing summer cocktail, but you can omit the alcohol. One batch will completely fill your blender, so if you need more, make multiple batches rather than doubling or tripling the recipe.

2 lb fresh or thawed frozen sour cherries
(1 qt), stemmed
1 cup fresh lemon juice
¾ to 1 cup sugar
1½ cups vodka (optional)
2 to 3 cups chilled sparkling water

Garnish: **fresh sour cherries with stems**

Blend cherries (including pits) in a blender at low speed until skins have broken down enough to brightly color liquid (some of pits will be coarsely chopped). Pour through a medium-mesh sieve into a 2-quart pitcher, pressing on and discarding solids. Add lemon juice and sugar (to taste), stirring until sugar is dissolved.

Pour 3 tablespoons vodka (if using) into each of 8 tall (10-ounce) glasses filled with ice. Add ½ cup cherry lemonade to each glass and top off with sparkling water.

Cooks' note:
• Sour cherry lemonade can be made 1 day ahead and chilled, covered

PHOTO ON PAGE 78

ISLAND RUM PUNCH

Makes 8 drinks
Active time: 10 min   Start to finish: 10 min

1 (12-oz) can guava nectar
1½ cups fresh orange juice
1½ cups unsweetened pineapple juice
1½ cups amber rum
½ cup fresh lime juice
8 drops Angostura bitters
Freshly grated nutmeg to taste

Garnish: **lime slices**

Stir together all ingredients except nutmeg in a pitcher. Serve over ice, sprinkled with a pinch of freshly grated nutmeg.

PINEAPPLE AND LIME COCKTAILS

Makes 6 drinks
Active time: 10 min   Start to finish: 10 min

2 cups chopped peeled and cored fresh pineapple (labeled "extra sweet")
½ cup ice water
2 tablespoons fresh lime juice
2 tablespoons sugar
¾ cup vodka

Garnish: **lime wedges**

Blend pineapple, water, lime juice, and sugar in a blender until very smooth. Fill 6 tumblers with ice and pour 2 tablespoons vodka into each. Divide pineapple mixture among glasses and stir.

Cooks' note:
• Pineapple mixture (without vodka) can be blended 1 day ahead and chilled, covered.

Each serving about 112 calories and less than 1 gram fat

non-alcoholic

BLOOD-ORANGE AND GRAPEFRUIT JUICE

Serves 6
Active time: 20 min   Start to finish: 20 min

3 cups fresh pink or red grapefruit juice (from about 4 grapefruit)
3 cups fresh blood-orange juice or regular orange juice (from about 11 oranges)

Garnish: **lime slices**

Stir together juices in a pitcher and add ice (if desired).

PHOTO ON PAGE 48

PLUM LIMEADE

Serves 6
Active time: 10 min   Start to finish: 10 min

Adding rum or vodka to this plum limeade makes a delicious cocktail. With or without alcohol, the limeade should be served immediately, since it will quickly darken if left standing.

1 lime, cut into 6 wedges and seeded
1 lb ripe red or black plums, quartered and pitted
1½ cups crushed ice
1 cup cold water
⅔ cup superfine granulated sugar

Garnish: **plum and lime slices and fresh mint sprigs**

Blend lime wedges (including peel) in a blender on high speed 10 seconds. Add pitted plums, ice, water, and sugar and blend until plums are puréed, about 15 seconds. Pour through a fine-mesh sieve into a pitcher, pressing on and discarding solids.

Stir limeade and serve immediately over ice.

ICED GINGER TEA WITH LEMON AND CLOVES

Makes about 12 cups
Active time: 10 min   Start to finish: 5¼ hr

This is a traditional homemade drink that's found all across West Africa. It's sometimes called ginger beer, though it's not alcoholic.

¾ **lb fresh ginger, peeled and coarsely chopped (1½ cups)**
5 **cups boiling-hot water**
1 **tablespoon whole cloves**
6 **cups water at room temperature**
½ **cup strained fresh lemon juice**
1 **cup sugar, or to taste**

Special equipment: **cheesecloth**

Purée ginger with ¼ cup boiling-hot water in a food processor, then stir together with cloves and remaining 4¾ cups boiling-hot water in a large glass or stainless-steel bowl. Let stand, uncovered, at room temperature 2 hours.

Set a medium-mesh sieve lined with 4 layers of rinsed and squeezed cheesecloth over another large bowl. Pour ginger mixture into sieve, then gather up edges of cheesecloth and squeeze to extract as much liquid as possible into bowl. Discard solids, reserving cheesecloth in sieve.

Stir in 4 cups room-temperature water and lemon juice, then let stand at room temperature 1 hour (to allow sediment to settle).

Ladle or pour ginger tea through sieve lined with cheesecloth, leaving any sediment at bottom of bowl. Add sugar and remaining 2 cups room-temperature water, stirring until sugar is dissolved. Chill in a pitcher until cold, about 2 hours.

Serve over ice.

CHOCOLATE EGG CREAM
Fizzy Chocolate Milk

Makes 1 drink
Active time: 5 min   Start to finish: 5 min

Many years ago, this delicious New York fountain drink was actually made with eggs, but it's been a long time since anyone's seen that version. If you are a serious egg cream lover, use a seltzer siphon to get the best foam.

½ **cup chilled whole milk**
   Chilled seltzer
¼ **cup chocolate syrup**

Special equipment: **a long-handled spoon; a seltzer siphon (optional)**

Pour milk into a 16-ounce glass and place spoon in glass. Pour enough seltzer (or squirt if using siphon) into glass to reach ½ inch below rim. (A snow-white foam will develop.) Pour syrup into center of white foam, then stir in syrup and remove spoon through center of foam.

TROPICAL SMOOTHIE

Makes about 4 cups
Active time: 15 min   Start to finish: 15 min

1 **(1-lb) ripe papaya, peeled, seeded, and chopped (2 cups)**
1 **ripe mango, peeled, pitted, and chopped (2 cups)**
5 **tablespoons fresh lime juice**
⅓ **cup water**
2 **teaspoons chopped peeled fresh ginger**
1 **cup coconut sorbet**
1 **cup ice cubes**

Blend together papaya, mango, lime juice, water, and ginger in a blender until smooth. Add sorbet and ice and blend until smooth.

259

MANGO LASSI

Serves 4
Active time: 15 min   Start to finish: 15 min

In Indian restaurants, lassi *is served with the meal, but we prefer this exotic "smoothie" in place of dessert. Look for the smaller, yellow-skinned mangoes, which have a more pronounced flavor.*

2½ cups chopped peeled mango (from about
    2½ lb very ripe mangoes)
¼ cup sugar
1 qt well-shaken buttermilk

Garnish: **lime wedges**

Purée mango with sugar in a blender until smooth. Add buttermilk and blend well. Force through a fine-mesh sieve into a large glass measure. Serve *lassi* over ice in tall glasses.

Cooks' note:
• *Lassi* can be made 6 hours ahead and chilled, covered.

Each serving about 210 calories and 2 grams fat

MOCHA MALTED SHAKE

Makes about 3 cups
Active time: 10 min   Start to finish: 1 hr (includes chilling coffee)

1 pt chocolate ice cream
¾ cup strong brewed coffee, chilled
5 tablespoons malted milk powder

Blend all ingredients in a blender until smooth.

Cooks' note:
• **To save time, 4 teaspoons instant coffee and ¾ cup cold water can be substituted for freshly brewed coffee.**

VANILLA STRAWBERRY COOLER

Makes about 1½ quarts
Active time: 10 min   Start to finish: 10 min

A vanilla bean is an extravagance that lends a note of sophistication to this drink, but we found extract is a fine substitute.

1 lb strawberries (1 qt), trimmed and halved
    (quartered if large)
1 cup fresh lemon juice
¾ cup superfine granulated sugar
4 cups water
1 vanilla bean, halved lengthwise, or
    1 teaspoon vanilla extract

Blend strawberries, lemon juice, sugar, and 2 cups water in a blender (in batches if necessary) 2 minutes. Scrape seeds from each vanilla bean half with tip of a knife into blender (or add extract), then blend with strawberry purée.

If desired, pour through a fine-mesh sieve into a pitcher to remove strawberry seeds, pressing hard on solids. Stir in remaining 2 cups water and serve over ice.

Cooks' notes:
• **Cooler can be chilled, covered, up to 1 day.**
• **Vanilla pod can be placed in a jar of sugar to flavor it.**

PEACH RASPBERRY SMOOTHIE

Makes about 3½ cups
Active time: 10 min   Start to finish: 4 hr (includes freezing)

¾ lb ripe peaches, pitted and cut into
    ½-inch wedges
1 cup water
1 cup fresh raspberries (8 oz)
¼ cup sugar
⅛ teaspoon almond extract

Freeze peaches in 1 layer in a large sealed plastic bag until frozen, about 4 hours.

Blend peaches with remaining smoothie ingredients in a blender until smooth. Thin with more water if necessary.

STRAWBERRY BANANA SMOOTHIE

Makes about 4 cups
Active time: 5 min   Start to finish: 5 min

1 lb strawberries (about 1 qt), trimmed
  and halved
1 ripe banana, cut into pieces
1 cup ice cubes
½ cup silken tofu
½ cup orange juice
2 tablespoons sugar

Blend all ingredients in a blender until smooth.

HONEYDEW CUCUMBER SMOOTHIE

Makes about 4 cups
Active time: 15 min   Start to finish: 4¼ hr
(includes freezing honeydew)

1½ lb piece ripe honeydew, seeded, rind
  discarded, and flesh cut into ½-inch
  pieces (3 cups)
1 (8-oz) cucumber, peeled and chopped
  (1 cup)
1 cup lemon yogurt
2 tablespoons chopped fresh mint
1 to 2 teaspoons sugar

Freeze honeydew in 1 layer in a large sealed plastic bag until frozen, about 4 hours.

Blend honeydew with cucumber, yogurt, mint, and sugar (to taste) in a blender until smooth. Thin with water if necessary.

PINEAPPLE ORANGE BATIDOS

Makes 2 drinks
Active time: 10 min   Start to finish: 10 min

Long before smoothies swept our nation, Puerto Rico and Cuba were whipping up their own fruit shakes, known as batidos.

¼ pineapple (labeled "extra sweet"), peeled,
  cored, and cut into chunks (1 cup)
¾ cup ice cubes
¾ cup fresh orange juice
2 tablespoons sugar
½ cup whole milk

Garnish: **pineapple wedges and orange slices**

Blend pineapple, ice, orange juice, sugar, and a pinch of salt in a blender until smooth. Add milk and blend until frothy. Serve immediately.

guides to the text

CREDITS

We gratefully acknowledge the photographers listed below. With a few exceptions, their work was previously published in *Gourmet* magazine.

Sang An: Steamed Corn Custards with Crab, p. 2. The Art of Cool, pp. 80–83. All photographs © 2002.

Quentin Bacon: Table setting, back jacket. Beet and Goat Cheese Salad, p. 6. Sizzle in the City, pp. 68–71. Feast of Fancy, pp. 104–107. All photographs © 2002.

Brown Cannon: Driving across the Golden Gate Bridge, p. 10. Photograph © 2002.

Miki Duisterhof: Cook Me a Rainbow, pp. 54–57. A Trip to Bountiful, pp. 92–95. All photographs © 2002.

Rob Fiocca: Individual Chocolate Raspberry Baked Alaskas, p. 6. Dinner Under Glace, pp. 62–65. Photographed at the Ice Hotel in Quebec. All photographs © 2002.

Dana Gallagher: Plain Good Amish Cooking, pp. 58–61. All photographs © 2002.

Lisa Hubbard: The Welcoming Table, pp. 46–47. A Grand Rising, pp. 48–49. One Enchanted Evening, pp. 50–51. Sunday Send-Off, pp. 52–53. Thanksgiving with a Twist, pp. 98–101. Baked Eggs and Mushrooms in Ham Cups, p. 114. All photographs © 2002.

Richard Gerhard Jung: Food Noir, pp. 22–27. A New Way to Grill, pp. 72–75. Splendor in the Grass, pp. 88–91. The Peaceable Feast, pp. 102–103. All photographs © 2002.

John Kernick: "Tosca" sign, p. 11. Pastry shop, p. 28. Booths at Tosca, p. 28. Molinari Delicatessen, North Beach, p. 28. Browser Books, Fillmore, p. 28. Golden Gate Bridge, p. 28. Washington Square park, North Beach, p. 28. City Lights, looking downtown from Columbus and Broadway, p. 28. Food shop, p. 28. Cable car, p. 28. All American, pp. 76–79. All photographs © 2002.

Ericka McConnell: Tropic of Casual, pp. 66–67. All photographs © 2002.

Rita Maas: Whole Stuffed Artichokes Braised in White Wine, pp. 6, 37. Carciofi alla Romana, p. 34. Deep-Fried Baby Artichokes Stuffed with Pepper Jack Cheese, p. 36. All photographs © 2002.

Victoria Pearson: Stuffed Baby Bell Peppers, p. 6. Table setting, pp. 12–13. San Francisco Celebration, pp. 14–21. All photographs © 2002.

David Prince: Less Is More, pp. 42–45. All photographs © 2002.

Jonelle Weaver: Out of Africa, pp. 40–41. Welcome to the Future, pp. 96–97. All photographs © 2002.

Anna Williams: Outdoor table setting, p. 38. It's a Breeze, pp. 84–87. All photographs © 2002.

Romulo Yanes: Berry Tart with Ginger Cream, front jacket. Cooking Class: Artichokes, pp. 32–33. Low-Fat: Play It Cool, p. 108. Low-Fat: Fall Harvest Dinner, p. 109. Eggplant and Spinach Lasagne Spirals, p. 110. Moroccan-Style Roast Cornish Hens with Vegetables, p. 110. Layered Cobb Salad, p. 110. Red Wine-Braised Short Ribs with Vegetables, p. 110. "Paella" Couscous Salad, p. 111. Duck and Wild Rice Salad, p. 111. Dinner for One: Home Alone, p. 112. Dinner for One: Be Your Guest, p. 113. All photographs © 2002.

SOURCES

Below are sources for the sometimes hard-to-find ingredients and cookware

INGREDIENTS

Andouille sausage—Specialty foods shops and Citarella (212-874-0383).

Broccolini—Specialty produce markets and many supermarkets.

Buffalo rib roast—Wild Idea Buffalo Company (866-658-6137; wildideabuffalo.com), Jackson Hole Buffalo Meat Company (800-543-6328; jhbuffalomeat.com), Arrowhead Buffalo Meats (877-283-2969; arrowheadsteaks.com), and D'Artagnan (800-327-8246; dartagnan.com).

Bulgur—natural foods stores and Kalustyan's (212-685-3451).

Bottled whole shelled roasted chestnuts and **marron glacés** (candied chestnuts)—specialty foods shops.

Dried Aleppo chile flakes—Kalustyan's (212-685-3451).

Dried *ancho* chiles—Latino markets and Kitchen/Market (888-468-4433).

***Ancho* chile powder**—Mexican markets, Chile Today—Hot Tamale (800-468-7377), and Kalustyan's (212-685-3451).

Chiles de árbol—Latino markets and Chile Today—Hot Tamale (800-468-7377).

Spanish chorizo (spicy cured pork sausage)—Latino markets and some supermarkets.

Pearl (Israeli) couscous—Middle Eastern markets, some specialty foods shops and supermarkets, and Kalustyan's (212-685-3451).

Boneless magret duck breast halves with skin—D'Artagnan (800-327-8246) and Hudson Valley Foie Gras (877-289-3643).

Smoked duck breast halves—D'Artagnan (800-327-8246).

Confit duck leg—some butcher shops and D'Artagnan (800-327-8246).

Frozen *edamame*—Asian markets, some specialty foods shops, and in the frozen foods section of many supermarkets.

Just Whites (can be substituted for egg whites, when not fully cooked, if salmonella is a problem in your area)—many supermarkets and New York Cake & Baking Distributors (800-942-2539).

Hoisin sauce (Koon Chun and Lee Kum Kee brands)—Uwajimaya (800-889-1928).

Habanero and Scotch bonnet chiles—Latino and Caribbean markets.

Japanese pickled ginger—Japanese markets and Uwajimaya (800-889-1928).

Kumquats—specialty produce markets and some supermarkets.

Fresh or frozen *kaffir* lime leaves—Asian and Indian markets and Uwajimaya (800-889-1928).

Bottled Key lime juice—Manhattan Key Lime Juice (212-696-5378).

Malted milk powder—supermarkets and The Vermont Country Store (802-362-8470).

Alphonso mango slices (preferably Ratna brand)—specialty foods shops and Kalustyan's (212-685-3451).

Maple sugar—specialty foods shops, farmers markets, The Baker's Catalogue (800-827-6836), and La Cuisine (India Tree brand; 800-521-1176).

Grade B maple syrup—The Baker's Catalogue (800-827-6836) and Dakin Farm (800-993-2546).

Mascarpone cheese—Italian markets, specialty foods shops, some supermarkets, and cheese shops.

Matcha (powdered Japanese green tea)—Japanese markets and some specialty foods shops.

Mirin (Japanese sweet rice wine)—Japanese markets, natural foods stores, and Uwajimaya (800-889-1928).

Nerigoma (Japanese sesame paste)—Japanese markets and Uwajimaya (800-889-1928).

Nori—Japanese markets and Uwajimaya (800-889-1928).

Old Bay Seasoning—specialty foods shops, fish markets, and some supermarkets.

Smoked paprika—Formaggio Kitchen (888-212-3224) and Tienda.com (888-212-3224).

Frozen passion-fruit pulp—Latino markets.

"Baby" bell peppers—specialty produce markets and Garden of Eden (212-255-4200).

Dried long peppers—Fauchon (212-308-5919).

Shelled unsalted raw (not roasted) pistachios—many natural foods stores and Kalustyan's (212-685-3451 or kalustyans.com).

Pistachio oil—specialty foods shops and Dean & DeLuca (800-999-0306).

Short-grain sushi rice—Japanese markets and Uwajimaya (800-889-1928).

Rice flour—some supermarkets, natural foods stores, Kalustyan's (212-685-3451), and The Baker's Catalogue (800-827-6836).

Rye flour—Natural foods stores and most supermarkets.

Shiro miso—Japanese markets and Uwajimaya (800-889-1928).

Fresh *shiso* leaves—Japanese markets and Uwajimaya (800-889-1928).

Soba—Japanese markets, natural foods stores, and Uwajimaya (800-889-1928).

Sweet soppressata—Italian markets and some deli counters.

Ground sumac—Middle Eastern markets and Kalustyan's (212-685-3451).

Tamari—Japanese markets, natural foods stores, and Uwajimaya (800-889-1928).

Tamarind concentrate—Latino and Indian markets and Kalustyan's (212-685-3451).

Wasabi paste (Japanese horseradish paste)—Japanese markets and Uwajimaya (800-889-1928).

White miso—Japanese markets, natural foods stores, and Uwajimaya (800-889-1928).

White truffle oil—specialty foods shops.

Wild rice—specialty foods shops and Kalustyan's (212-685-3451).

COOKWARE

Barquette molds—some cookware shops and Bridge Kitchenware (800-274-3435).

Hardwood charcoal—hardware stores and some specialty foods shops.

Charlotte molds (5-oz)—Broadway Panhandler (866-266-5927 or 212-966-3434).

Madeleine pan with 20 miniature (½-tablespoon) molds—cookware shops and Bridge Kitchenware (212-688-4220).

Mandoline **or other adjustable manual slicer** (such as the Japanese Benriner)—many cookware shops. Benriners also found at Asian markets and Uwajimaya (800-889-1928).

Julienne peeler—some cookware stores and Chef's Catalog (800-884-2433).

INDEX

Page numbers in *italics* indicate color photographs
☺ indicates recipes that can be prepared in 30 minutes or less
↘ indicates recipes that are leaner/lighter

INDEX

TABLE SETTING ACKNOWLEDGMENTS

Any items not credited are privately owned.

San Francisco Celebration

Pages 12–13: Rattan dining chairs—The Far Company (415-553-7774). Table, dinner plates, and bowls—Alex Marshall Studios (415-383-1662). "Alton" flatware—Williams-Sonoma (800-541-2233). Linens—The Gardener (510-548-4545). Belgian wineglasses and decanter—La Maison de la Bouquetière (800-884-8875). Pomegranate and mandarin dupioni silk tablecloth fabric—Forgotten Shanghai (415-701-7707). *Page 17:* Plate—Alex Marshall Studios (415-383-1662). Indonesian teak tray—Meru Design (415-431-6378). *Page 21:* Dessert plate—Alex Marshall Studios (415-383-1662).

Food Noir

Pages 22-23: Drinks trolley by Jacques Adnet—Alan Moss (212-473-1310). Puiforcat saltcellar, cocktail stirrers, Martini glasses, and mirrored drinks tray—Deco Deluxe (212-472-7222). Silver ceramic cocktail plate—Takashimaya New York (800-753-2038 or 212-350-0100). *Page 25:* Mother-of-pearl shell—Takashimaya New York (800-753-2038 or 212-350-0100). Plates and Georg Jensen "Parallel" flatware—Alan Moss (212-473-1310). Silver glass—Maya Schaper Cheese and Antiques (212-873-2100). *Page 26:* Black-banded plate—Michael C. Fina (212-557-2500). Flatware and wineglass—Deco Deluxe (212-472-7222). Lindstrand vase—Alan Moss (212-473-1310). *Page 27:* Etched-glass ice cream bowl and plate—Depression Modern (212-982-5699). Ebony flatware—Deco Deluxe (212-472-7222). Chair—Skyscraper (212-588-0644).

Cooking Class: Artichokes

Page 36: Platter—Lawrence Essentials (212-481-0042).

Out of Africa

Page 40: Emile Henry ramekins—Broadway Panhandler (212-966-3434). *Page 41:* Linen napkin and tablecloth—for stores call Area (212-924-7084).

Less Is More

Page 42: Platters and decanter—La Cafetière (866-486-0667 or 646-486-0667). Knives—Aux Belles Choses (504-891-1009). Linen napkins—Kim Seybert (212-564-7850). *Page 44 (top):* Soup bowl—Crate & Barrel (800-323-5461 or 212-308-0011). *Page 45:* Goblets—La Cafetière (866-486-0667 or 646-486-0667).

The Welcoming Table

Pages 46–47: Carafe—Nicole Farhi (212-223-8811). Wineglasses—IKEA (800-434-4532). Faux fur throw—Pottery Barn (800-922-5507). Gray knitted scarf—J. Crew (800-562-0258). Gray knitted hat—Banana Republic (888-906-2800). Blue silk cushion—Troy (212-941-4777). Shearling patchwork cushions—Room Interior Products (212-847-8488, ext. 109). *Page 47 (top):* Bowl—Rosenthal (800-804-8070). *Page 47 (bottom):* Light blue plate—Mood Indigo (212-254-1176).

A Grand Rising

Page 48 (top): "Irma" European quilted pillowcase, "Irma" QS quilt, white and natural pillowcases, "Trim" white DS sheets, standard pillowcase with blue detailing, and "Sky" linen place mat—Area (212-924-7084). Knitted rabbit—Lake (646-654-0129). Juice tumblers—Crate & Barrel (800-996-9960). Tse & Tse carafe—Zinc Details (415-776-2100 or 510-540-8296). *Page 48-49:* Whitewashed wooden tray—Calvin Klein Home—(212-292-9000 or 877-256-7373). Oval wire rack—French General (212-343-7474).

One Enchanted Evening

Page 50 (top): Candles—Pottery Barn (800-922-5507). "Sand" dinner plates and shallow bowls—Nicole Farhi (212-223-8811). "Willow" cutlery—Crate & Barrel (800-996-9960). Wineglasses—ABC Carpet & Home (212-473-3000). Natural place mats and white linen napkins—Area (212-924-7084).

Sunday Send-Off

Page 53: Ladybug boots and frog boots—Restoration Hardware (877-747-4671). Sheepskin slippers—Ugg Australia (uggaustralia.com). Handmade toys—Lake (646-654-0129).

Cook Me a Rainbow

Pages 54-55: "Ashford" extending white oval table and "Napoleon" white chairs—Pottery Barn (800-922-5507). Embroidered white linen tablecloth—Sferra Bros. (732-290-2230). "Regence" pitcher and twin shell centerpiece—Romancing Provence (212-481-9879). Water glasses—William Yeoward Crystal (212-532-2358). Victorian etched small glasses—L. Becker Flowers (212-439-6001). "Lafayette" wineglasses—Baccarat (800-777-0100). Georg Jensen flatware—Michael C. Fina (800-289-3462). *Page 55 (top):* Footed serving platter—Romancing Provence (212-481-9879). Napkins—Sferra Bros. (732-290-2230). *Page 56 (top):* Provençal chairs, circa 1910—Aix Antiques (212-941-7919). *Page 56 (bottom left):* Dinner plate—Romancing Provence (212-481-9879). *Page 56 (bottom right):* Royal Copenhagen "White Half Lace" soup bowl and footed bowl—Michael C. Fina (800-289-3462). *Page 57:* White dessert plate—Romancing Provence (212-481-9879).

TABLE SETTING ACKNOWLEDGMENTS

Plain Good Amish Cooking

Page 58: English wheat-patterned clay plate, circa 1925—Aero (212-966-1500).
Page 59 (left): French white ceramic mixing bowls—Aero (212-966-1500). Cream bowl—Simon Pearce (212-334-2393).
Page 60: "Direction" pilsner glass—Crate & Barrel (800-996-6696). Round dinner plates—Simon Pearce (212-334-2393).

Dinner Under Glace

Pages 62–63: Votive holders, forks, spoons, and knives—Ad Hoc (212-982-7703). Linen napkins—Dransfield & Ross (212-741-7278).
Page 65: Dessert wineglasses—Crate & Barrel (800-996-9960). Gratin dishes—Broadway Panhandler (866-266-5927).

Sizzle in the City

Pages 68–69: White tumblers—The Terence Conran Shop (866-755-9079 or 212-755-7249). "Parker" wineglasses—Calvin Klein Home (800-294-7978).
Page 69 (top): Martini glasses—Williams-Sonoma (800-541-1262).
Page 71 (top): Weber "Performer" grill—Weber Stephen Products (800-446-1071).

A New Way to Grill

Pages 72–73: Slate table—Treillage (212-535-2288).
Page 74: Dinner plate by Hakusan—Sara (212-772-3243).
Page 75 (top left): "Niyaz" table runner—Anichini (212-679-9540).
Page 75 (bottom left): Oval underplate by Christiane Perrochon—Takashimaya New York (800-753-2038 or 212-350-0100). Orange linen mesh napkin—Anichini (212-679-9540).
Page 75 (bottom right): Tray plates—In The Market (212-255-6290). Glass and silver vintage spoon—Takashimaya New York (800-753-2038 or 212-350-0100).

The Art of Cool

Page 80 (top): Ceramic 9-inch salad plate, dark-wood chopsticks, and periwinkle and natural woven placemat—Ad Hoc (212-982-7703).
Pages 80–81: Wooden "Yakisug" tray, floral sauce dish by Atsu Mashikofu, round silver bowl, and bamboo chopsticks by Susutake Seseragi—Dean & DeLuca (212-226-6800). Chopstick rest and gray and white flecked ceramic bowl—Sara (212-772-3243). White spoon—Takashimaya New York (212-350-0100).
Page 82: Green star and red spotted napkin—Ad Hoc (212-982-7703). Lotus 4-inch bowls—Fish's Eddy (212-420-9020).
Page 83: Gold leaf teaspoon—Takashimaya New York (212-350-0100).

It's a Breeze

Page 85 (bottom): Glass—Takashimaya New York (800-753-2038).

Splendor in the Grass

Page 88 (left): Andrea Stewart handbag—Saks Fifth Avenue (212-753-4000).
Page 89: "Bento" bamboo basket—Takashimaya New York (800-753-2038).
Page 90 (bottom right): Christiane Perrochon bowls, Ercuis spoon, and Murano water glass—Takashimaya New York (800-753-2038).
Page 91: Basket—Saks Fifth Avenue (212-753-4000).

A Trip to Bountiful

Page 93 (bottom): Centerpiece—L. Becker Flowers (212-439-6001).

Welcome to the Future

Page 96: Oval platter and pale amber salad plate—Crate & Barrel (800-996-9960). Frosted glass square plate and octopus bowl with silver interior—Dean & DeLuca (212-226-6800). Square pearlescent dish and round clay dish with silver interior—Aero (212-966-1500).
Page 97 (top): "Kasumi" oval glass serving plate—Aero (212-966-1500).

Thanksgiving with a Twist

Page 98 (top): "Honey-moon" plates and bowls—Rosenthal (800-804-8070). Flatware and wineglasses—Armani Casa (212-334-1271). Silk runner—Simon Pearce (212-334-2393). Lucite cube candle holders—Room Interior Products (212-847-8488). Alvar Aalto vases—MoMA Design Store (800-447-6662).
Page 98 (bottom): Rectangular platters—Global Table (212-431-5839).
Page 101: White ceramic platter—Aero (212-966-1500). Sterling-silver cake server—Takashimaya New York (800-753-2038 or 212-350-0100). Square white plate—Global Table (212-431-5839).

The Peaceable Feast

Page 103 (top): Olive linen place mat (used as a napkin)—Takashimaya New York (800-753-2038 or 212-350-0100).

Feast of Fancy

Page 104 (top): Jean-Louis Coquet "Samoa" salad plate and dinner plate—Lalique North America (800-993-2580).
Page 104 (center): Jean-Louis Coquet "Samoa" soup bowl—Lalique North America (800-993-2580).
Page 105: Dessert stand—Dean & DeLuca (800-999-0306).
Page 106: Vintage silver platter—Michael C. Fina (800-289-3462).

Six One-Dish Dinners

Page 110 (top right): "Luna Mahogany" porcelain dinner plate—Calvin Klein (800-294-7978).

Dinner for One: Be Your Guest

Page 113: Ceramic square dinner plate and textured paper place mat—Armani Casa (212-334-1271).

If you are not already a subscriber to *Gourmet* magazine and would be interested in subscribing, please call *Gourmet*'s toll-free number, (800) 365-2454, or e-mail subscriptions@gourmet.com.

If you are interested in purchasing additional copies of this book or other *Gourmet* cookbooks, please call (800) 245-2010.

tagliatelle